WRITERS TALKING

WRITERS TALKING

Nigel Gray

CALIBAN BOOKS

© Caliban Books
First published 1989
by Caliban Books
17 South Hill Park Gardens
Hampstead, London NW3

ISBN 0 85066 009 3

Typeset by Clerkenwell Graphics,
13-14 Vandy Street, London EC2A 2DE

Printed and bound in Great Britain by
Wheaton & Co. Ltd., Exeter, Devon

CONTENTS

INTRODUCTION

When we read a book, to a certain extent we get to 'know' the author of it. When we enjoy or respect the book, most of us feel we would like to know the author better. There are questions we would like to ask about the author as a person as well as about his or her work. In these interviews I have endeavoured to be a representative of the reader: a person welcomed by these writers as a companion, yet someone whose curiosity was not dulled by intimacy. My hope too is that, through these pages, I can introduce readers to writers they have not yet 'met'.

In some ways this book is a key to a treasury of fine literature; but it is important for readers to bear in mind that these are not 'literary' pieces in themselves – they were not written, but spoken. They have been extensively edited of course (and I have edited myself out of them because I see my role as 'ear' rather than 'voice'), but I hope they retain some of the spontaneity of the live conversations. They were not intended to be journalistic or academic interviews, but rather an attempt to give a sympathetic picture of the writer, at home, at ease, chatting with a friend. Nevertheless much is lost. I regret that it is not possible to pass on the laughter I shared often with these writers; they seem more sombre here than was actually the case. I learned, from editing this book, that much humour depends on nothing more than a tone of voice; and the flattening out of the voice to the shallowness of printers' ink on paper diminishes communication. Indeed, printed words can often say the opposite of what has, in fact, been said. There was no alternative but to cut out many of the jokes and much of the fun. There are other lost pleasures too, such as mimicry, and other performance and story-telling skills.

Reading through the manuscript, I was particularly struck by two recurring topics: war and education. Four of these writers were fathered by men who somehow survived the carnage that was the First World War. As well as being reminded of its crass obscenity,

2

one cannot help but wonder what vast reservoir of talent was lost through that criminal decimation of European manhood. Four of the writers were public school pupils, and three are vociferous about the damage of one sort or another that that system inflicts upon its victims (and consequently upon this country). On the other hand, none of the remaining five British writers would have been able to enjoy more than a very elementary education had it not been for the radical decency of the 1945 Labour Government. That is an important fact to bear in mind as we watch Thatcher and her henchmen demolishing the civilised structures that that government built. And although writers in the British Isles are not looked to for wisdom in the way that they still are in some South American countries, the present Labour Party might take note of the universality of regret shown here for what has happened to it since those courageous days of its early maturity.

I should perhaps say something about how this book came to be. In 1983 a small publishing firm owned by Sinclair (the Sinclair of minuscule car and computer fame) and a man called Browne (whom I dubbed 'Aboulia Browne' because of his difficulty in making decisions) accepted two of my books for publication: *Life Sentence*, a collection of stories; and *The Worst of Times*, an oral history of the Depression. I then proposed to them the idea of a series of books of interviews with writers. After much discussion and many changes of mind it was decided that we should start with the simultaneous publication of two books, one comprising ten male writers and one comprising ten female. The thinking was that there is a particular market for women's authors, and this division would enable the marketing and sales people to take advantage of that fact. Sinclair Browne promised me a good advance and expenses. The obvious place to start, I thought, was with people I knew well and liked, whom I knew also to be interesting conversationalists. (Writing well, after all, is not always synonymous with talking well.) Consequently I set to work on the interviews which gave rise to this book.

In the event, Sinclair Browne ceased trading in the spring of '84, the very same month that Life Sentence was published, or rather, almost published; by which time I had completed most of the interviews included here. The contracts on the three books were never honoured: not a penny was paid. *Life Sentence*, and *The Worst of Times*, were soon brought out by other publishers; but *Writers Talking*, despite its merits, languished for the most part in my filing cabinet. Publishers who saw it rejected it on the grounds that there weren't any women in it!

Maybe, if the book does well, I will be commissioned to do the sequel and thereby be able to atone for my seeming sexist sin. Talking to ten women writers would be no hardship – it would be pure pleasure, and I have my list of desirable candidates already drawn up.

In fact, it was through listening to women that I discovered I was someone people would talk to. I used to work as a baker's roundsman, and I had many 'tea calls'. My customers would tell me about their lives and their troubles. I was sometimes, I suppose, a sort of substitute for social worker or priest. Then, in the heady days of late hippiedom when 'encounter groups' were all the rage, I used this talent, if I may call it that, to give amateurish therapy to people in need. I don't think I ever did a great deal of harm, and sometimes I feel I did some good. Talking to someone who was a good listener, who was sympathetic, non-judgemental, perceptive enough to put in a germane question here and there, or make a necessary challenge, seemed to be something most people needed in their attempts to heal themselves. I suppose it was not a great step from there to carrying out the interviews which comprise *The Worst of Times* – a little book I feel pleased to have done. And it was not such a big step again from talking to strangers, to talking with friends, the friends included here.

There are many differences, obviously, between the various writers in this volume. But I was also struck by two characteristics which, unless my intuition is incorrect, they share; characteristics which may not be readily discernible in the interviews. One is this: however apparently forthcoming they were, I always felt that they remained guarded, as though there was some precious core to themselves they were frightened of sharing, or losing. In the same way I have heard of primitive people who did not like being photographed, feeling that the photographer would be stealing some part of their soul. The other is something which may be more apparent in some of the photographs than in the words: an aura of loneliness, of deep sadness, however cheerful their public face. I wonder if these are necessary ingredients in what it is to be an artist – part of the price an artist has to pay?

Finally, in introducing this rogues' gallery, I will turn around one of Peter Vansittart's closing comments – that literature shows that

4

nothing is either ordinary or extraordinary – and say that I hope this book will show that the best of our writers are both ordinary, and extraordinary.

Nigel Gray, Northampton, February 1988.

Chapter One
BRIAN ALDISS

As good a way to start as anything is with resentment. My parents decided to send me away to a prep school at the age of eight. At the age of eight you're still on nodding terms with your teddy bear. It was a severe ordeal to go to this place and be incarcerated without toys, to be separated from your parents, to go through this whole rigmarole of a school that was obviously a descendant of Dotheboy's Hall – the conditions were awful. We were not so much cruelly treated as neglected. I don't think that sort of school exists anymore. We've passed laws since then. In those days they could do what they liked with you once they'd got you in their power. It was a money-making concern for the old bugger who ran it, and everything was done on the cheap.

He was a lazy man. When he didn't feel like working he'd come in and say, 'Well, boys, you've been doing jolly well – it's a holiday for you today.' Everyone would groan: it meant we were kicked out of his shambling house and we would have to spend the day in the field. He had a lad-of-all-trades working for him, and at mid-day the lad would bring out a Quality Street tin of sandwiches with gristly meat in. It was shockingly primitive and there was nothing to do really but bully each other.

The only good thing was that we were allowed a small garden. In the spring term, you bought, out of your pocket money, penny packets of seeds, and planted them. With any luck they'd be coming up in the summer term and you could ward off starvation by eating your tiny carrots and spring onions. It was subsistence level agriculture; and so, very early on, I learned to love gardening and respect agriculture, because I practised it myself. Your little strip of garden was an essential part of life. The local stone had got veins of what they call 'fool's gold' in it (pyrites of some kind), and we would ornament our paths with these stones, and the tougher you were, the more gold you had – a microcosm of real life! We would get an old bit of concrete or something (our 'thrones' we called them) and we would sit there watching over our bit of garden. It's grotesque to think of it now, but that's what we did.

No one paid the fees demanded in the prospectus; you could do a deal and get there for less. The objective of the school was to teach you to 'be a gentleman' (that awful phrase), and of course it turned out a lot of absolute scoundrels. The owner's name was Fen, and he had an assistant master called Knowles; the two of them taught us everything. While I was there, Knowles was sacked – he didn't want to get up one morning, he had a hang-over. Many of the boys liked Knowles – I didn't. I suppose, in a way, I preferred the oily Fen, until at a certain point he administered a most vicious beating. One of the boys was given twelve strokes on his bare bottom. I suppose there were never more than twenty of us at this school (only twenty suckers of parents could be found) and I can remember us all being sick or fainting or trying to run out. The boy involved was expelled. Who knows what the poor kid did. Perhaps he tried his first cigarette, I don't know; but it remains an early example in tyranny.

You were not allowed toys at the school, but I had *some* resources. I had a microscope. (That was classed as a scientific instrument.) I used to spend a lot of time observing people's spit and things through this microscope, and looking at people's hair. I was instrumental in delivering an awful fate to one of the boys because I took a strand of his hair, and we looked at it under the microscope. There was something moving on it! From then on he was a kind of leper. (We probably all had things that moved on our hair – considering the awful state of hygiene.) I had a little pocket telescope, with which I used to look at the moon and stars. And I had a toy I could hide in my pocket: a little kaleidoscope. I suppose it was about as long as a teaspoon. And I owned a pocket torch. I was terribly homesick for my first three terms, and so at night, to stave off the misery, I would go down the bed and look into my kaleidoscope for hours, just turning it round watching the patterns tumble, with the torch at the end of it. It's curious to think now that there were these three objects which aroused my interest – the interest in science, the interest in astronomy, and also an awakening aesthetic sense. I was also hooked on dinosaurs, and in fact my shrewd commercial sense was also born then. Because I knew more about dinosaurs than the other boys (though that was very little) I used to give them lectures on 'prehistoric monsters' for a penny a time. This was actually a hypothetical fee – I can't remember anyone actually paying me, but the principle was established that one shouldn't give anything away for nothing. So those really were (in the hideous phrase) the formative years.

At the age of eight I'd already started writing stories and making and illustrating little books. (I'd learnt to read at kindergarten, and I was very fluent.) I wanted to communicate, and as soon as I'd written the stories they'd be passed around. The other chaps didn't complain – they read the damn things. The other consolation was something that Fen grandly called 'the library'; in fact it was a few shelves of books. One book in particular, *Prisoners of the Sea* , I loved. Every term I would get back, bag it, and read it again; and since I was stuck there for three years and read it every term I suppose I had it by heart. It was written by Mrs Florence Kingsley; it was about the Huguenots and the terrible ordeals they went through. (Funnily enough I've managed to acquire a copy in the last year. It's not a bad story – I can understand why I was enchanted by it.) Later in life you can look back and see the genesis of many things. I think it's too neat a way of summing it up to say, 'Here's where it started,' but there's no doubt that a lot of good and bad character traits were formed there and then in that prison of a school.

My family were tradespeople – big fish in a little pool. We lived in a boring little town in Mid Norfolk where my grandfather had his shop: furnishers, drapers, men's outfitters, undertakers, removers. There were tailors on the premises who actually sat cross-legged and would make you up a suit. My grandfather's foremen were his two sons: my uncle and my father. That shop was the paradise I was exiled from. It was a marvellous place. It was like living in Gormenghast. It formed a complex series of rambling buildings with all kinds of odd people cached away making hats, or suits, or bits of furniture, or stoking great subterranean boilers. I had the free run of this place, and I could escape. I was small – I could hide in cupboards. There was a warehouse with rooms full of coconut matting and lino, and you could get in between them and have dens and play pirates and God knows what. The staff would always fool around when they could – knotted dusters would be thrown. It was pure joy. We had a flat over part of the shop; my parents would think, 'If he's not in the house, he's in the shop.' They could never keep tabs on me, so freedom was always on hand. Just outside the town was a heathland – a place called the Nettard. I knew that heath.

(Dumping Green was nearby where George Borrow was born. 'The wind on the heath, brother. Life is sweet, brother.') Those early years were full of excitement and freedom and fun. Came school – I returned home for holidays, but I was estranged. There was a kind of division, and paradise was spoilt. But in those early days it always seemed to me that I was the luckiest of children to have this marvellous place to explore.

My mother didn't *do* anything. She just swanned around looking after the house. We had maids and we lived quite well. Mother was supportive of my father because he worked all the time. I don't know if she realised how awful my school was. One doesn't, at the time, say anything. There's an extraordinary secrecy to small boys, and loyalty to you-know-not what. You never split. Later, when I did mutter something about it, my parents said, in that horrific phrase, 'It was for your own good.'

My grandfather was the archetypal self-made man; there's a lot of my grandfather in me. He was a tough old bastard. He was always referred to as 'the Guv'nor'. My father and my uncle always addressed him as 'Guv'nor'. Even my mother would always say, 'Guv'nor' – It was never grandad or anything of the sort. He ruled his business with a fairly active rod of iron, so I guess that was how he ruled his three sons. He sent them all off to Bishop's Stortford, and the eldest son, Nelson, died there. Nelson was good at rugger, and on the evening before an important match he reported sick with terrible stomach pains. They said, 'Nonsense, you're trying to get off the game.' I suppose the sister gave him a spoonful of brimstone and treacle or whatever, and he died of peritonitis at the school. That didn't deter my grandfather from sending, in their turn, my uncle and my father there too. It's always seemed to me a peculiar kind of insensitivity.

After my prep school I was sent to two minor public schools. I would never send my sons to board. The generation gap, as I understand it, was a phrase much circulated in the 60s, but it certainly existed before that. I can talk to my kids, we swear, we talk about sex or whatever – all things that were *verboten* in my time. My father and I had little communication. I think he thought whatever he'd gone through was the proper thing for me to go through. They had no sensibility. They were extraordinarily innocent; I suppose some would say ignorant. My family suffered from rotten teeth. My parents had a tin of Old-English humbugs by their bed. They liked to jump into bed and have an Old-English humbug before they went to sleep. First thing in the morning my father would get up and light a cigarette. He'd be shaving, and while he was coughing and hacking he'd be saying, 'The first of the day – the best cigarette of all.' It was killing him! They had this awful, damning *innocence*. Innocence is not a very good quality.

At public school I was good at holding my own, but I was never happy. It always astonished me at the beginning of every term to see how cheery and buoyant everyone else was. Perhaps, like me, they were putting on the cheeriness, but I don't think so. The first public school I went to, age eleven, was Framlingham in Suffolk. I owe Framlingham no affection at all. I was quite popular there because I was eccentric. I was known as 'The Professor'. I used to buy aeroplanes before the war for sixpence, powered by elastic bands: you wound the prop round and round and the plane flew beautifully. When one plane was buggered up, I fixed it in my locker so that when you opened the door a propeller started whirring and lights came on, and so on. I made various little gadgets like that. But I didn't like the school.

Another reason I was popular was because I became a story-teller. We had a large dormitory and the rule was, very strictly, that after lights out there was no talking. But there was a tradition of story-telling, and we would go round in turn; everyone would be forced at the peril of being beaten up, to tell a story. Most stories were fairly awful, and the champions who eventually emerged from these marathons were a great friend of mine called B. B. Gingell, and me; we would tell stories till the cows came home. But Gingell was a nature buff. His stories would be about badgers, or beavers, or lame cockerels. I had the edge on him because mine would be about adventures on other planets, or terrible threats to the earth, and that kind of thing. I found a knack of spinning it out for half an hour and getting to an exciting point before saying, 'Well, I'm tired now – more tomorrow.' They'd all shout out, 'Aldiss, you bastard – more! More!' 'No, no. I'm too tired. I'll tell you the rest tomorrow.'

Throughout the 30s I was reading a magazine called *Modern Boy* It had all kinds of stories which appealed to boys: motor racing; pirates; trading in the South Seas; school yarns; and in particular the adventures of the marvellous Captain Justice, written by Murray Roberts. I mainly relayed Captain Justice stories, but I camouflaged them, or made them something else, or embellished them in many ways. One always, I think, begins in a derivative way. What I did learn was the art of keeping people's attention, the art of suspense – I could drag a story out all term if they wanted it. (It makes it sound like *The Thousand and One Nights*.) It was a very hazardous calling because the housemaster had a listening hole in the door. He would burst in and say, 'Who was talking?' A horrible silence. 'Come on – who was talking?' And so I'd sit up in bed and put my hand up. 'All right, Aldiss, get up! Who else?' No one else would own up. 'All right, Aldiss, you're for it!' He'd take me down to his study and cane me in my pyjamas. Those beatings were really the first rewards I ever got for my art – after such beginnings one learns to fear the critics less.

Then there was the great Aldiss family quarrel. My grandfather had died and left the business to his sons, who were always at loggerheads – absolutely Cain and Abel stuff. In the battle that ensued my father was bought out, and we left Norfolk in a cloud of goat dung and went to live in Devon. That was coincident with the beginning of the war in 1939. I was sent to a school on Exmoor: West Buckland. It was a school where, although they'd *heard* of Oxford and Cambridge, no one ever thought of going on to university. They were farmers' sons, or they were going to be country solicitors, or, like me, they were wondering what the hell they were going to do. But that was a different school altogether from Framlingham.

West Buckland is on the edge of Exmoor and it has eighty-eight inches of rain a year – it comes straight in off the Atlantic. God, it rains there! So, in a way, there was not the division between the staff and the pupils that, on the whole, in those days existed. We were united against a common adversity. The spirit in that school was good. At weekends you could get sandwiches and clear off to wander all over Exmoor; if you were hardy enough you could swim in the little pools and streams (which were absolutely freezing). The temperature up there was enough to delay puberty for a couple of years.

At this time I was writing pornographic crime stories. They were very popular. I'd done away with all this nonsense of trying to charge money – I just enjoyed the popularity. At the end of term, my great friend Bowler and I used to take these precious manuscripts in a square Huntley and Palmer's biscuit tin and bury them in a rabbit hole in the plantation, so we could get them back next term. We daren't take them home. I was fifteen when I went to West

Buckland. By that time I was more mature and had acquired an
ambition to be a writer. My father's disaster had been my release.
To work in an outfitter's was the last thing I wanted. I never was
interested. The idea of fitting anyone up in clothes did not turn me
on one little bit. And yet, as a dutiful, compliant son, I would have
done it. When we left Dereham it was a great relief.

I had a subversive streak in me. The more they beat me at school
the more subversive I was. At West Buckland, when I was feeling
my strength, I had a vendetta with the headmaster, whom I loathed.
He would say, 'Oh, I know you – you're a comedian. Well, we can
see about that.' It was not regarded as a good thing to be at all funny.
Indeed, it was often made very painful for you if you were. But we
had an English teacher called H. C. Fay, a splendid Irishman who
moulded himself somewhat on G. B. Shaw. Crasher Fay – he wore
great boots – was enormously tall and appallingly bald. He was a
kind and humorous man and when he got the idea that I was writing
stories I was allowed the first privilege I ever earned: instead of the
weekly essay on visits to the dentist and hot-water bottles and all the
rest of it, I was allowed to write a story for him.

It's terrible to be encouraged – you immediately get swell-headed
and absolutely above yourself. I remember one Monday morning
when he was reviewing our efforts, he said, 'Now we have Aldiss's
story.' He put it down on the desk and there was an awful silence.
Everyone waited. Then he looked at me and said, 'We won't go into
this story, Aldiss, but I warn you, if you keep on like this you're
going to be another Evelyn Waugh.' I suppose he had a particular
hatred for Evelyn Waugh, but I adored Waugh's books – it was the
most encouraging bit of damnation I ever heard.

I was avidly reading Evelyn Waugh, Aldous Huxley, H. G. Wells,
Jules Verne, and a host of novelists whose names are now forgotten,
like Patrick Hamilton, who wrote *Rope* and *Gaslight*. And I liked
the novels of A. J. Cronin, most of which seem to me now
unreadable (with the possible exception of *Hatter's Castle*). When
we got Cronin's *The Stars Look Down* in the school library it was
very popular. There was one particularly sexy page that the
headmaster removed. In the sixth form – it sounds terribly snobby,
but we were actually fond of Shakespeare. We were studying *Julius
Caesar*, and I did a version of Julius Caesar in modern dress written
in gangsterese. How does it begin: 'Hence home, you idle creatures.
What, think you this is a holiday?' And my version went something

like, 'Say, you guys. What're you hanging around here for? Come
on. This ain't no vacation!' It was grotesque when one thinks of it.

At West Buckland there was little division between the studious
types and the sporty types. It was a peculiarly decent school, for
reasons I cannot determine. One played all the games, rugger in
particular. It was a great school for running. I loathed the runs. We
used to run all over Exmoor and it was always pissing with rain. They
worked up throughout the spring term to a twenty-mile killer. At
the same time the sixth form was quite civilised. For some reason
our rather horrible headmaster employed an art master called Mr
Lyons-Wilson. Mr Lyons-Wilson had rather an affected voice, but
he did know his art discrimination. He was a very eccentric figure:
he would come in a suit and an Anthony Eden hat, rather dressed
up – not like your average art master. He was extraordinarily good
and extraordinarily enthusiastic; and instead of violently taking the
mickey out of him as you would expect, this rather hoodlum-like lot
of young lads adored Lyons-Wilson. It was a good school – though
rather rough: there were no taps in the dormitory for instance – we
had bowls of cold water, and in the winter you'd have to break the
ice before you washed. It made you hardy.

It was a relief after all that to escape into the comparative safety
and comfort of the British army. We were precisely of that
generation which could see the war was going to be over soon: we
were torn between hoping to save our skins, and not wishing to miss
this enormous sideshow – this great initiation rite, THE WAR. I was
very fortunate to get in on the tag end of it. I was trained rather
rapidly and shunted abroad to fight. I arrived on Indian soil in 1944
just before my nineteenth birthday, and in no time was whipped out
to Burma. I was not 'officer material'. I wasn't interested. I didn't
want to command people. I could see it was, in a sense, easier to be
an officer, but I didn't think it was my role in life.

I suppose 'joining up' marked the birth of my political awareness.
Dereham was a strongly Conservative area, but there were a few
Liberals around. My grandfather was a local JP who campaigned for
the Conservative Party. When there was an election I was allowed
to stay up late, and sit in the front of my grandfather's car with him
while he drove electors to the polling station. We were on the
outskirts of Dereham one evening (if you weren't in the High Street
you were on the outskirts of Dereham) going down this lane, and a
figure came staggering along towards the car (there were very few

cars in Dereham which was still in the heady afterglow of Victoria's day), and the figure was so horrified by the sight of my grandfather's car approaching that he fell over into the ditch, his two little legs waving in the air (all rather Monty Pythonish), and then disappeared. I was startled by this and didn't realise it was just your ordinary drunk. I said to my grandfather, 'Who was that, Grandad?' He said, 'A Liberal,' and drove on. And so one felt immediately attracted to the Liberal cause.

After such a petit bourgeois upbringing, once you went into the army one of the shocks was to meet guys from the real world. I think that's why I'm grateful to the army, despite all the horror of the institution and what it was supposed to be doing. I'm grateful for the wide spectrum of people I met. It was enlightening for instance to find the hatred of the Welsh lads for Churchill. They all believed as gospel, that Churchill ordered the troops to fire on the striking miners in Tonypandy. I've still not found out whether it's true – you read conflicting reports: the Tories say he didn't, of course. But the bitterness of those lads, whose fathers had all been out-of-work miners, in the same lousy situation that we're faced with now, was unforgettable. It's awful to think of it repeating itself.

A lot of my education was conducted on the march, as it were. I was called up to Norwich, and our squad was given a heavy bashing. There was only one other guy who'd been to public school, a minor public school rather like mine, Eddie Breeze. And there was a delightful fly-boy from Birmingham, a good Brummy whose father had a bicycle shop, whose name was Lions. Lions could look after himself. So could Breeze and I because we'd had this horrid training – it was *easier* in the army than at public school. But the other poor guys were lost. A lot of them had never been away from home before. They were homesick; they were cursed out all the time; they couldn't make their beds (mummy had always made their beds). The army was a nightmare for them. For us it was fine. At six o'clock prompt, Breeze and Lions and I would be bullshitted up, and out to the gate and down into town.

To be honest, I'd always felt that I was disowned by my parents. As a small child I was threatened, if I did anything wrong, with the withdrawal of love. My mother would say, 'Then I shan't love you any more.' And she would run away. She'd just blow, sometimes taking my baby sister with her, just to frighten me. It works. It's a most cruel thing to do to a child. It's better to give them a slap –

they know that's done in anger and it's over. But the threat of withdrawing love is a very damaging thing. I thought that my incarceration in all those schools was the fulfilment of the threat. I was depressed for a lot of the time – until I got in the army. I went to the Far East and thought, 'Well, all right, to hell with them. I'll live my own life from now on.' That was a kind of freedom.

I had four years out in the Far East. One learnt to grow up and enjoy all the pleasures and vices of adult life far from any supervision. There was also the chance to see the kind of lifestyle that Asiatic races enjoyed. And the sun shone most of the time. You were out in the monsoon, it would turn off like a tap, your clothes would dry on you; everything would be fine again. I thought the climate was great. I loved the place, though, as common soldiers, we were treated like dogs. I was a signalman – I was communicating, in a way, even then. One was sandwiched between what we know as the British Raj and the Indians. And who are the soldiers' friends? – priests and whores. We lived on a kind of dirt level. I liked Burma a lot. Then spent a year in Sumatra. I liked the people there immensely. Life was rather good there – better in some ways than in England. And I did form a resolve that I would come back to England and write a novel to tell people what it was like. I had written a few short novels in the army, but that was when I first had a serious purpose. The novels I wrote were in manuscript. I'd hand them round, just as I'd handed round my novels at school. Everyone read them, and they just got lost.

When I came back to England, the England I knew as a kid had gone. I got back here in '48; by that time it was a harsh, gritty, post-war world. My parents were moaning because they couldn't hear Kevin O'Connor or Suzette Tarry on the radio. They wanted life to go back to the 30s.

When we'd first gone to Devon, my father had bought a sub post office and grocers – a little corner shop, where he worked all hours for little reward. Then he got a rather better job in an outfitter's shop – it was what he knew how to do. But the fact was that the poor man never recovered from the family catastrophe. It overshadowed his life. We'd rattled around in the social strata considerably. And one thing that bloody Fen taught me was to be a snob. For instance, at school I would never admit that my father managed a sub post office. (Oh dear, it's humiliating to say it, but I never would admit that.) But then equally, in the army, I would never admit that I had been to public school. It's awful to be young. It's much better to be old and be able to say these things and think, 'Fuck it – people either like it or they don't.'

When I was demobbed I went back to Devon. There was only one family route open to me. My mother's family came from Peterborough. They were the nice branch of the family. They were all that the Aldiss's weren't! Two of my uncles, of whom I was very fond, were partners in a little architect's business. Some of the uglier chapels around Peterborough were built by my uncles; a lot of the sluice gates on the Nene were their work. I used to drive with them around the fenland and see that all the sluices were working, and all that sort of thing. After the war they were keen to have me in the business, but I could only see seven years of exams ahead, and, Christ, I didn't want to go back to schoolwork. About the only job you could do in North Devon was to be a ploughboy. I didn't see myself in that role. I suppose if you wanted to take a psycho-analytical view, you would say that I was really a displaced person – much more so than I realised. I didn't know what the hell I wanted, I didn't know where I was in society. And so I was an absolute natural for a writer.

Sidney Harper was an old fellow who had a second-hand bookshop in Barnstaple. I saw quite a bit of him. He was prepared to chat, in the way of most booksellers, and so I said to him one day, 'Why don't you give me a job?' He said, 'Look at the people working in the shop – they're all spinsters who can live on an oily rag.' But he had a bookseller friend in Oxford, a chap called Sanders, so he said, 'Go and see old Sanders – he always wants assistants.' Well, now I know why – Sanders was such a rogue no one would stay with him. Anyway, I got the train up to Oxford and came to see Sanders, and he said, 'When do you want to start?' I said, 'I'll start now if you like.' That very day I began sorting out books.

Oxford was actually the first English city I'd ever known. I was familiar with the back streets of Calcutta, Bombay, Hong Kong, Singapore, all those great, romantic, steaming, whoring cities. I was charmed by Oxford and thought it was marvellous. Sanders was a humorous man. He was very fond of Oxford. He knew Sidney Harper because he was a Barnstaple man too. He'd started life selling newspapers on Barnstaple station for W H Smith. He had a kind of fellow-feeling for me, slightly mitigated by the fact that he was the Artful Dodger grown up.

I kept writing my Sumatra novel, and it never worked – I didn't
know how to construct a novel. So I wrote short-stories. They're
easier. They take up less time. It was a great relief when I left
Sanders, because I used to work like a dog there till seven or eight
every night. I got a job in Parker's, part of Blackwell's empire, and
there everyone downed tools very promptly. That was much better.
Also one could do a lot more furtive reading in the shop.

Then I became lucky: we used to see the organ of the book trade,
entitled, with God knows what subtlety, *The Bookseller* , and I did
some articles for the editor. Then I wrote to him and said, 'What
you really want is a comic diary about day-to-day life in a bookshop,
and I'm sure I could do that.' So I produced a column about a
fictitious bookshop called Brightfount's. That column ran for two or
three years. Eventually Faber wrote to me and said, 'We're all your
fans. Would you consider turning your column into a book?' And so
I got into publishing in that underhand way. Since all booksellers
knew *The Brightfount Diary* and liked it, they stocked the book. It
was very funny to be working in Parker's when the book was
published. Parker's cautiously ordered twenty-five and put one in
the window. All the copies sold, so they grew bold and said, 'OK,
we'll have a whole window full.' They ordered two hundred and fifty
and sold them all. So from then on there was no stopping me.

1955 was a very happy year for me. My first story had been
published in 1953 in a science fiction magazine. In 1955 my first son,
Clive, was born; I won an *Observer* competition for a short-story;
and *Brightfount's* was published and was a modest success.

Although there's a sense in which I was dedicated to the idea of
writing, there was also a sense in which I regarded it as a lark. I
constructed my early stories while I was cooped up in the bookshop,
and then went home and wrote them out. What I loved about the
science fiction field was its tremendous diversity. One could do all
kinds of things with absolute liberty. There's a quality about those
early stories which I can recognise now as the mind at play. What
was lacking, I suppose was some kind of commitment. I had
commitment only to the written word – and that I've still got.
Although I now write about matters I regard as important, the most
important thing is the writing itself. Perhaps if you don't feel that,
you become a propagandist. That was the great falling-off of H. G.
Wells. At the beginning of his career, he was a writer of mythopoeic
power. Later on, he began to turn into a proselytiser, a

propagandist, a journalist – all things at which he was accomplished, but the writing suffered. And since I owe a debt to Wells, I've taken that example to heart.

I started well with two novels, *Non-Stop*, and then, shortly thereafter, *Hothouse*. Those two novels have been in print now for twenty-five years, and they retain a kind of joyous invention. But then I was in trouble: my first marriage was breaking down, and I lost my direction. I was living in one room and drinking a lot, and sort of enjoying life on one hand while suffering hell on the other. I was writing rather badly. I'd given up the bookshop. I waved it goodbye as soon as I could. My first novel was published when I was thirty, which some people regard as rather late. There were one or two falters along the way; then I got my personal affairs sorted out. I bought a little terraced house and there I wrote with increasing assurance: *Dark Light Years, Greybeard, Probability A*.

Dark Light Years was very important to me. It was the first book I wrote in anger instead of in a sort of enchantment with the written word. That was 1963 – the time when Dr John Lilley aired his theory that dolphins had the same brain/body ratio as human beings, and thus a similar kind of intelligence, and therefore one could communicate with them. Lilley's way of achieving his aim was to haul the dolphins out of their natural element, strap them to a laboratory bench, cut away the skin on their skull, and sink electrodes into their brain. This seemed to me so characteristic of the way that bloody mankind barges about the world that I had to find a way of satirising it in science fiction.

Dark Light Years is the only novel I've written in a month. I took another month correcting it. Something of the fervour with which I wrote it shows in its brisk, galloping pace. I spoilt it here and there with rather too easy jokes, but it remains a novel with a lot of bite. It was picked up later by an American critic who said it was the second best science fiction novel about the Vietnam war. When I read that I laughed and thought the man was out of his mind. But when I thought about it, he had a point. Science fiction has a strong metaphorical content. That's one of the reasons you write it. It's a way of holding up a mirror to the present day; if you read *Dark Light Years* in an American situation, unhappy with the Vietnam war, you immediately apply the metaphor to your own condition. I've had that experience with other books, where the metaphorical content has allowed the novel to slip easily into another culture and be read on a different level. For instance, *Non-Stop* which is about an interstellar voyage covering many generations, was translated into Polish a few years back, when it became the second quickest-selling science fiction novel ever published in Poland. The metaphorical content could be applied to the Polish situation – being incarcerated in a horrible machine and not knowing where it is going is a political as well as a technological experience. You only need one or two such instances to see that you've seized on something powerful. Unlike the ordinary, narrow, English novel, science fiction can speak to people everywhere. The realisation changes your mind. In a way *Greybeard* was part of the change of mind. I wrote several novels quite rapidly because I had no other responsibilities. I wrote *Report on Probability A* at that time. *Probability A* was regarded as extreme and no one would publish it until several years later.

In 1964 I bought a second-hand Land Rover, got a commission from Faber and permission from the Jugoslav authorities, and went with Margaret – now my wife – to Jugoslavia for six months, to produce a travel book. That was really educational; in many respects, Jugoslav society in 1964 was more open than people outside would suspect. You could ask what was going on and get a good grasp of things in a way that would be much more difficult in say, Italy. People were accessible, and would talk to you. Somehow, that dusty summer, there seemed to be a charge about the atmosphere, a magic: on the one hand Jugoslavia was on the wrong side of the political fence, and on the other hand here was this beautiful land, fought over for God knows how long.

We passed houses with big slogans painted across them: MISMO HRVATI – ('We're Croats': Don't kill us, we're not Italians); and, HOCIMO TITO I SAMO TITO – ('We want Tito and only Tito') – life insurance slogans. Everything was pared to the bone. There wasn't much to eat, but there was plenty of strong red wine to drink. It was very exciting, and as in the Far East, life was very simple – I wanted to get back to that. And indeed, back we did get, living in our Land Rover for six months like gypsies. But we had extraordinary freedom. We carried one letter from Belgrade typed in Cyrillic, growing more and more tattered, and it got us everywhere. We travelled right up to the north, to the Vojvodina and the border with Hungary, and right down to the south to the frontiers with Greece, Albania, Bulgaria. Jugoslavia's a wonderful country. The amount that I learned politically was enormous. The historical background was very interesting because Jugoslavia contains so many histories within its frontiers. I've benefited ever since from the Jugoslav trip. It gave me a reservoir of knowledge and history. Even in my latest novels, in Helliconia, often concealed, there are bits of early Serbian history, little bits of scenery that I've carried out of Montenegro. *Cities and Stones* was my only travel book – we then got married and had kids to bring up.

Jugoslavia made me impatient with science fiction, and I got rebellious. The whole Swinging 60's drug scene was developing. I wrote *Barefoot in the Head*, which is about Europe being wiped out by psychedelic drugs. We'd been doing a lot of travelling, buzzing around Europe – we were very free – and a lot of *Barefoot* began as travel notes I'd written at the time. Since it was about people who were wiped out on drugs, the novel was written as though in a kind of drug trance, so that it's got a special language (which critics insist on calling Joycean). Then *Report on Probability A* was published. Those two novels really put me at odds with the science fiction field – many readers just want 'more of the same', not experiment. They wanted me to go on doing *Non-Stop* and *Hothouse* for ever.

Probability A was much influenced by the new novel in France, by Robbe-Grillet, Michel Butor, and Marguerite Duras. I saw a way of escaping from the formal standards of the bourgeois novel (which standards apply on the whole to the ordinary science fiction novel). *Probability's* characters are referred to only by initials; they're hardly characters. There's no dénouement. There are none of the ordinary upholstered delights and comforts of the novel. At the end I went through the text, carefully deleting adverbs and adjectives. I missed a few, it's true – but spare writing was my objective. When you get to the end of a novel you remember the vision that was yours before you started writing; somehow some of it's evaporated, sometimes a rather large part of it. In the case of *Probability A*, I nearly achieved what I set out to do. But it was so limiting – basically I'm still the guy who started out in the dormitory telling stories. I can't resist telling a story. So I abandoned the nouveau roman approach. It was, for me, an experiment along the way – a very valuable one: it made me more aware of my capabilities. For once the critics were nicer than the readers. Normally critics are so shitty, while the readers will still enjoy, but on this occasion the critics applauded. *Probability A* has stayed in print ever since, despite the lambasting I got from my fans at the time.

I compounded my heresies with *Barefoot in the Head*, which requires more concentration than *Probability A*. I got abusive letters and hassles, and I thought, 'Well screw that – the world's bigger than science fiction. I can get along without SF.' When I was writing *Barefoot* I thought I was going mad doing all the psychedelic thing. So Margaret said, 'Take a rest from it. Do something else.' 'Good idea,' I thought, and so I wrote *Hand-Reared Boy*.

The Hand-Reared Boy didn't take long. It's a slender novel, full of feeling, and it hit certain nails on the head. Everyone in the late 60s was in a self-congratulatory mood, saying, 'Oh, God, we're so liberated. We can talk about sex, and do it any way we like.' But I thought, 'You don't have to dress up for masturbation, yet no one's got a good word for it – I'll write a novel about masturbation.' Happily, I have a good literary agent. He fought tooth and nail to persuade someone to publish *Hand-Reared Boy*. I think it went to fourteen publishers before it was finally accepted. It was immediately successful. So I thought I should turn to social satire – I'd put all I knew about writing science fiction into *Barefoot in the Head* and maybe I'd shot my bolt. I wrote two more 'Stubbs' books, one of which, thirty years late, was my Sumatra novel, *A Rude Awakening!* I was a bit disappointed afterwards – I don't think I did the reality justice. *A Soldier Erect*, which is about India and Burma, is much better. A grouchy old general was asked on the radio recently if he could name a war novel where the author had 'got it right'. He said, 'You should try Brian Aldiss's *A Soldier Erect*.' I felt very proud about that. You tend to think that such things get forgotten. The science fiction novels always live on, and there's always a new readership, but you're never sure about the other ones.

I decided that before I forgot my knowledge of the science fiction field I'd write a history of it. So I embarked on the book that became *Billion Year Spree*, which took me three years of concentrated work. That was very successful, thank God, and warmly received in the States. Of the multitudinous books discussed in *Spree*, to my mind the richest and most radical is Mary Shelley's *Frankenstein*, and in a way one of the most neglected. You have to paddle a long way up the Amazon before you find someone who hasn't heard of Frankenstein – and yet you have to go equally far up the Congo before you find someone who's actually read the book. People take it for granted. It is an extraordinary thing that this girl of eighteen, self-effacing Mary Shelley, should have written her beautiful novel under the shadow of the two poets, Byron and Shelley, on whom all the attention has been concentrated. At first the public believed Shelley had written it. I begin *Billion Year Spree* by saying that this is where science fiction began – with Mary Shelley's *Frankenstein*.

In the early 70s I gave up the literary editorship of *The Oxford Mail*. I'd been doing it for fourteen years: with having all the books to re-read for *Billion Year Spree*, the job was just too much, so I went in and said goodbye. That was the end of my association with any kind of office or institution, and it was difficult to adjust. Life was very pleasant at *The Oxford Mail*. People would go down and have a pint in the pub over the lunch hour – it was all very sociable. But I was determined to write, and that's what I did. I then wrote *Frankenstein Unbound*, and everyone said, 'Aldiss is back on form – he's writing a real science fiction novel again.'

Before we say goodbye to the 70's I'll mention *The Malacia Tapestry*, my favourite among my novels. I wanted a Utopia. Things were getting very dystopian and I felt that some sort of vision was needed. It should be possible to create, at least on paper, a better world – but I suppose I just wasn't built for it. The best kind of political organisation I could think of was the city state with an enlightened despot in charge. But my books were always about underdogs, and I realised that if you were an underdog in a city state it wouldn't be any more comfortable than anywhere else, enlightened despot notwithstanding. So I invented a magical state called Malacia, which is Italianate, I suppose, or Ragusan, and the novel slowly developed round it. I caught hepatitis at that time and was fairly ill. I was not moving about much; so the book has a kind of static quality, which I think is very satisfying in an artistic way. I designed the story like a tapestry, so that it is a series of still-lives rather than a continuous novel. It concerns the difficulty of being any kind of artist. The book's full of all kinds of rogues – historians, painters, musicians, actors and so on. Malacia is still in print and in fact it's just going to be re-issued in paperback with a different cover. An indifferent cover, I should say.

One has great difficulties over covers with publishers. Jonathan Cape are good. I based a lot of the Malacia story on etchings of G. B. Tiepolo. When I'd finished the manuscript it looked so long and boring that I photocopied some of his little etchings and shuffled them at random among the manuscript to cheer the reader up every

now and again. I also put one on top as a kind of cover. Tom
Maschler was very enthusiastic about *Malacia* and said he wanted to
use the Tiepolos in the book. He told me it was the first time that
Cape had published a novel with illustrations in the text. Cape also
used a Tiepolo for the cover. It's a marvellous cover – an etching of
three magicians burning a snake on an altar, with the title in brown.

When it came to the paperback, I happened to visit the publishers
just as they'd received the proof of their cover, and when I saw it I
said, 'Oh God, it's awful. What *is* this thing? It has absolutely no
relevance to the novel.' They said it was the artist's own
interpretation. It was preposterous. I've saved a copy for the black
museum. Eventually they devised an alternative. It featured a cock-
eyed beast. I said, 'This is horrible too. Why are you doing all this?
Why don't you do what Cape did and use a Tiepolo?' They said,
(one more palsied publishers' excuse), 'Well, you see, Brian, the
Tiepolo's only black-and-white and no one would think we'd spent
enough on it.' I said, 'Christ, give it to me – I'll colour it for you!'

The argument dragged on, and the art director phoned me irately
one day and said, 'Look, Brian, if you're going to make all this
difficulty we're going to have to do a plain typographical cover.'
'Great,' I said. 'Fantastic. The idea of the century! Do a plain
typographical cover!' In the end they even wriggled out of that and
inserted a little monster. So *Malacia* in paperback has been badly
treated, and now they've got a new cover which I suppose is better
– I daren't complain anymore. It's amazing how publishers seem not
to know their business. Cape are marvellous on the whole; some of
the others are intensely dim.

So much for the 70's. Before the 80's arrived, Aldiss got
ambitious, and decided he wanted to do something which would
reflect the world. Redeem it, perhaps. Who knows? So I started
work on *Helliconia*, which my dear wife is typing out upstairs at this
very moment. Seven years have passed while I've been exiled on
Helliconia. The idea of it being an allegory got lost as I went along,
advisedly. But in the third volume, *Helliconia Winter*, I return more
openly to the world situation as I see it. Perhaps that might be
regarded as an artistic blemish, but as things are at the moment, one
should, in however small a way, speak up. *Helliconia Winter* is
equated with a nuclear winter because we have those obscene
nuclear weapons hanging over us. It's an awful position that we've
got ourselves in through aggression or xenophobia or whatever it is

in mankind – something wrong in the head (just as I felt when I wrote *Dark Light Years*). So *Helliconia* is not pure story; it comes, at least in the last chapters, with a strong tonic of message. I've finished the final volume. That is to say, I've done four drafts, and I'm going through Margaret's fair copy, mucking it up again, still making the last, last changes.

Next year I may do an *Encyclopaedia of Helliconia* because I've coaxed so much good advice from scientists, historians and so on, that I would like to collect it into a volume. It should be interesting for students as well as general readers. Meanwhile I've got three other books that might materialise.

The way I work varies according to the book, or according to what I'm doing. Much of the time one is not actually writing a novel or a short-story – answering correspondence consumes so much time. Once, if I didn't feel like working I'd take a month off. In the 60s I took a more light-hearted view. Now, I am much more dedicated to writing and I work very hard. I don't often take days off. I work six days a week. At the moment I'm getting up at six in the morning. That's not the best way to go about things, but *Helliconia* has been an enormous sack to have on one's back.

You never wait on inspiration. You sit down and you write and you see what comes out. You free-associate or whatever you do. It's really a matter of always having something that you want to write about. So often, at the end of the day, I've exclaimed, 'I've had enough – I want to go to bed.' I get into bed and put my head down on the pillow and immediately there goes the next paragraph in glowing letters. I say, 'Oh God!' and I climb out of bed and crawl back to the typewriter. Another time, I'll tell the family, 'I've nearly got to the end of the novel, then we'll go away on holiday.' And the day after I've finished the novel, I remember a marvellous something which I must write before we leave. The precious gift of logorrhoea! But the fact is, I have a burning ambition to write a good novel.

I've never been too financially orientated, thank God. I've seen so many writers writing for money; if they don't make any money they haven't had any pleasure. Generally, when I'm writing a novel I'm longing to get back to it as soon as possible after breakfast. Occasionally you feel you're on the wrong track and then you feel estranged from your work. Then suddenly you can see it was a false note in that last chapter – or a character that was the wrong character. It also happens – this sounds naïve – that certain characters appear with whom a writer can do no wrong. You then have to amend what you intended and address yourself to changing your early sections to create a suitable place for those characters to live and move in.   ·

With *Helliconia*, It's the only time I've arranged a contract for a novel before writing it. To retain my independence I used to write my novel first and then submit it. But with an ambitious trilogy, more formal arrangements were necessary. Under the terms of the contract I had eighteen months to write each volume (running to about 170.000 words, and in the case of *Helliconia Summer* with about forty speaking parts). With the final novel, *Winter*, I couldn't operate on such a demanding timetable: I've taken two years. Someone wanted to commission a biography of H. G. Wells, but fiction is my métier. It's exhausting enough having done *Helliconia*. I must now convalesce a bit and write something modest. Three characters: two neighbours and a dog squabbling over a bicycle, that's my idea for my next novel.

I have been independent now, leading the lion's life or the Jackal's life, whichever it is, for twenty-five years. I have produced a novel just about every year, together with nine collections of stories and many edited anthologies. All writing is a matter of luck as well as skill. When I began to write science fiction, either no one had heard of it, or the novels they had heard of and enjoyed they decided were therefore not science fiction; so it didn't look like a promising mode to pursue. But I arrived as the tide was turning. I suppose, in this country at least, I helped it turn.

I set great store by my short stories. I've got a collection coming out at the end of this year, *Seasons in Flight*. They're not science fiction, and I don't think you would rank them as fantasy; nor are they everyday stories. They're fables. They have... tranquillity. It's a bit of a new departure. I was at a pub recently with a friend. He was holding forth about the merits of Kipling's stories. He then said to me, 'I was thinking I'd write a short-story.' And he leaned forward over the beer-stained bar and said, 'Have you ever tried your hand at a short-story, Brian?' With eight collections in print, I thought that was a bit *de trop*.

I don't really have a fixed position in society. Such rootlessness can be turned to advantage by a writer, and I believe that, as far as possible, I have turned it to an advantage. I've come to terms with that feeling of being disowned by my parents, but my position is that

of a satirist. There are a number of targets that you want to hit
without wanting them to go away. In fact a satirist is rather a
conservative creature in that respect. I don't really identify with the
working-classes (at one time I did). I don't really identify with the
middle-classes either, although that's how I would be categorised.
I'm madly impatient with the Labour Party at the moment, but I'm
a socialist with a small "s". I guess there are thousands of people like
that. I have a strong feeling for the East, the places where they don't
paper over the cracks, where life and death are visible on the streets
– perhaps because there is so much hypocrisy in English life.

I'm divided about Arts Council support. It seemed to me, when I
was on the Arts Council Panel, that there were grants going to
people who were absolute layabouts and not prepared to do anything
very much at all. The thing was that there was no accountability. If
they gave a chap £2,000 to get on with his next novel, shall we say
a novel about bull-fighting in Andorra, there was never a time when
they went back to him and said, 'What about your bull-fighting
novel, old chum – did you ever finish it?' That seemed to me to be
wrong. But it seems right that authors should be supported; that new
ones should be encouraged; that old ones – when their roof falls in
– should be given a grant. When you consider the amount of support
the other arts get, you realise that authors are left to rot. On the
other hand, no one owes you a living as a writer. You chose it. What
has the ordinary writer but his precious independence? Fame? – No.
Wealth? – No. Respect? – Scarcely.

One of the ways to support writers is to subsidise magazines; then
the market is there. The Arts Council was extremely good about
Mike Moorcock's *New Worlds* in the 60s. That got a fairly hefty
grant, and there's no doubt that the magazine did bring forth a lot
of good work. There was, for almost the one and only time, a living
market for British SF writers. Now we have a magazine called
Interzone; that has a grant, but it hasn't got the red corpuscles
Moorcock's magazine had.

Writing remains a hazardous, lonely trade, and will always be so,
with disappointment at the end of the trail for many. I enjoy the
independence it brings, and consider I have been lucky; but I have
never failed to write something every day throughout the last thirty
years, whatever was going on in the greater world outside my study.

* * *

When I was a kid in East Dereham, by some miracle – I cannot think
how it came into my hand – I read Zola's *Germinal*. I thought of it
just now when calling myself a socialist with a small "s". I owe that
to Zola. I thought *Germinal* was a marvellous book. I suppose I can
hardly have understood it – I was eight or nine at the time. But I'll
never forget the impact of reading *Germinal* for the old principle of
what they call, 'seeing how the other half lives'. Then I went on to
read *Earth*. I thought those were tremendous novels.

About the same time, I read *Vie de Bohème*, by Murger. I can't
think where that came from either. It's the novel on which *La
Bohème* is based. It seems curious to think of those books
circulating in East Dereham, but it was so. I loved *Vie de Bohème*
simply because it's about the free and easy, down at heel, immoral
life of the artist – which I've never quite managed to live. No one in
Vie de Bohème works in an outfitters. To think of all those lovely
Parisienne girls languishing in attics!

One hopes that one's books don't show their debts too nakedly,
but I'm sure you wouldn't have to go over mine with a magnifying
glass to see the influence of Hardy. That's one thing I owe to Virginia
Woolf. I don't much care for her novels, but I love her essays in *The
Common Reader*. Woolf introduced me to Thomas Hardy. Once I'd
read *The Mayor of Casterbridge*, I went back and read all of Hardy's
novels. I think he's an extraordinary author who produced at least
six brilliant novels that you would read at any time. His best novel
is *The Mayor of Casterbridge*, with its slow grinding of fate. It's very
powerfully done. *The Dynasts* is, in many respects, a kind of science
fiction play – an amazing drama of the Napoleonic wars with a
superstructure of the spirits and the Imminent Will who manipulates
human beings like puppets. It suggests that life is a series of
circumstances without ethical or moral implications. A very bleak
view of humanity. At the end, the possibility is offered that, like
humanity itself, the Immanent Will is evolving towards a more ethical
structure and will eventually form a bond of compassion in his
dealings with the human being. It's an extraordinary concept based
on Hardy's close interest in evolution.

One's reading also included a whole mass of books that would
roughly be categorised as crap. You get something from all such
books or you wouldn't read them. I certainly got something from
the novels of A J Cronin. They don't have anything to offer me now,
but when I was sixteen and seventeen, books like *Hatter's Castle*,

and *The Stars Look Down*, with their rather dark view of existence, had a great effect on me. I felt that I was living a very sheltered life and that here were books which told me something about how real people lived and suffered. I may not have projected our family as a happy one, although in many respects it was, but if there was suffering it was not allowed to emerge – it had to be suppressed. It's so much better, if you have to suffer, to be *able* to suffer – to suffer without artifice. That's vital. Some of my early books could be seen as a kind of vocalised agony. Barthes said that all any text can do is say, 'There is birth and there is life and there is death,' and in a sense I think that is true. I think that whatever you write, you must try and deliver the truth about life. I know writers who would say the reverse is true – that a novelist is paid to tell lies. I don't believe that. I think you're honour-bound to try and deliver the truth as you see it. Fortunately there are thousands of truths.

I love Aldous Huxley's novels, despite the preachments they contain. Huxley gives you a glimpse of the Garsington Manor type of life, and of the intellect. I was very pleased to see that Anthony Burgess, in his book *Ninety-Nine Novels* included three novels of Huxley's. Huxley is neglected, and Burgess allowed no one else three novels. My favourite is that cruel jest, *After Many a Summer*.

I liked D. M. Thomas's *The White Hotel*. I was a Booker Prize judge the year that *White Hotel* was up against Salman Rushdie's *Midnight's Children*; I still think that *The White Hotel* should have won. It's an ingenious knot-garden of writing, and despite the way it is segmented one does have a feeling by the end for the poor suffering woman, Anna. I appreciate, judging by Thomas's other novel, that he has difficulty in constructing a coherent novel pattern, but in *White Hotel* he transcends mere coherence. I like the sense that Freud, as one of the characters, will care for and help a single individual if he can. Ranged against him is the horrible Nazi killing-machine which has no feeling for the individual at all. I liked the sexiness in it, and the harshness and cruelty in it. It's a powerful and moving novel.

I thought Will Boyd's *A Good Man in Africa* was marvellously funny. God, you're so grateful for a funny novel. I think I'd have written more funny novels if it hadn't been for Kingsley Amis and *Lucky Jim*, which came out just as I was starting. The thought of being classified for twenty-five years as a second Kingsley Amis – Oh no, no! Boyd has tremendous force and éclat, and also is not afraid of being grim. *The Ice Cream War* is a good book, well coordinated, a splendid piece of writing which reduces war to the awful grim farce that war often is.

I liked Olaf Stapledon's two big novels, *Last and First Men*, and *Star Maker*. Stapledon reduces all the suffering on Earth to a distant perspective – you are looking at Earth through the wrong end of a pair of binoculars. His books have something that *The Dynasts* has – this idea of looking down a microscope and seeing mankind seething around at the bottom of the bucket.

George Orwell's writing was so good. One was grateful for his perpetual stream of criticism of society. He was a good man, and he wrote lucidly.

Any writer is under a debt to all previous writers, really. If you believe that civilisation is better than barbarism, however awful civilisation is, then literature is essential. Most of science fiction is about things breaking down and shows how fragile civilisation is. It's a very frail construct which has been under siege since time immemorial.

What you essentially derive from a book is the sense of a dialogue between you and the writer. There is, after all, an art of reading as well as an art of writing. Maybe it is already lost. Our teenagers have to be forced to put their noses in a book. The children of my first marriage were still of a reading generation. They had television, but they hadn't lost their heads in the set as kids have now. It's like the way people are losing the habit of reading a newspaper for news and taking one only to play bingo or whatever.

Literature is still the basis of our culture and I think will remain so. I can't really see that there's a better means of communication (but that's because I'm time orientated – perhaps another generation will think differently). There is nothing like the personal voice: that sense of intimacy which you have with an author. You don't get it anywhere else. It's rather like being educated by a wise man, an ideal tutor, who is with you most of the time and will converse with you. That's a different thing from having facts stuffed into you and being unable to respond as is the case with television. Good literature evokes a response that television doesn't. In a way I hate saying this because I also know how much I get from television. I wouldn't be without it, as I wouldn't be without the cinema. What one hopes is that all these arts will flourish together. In the last eight years the standard of the British novel seems to have improved and become more exciting. I wouldn't despair about the state of the novel: but I do despair about the state of the reader.

Oxford, July 1984

NIGEL GRAY'S COMMENT.

Brian Aldiss is a natural raconteur (a quality less common than one might expect among novelists). Physically, a big man, he is friendly, good-humoured and entertaining. I first read him in *The Hand-Reared Boy*, and wondered if this brave and amusing man was the same Brian Aldiss as the world-famous SF author. Here he was, on the one hand, introducing into the British novel an unmentionable area of human life which, though universal, remained far from respectable, while on the other, doing more to make science fiction 'respectable' than any other British writer.

I was first introduced to Brian by the actor and theatre director extraordinaire, Ken Campbell. I was acting in Ken's amazing, twelve-hour science fiction extravaganza, *Illuminatus*. Brian not only had the stamina to sit through the production, from 10 o'clock one Sunday morning till 1.00 am the following day, in a dusty old Liverpool warehouse, but remained a delightful and encouraging companion (during a succession of intervals in a nearby drinking cellar) to the bitter end.

By chance, the last time I saw him was when he appeared with Ken in a performance of his own stories. The evening was memorable partly because Ken arrived almost too drunk to stand up (fortunately he was required to be, for the most part, seated). A lesser man than Brian might have been angered or outraged at the rather bizarre execution of his text that followed, but Brian remained as unruffled, tolerant and genial as always. 'He's got a new play opening in a few weeks,' Brian told me. 'He's under a lot of stress.'

Since my interview with Brian, *Helliconia Winter* has been

published. And after Brian's eight Helliconia years he felt a need for his fictional reservoirs to refill. The sustained effort had left him physically as well as imaginatively drained, so he turned to an ambitious non-fiction scheme. *Billion Year Spree*, published in 1972, had proved controversial and had made him some enemies. Undeterred, he resolved to revise it and bring it up to date. The SF field had grown and changed immensely in the intervening years, and to handle the formidable amount of work he teamed up with David Wingrove.

Trillion Year Spree was published in 1986 by Gollancz. He moved to Gollancz from Jonathan Cape after publication of the *Helliconia* novels mainly because of their lack of support for the *Helliconia Encyclopaedia* project (something he and David Wingrove had been striving vainly to launch for a number of years).

Meanwhile, on his travels, Brian had met a small publisher starting up business in Seattle, Serconia Press. They published two collections of essays on travel and literature, one of which included *The Glass Forest*, a brief autobiography. This autobiography, Brian came to believe, was a mistaken interpretation of his life. He was guided to this understanding by a remarkable dream, and by coming across a French saying which claims that we are neither so happy nor so miserable as we think we are.

This led him into retrospective waters, in which he is still swimming. On New Year's Day 1987 he began a complex novel, *Forgotten Life*, which tells of the relationship between two brothers, one dead, and the marriage relationship of the living brother. Now, as I write, in February 1988, it is nearing completion. And a new SF novel is already in the planning stage.

Brian has worked hard on behalf of all professional writers through his long involvement with the Society of Authors and the Arts Council Literature Panel. He has received many honours for his work including the following: Hugo Award, '62; Nebula Award, '65; Ditmar Award, '70; BSFA Awards, '72, '74, '83; James Blish Award, '77; Prix Jules Verne, '77; John W Campbell Memorial Award, '83.

Brian Aldiss was born in East Dereham, Norfolk, on August 18th 1925.

Brian Aldiss's Book Choice:

Germinal Emile Zola
Earth Emile Zola
La Vie de Bohème
   Henry Murger
The Mayor of Casterbridge
   Thomas Hardy
The Dynasts Thomas Hardy
Hatter's Castle A. J. Cronin
The Stars Look Down
   A. J. Cronin

After Many a Summer
   Aldous Huxley
The White Hotel D. M. Thomas
A Good Man in Africa
   William Boyd
The Ice Cream War William Boyd
First and Last Men Olaf Stapledon
Star Maker Olaf Stapledon
Collected Essays George Orwell

Books by Brian Aldiss:

Fiction:

The Brightfount Diaries
Non-Stop
The Male Response
The Interpreter
The Primal Urge
Hothouse
Dark Light Years
Greybeard
Earthworks
The Saliva Tree
An Age
Report on Probability A
Barefoot In the Head
The Hand-Reared Boy
A Soldier Erect

Frankenstein Unbound
The Eighty Minute Hour
The Malacia Tapestry
Brothers of the Head
A Rude Awakening
Enemies Of The System
Life In The West
Moreau's Other Island
Helliconia Spring
Helliconia Summer
Helliconia Winter
Ruins
Cracken at Critical
Forgotten Life

Short story collections:

A Brian Aldiss Omnibus	*Intangibles Inc.*
Brian Aldiss Omnibus 2	*The Moment of Eclipse*
Space Time And Nathaniel	*Comic Inferno*
The Canopy of Time	*Last Orders*
The Airs of Earth	*New Arrivals, Old Encounters*
Best SF Stories of	
Brian W. Aldiss	

Non-fiction:

Cities and Stone:	*The pale Shadow of Science*
A Traveller's Jugoslavia	*And the Lurid Glare of the Comet*
Billion Year Spree:	*Science Fiction Art*
A History of Science Fiction	*This World and Nearer Ones*
Trillion Year Spree	
(with David Wingrove)	

Poetry:

Pile (a poem)	*Farewell to a Child (Poems)*

Chapter Two
PAUL BAILEY

I come from a working-class, South London family. My father was a road-sweeper and dustman. My mother worked in service all her life – until she was well into her late seventies in fact. Doing a day's work was the most important thing in her life. My father was much older than my mother (she was his second wife). It was very odd having a father who had fought in the First World War (about which he never spoke). I felt very self-conscious as a boy because all the other boys in the school had youngish-looking parents and I had a very old father. He died when I was eleven. It was he who encouraged me to read, strangely enough. He used to read to me from *Nicholas Nickleby*. No other books – just that one. I don't know where he'd got the copy from. He didn't read it as a sequence; he just read funny bits out of it. Otherwise there were no books in our family. Most of the books that I had as a child were things passed on to my mother from people she worked for. That's how I came to read *Alice in Wonderland* and things like that. Otherwise it was just *The Dandy* and *The Beano* and those sort of things. My father read *The Daily Herald*. Apart from that I can't remember him reading anything. It was the radio generation. (Television was in its infancy – and we couldn't have afforded one anyway.) It wasn't until I went to my second school (a grammar school which later became a secondary modern) that I started reading seriously. I was encouraged by the English master to read all sorts of things outside what we were reading at school. Listening to classic books enacted on the radio was a wonderful encouragement to read too. When we did Shakespeare at school, saying all that wonderful language, that gave me a kick; that kind of language still does give me a kick. It's like great music to me, and when I'm really in the doldrums I still pick up poetry rather than anything else – although I realise that the novel is the great art form.

I was the afterthought of the family. My mother had me after what she thought was the change of life. My brother was already grown

up by the time I was a small boy. It was my dad I spoke to more as
a child. We used to go for long walks together. It was he who took
me to the zoo and places like that. We were a staunchly socialist
family – my father hated Conservatives. He hated Churchill too (it
was a working-class attitude of that period, certainly in South
London – unlike the kind of adulation with which Churchill is now
talked about); he saw Churchill as a warmonger. My mother was a
bit of a snob because she worked in high-class service. My father
used to send her up about the nobs and toffs she worked for.

My dad had two children by his first marriage. One of them
attended his funeral. It's very odd to suddenly meet your half-
brother who's fifty when you're eleven; I've never seen him since. I
think my father probably was an intelligent man: the two children
by his first marriage were exceptionally intelligent and went on and
did very well. I don't know anything about his early life. He came
back from the First World War and found that his wife was having
an affair with another man so they divorced. With my mother it was
a sort of closed subject, so there was a great area of mystery about
him. In fact I'm now trying to write about it. I've invented a father
who lives to be ninety-seven. I know what it's like to be without a
parent – I'm now trying to imagine what it would be like to be cursed
with a parent who goes on and on forever and just refuses to die.

After my father's death it was perpetual warfare with my mother
to do what I wanted. She was going out to work and during the long
summer holidays I was plonked on an elderly Scottish couple. I think
this is where my (some people say, morbid) interest in old age comes
from. When I came to write about old people I didn't ever see them
as a sort of separate species – as a child I'd been surrounded by old
people.

My brother and my sister have been very much content to do as
my mother said: 'Don't think above your own immediate horizons.'
We were told this as kids and I fought with her ferociously about it.
When I went to the grammar school, which was a marvellous school,
I was encouraged to act. I was in the school play every year, always
played the lead, and by the age of thirteen I'd developed an ambition
to become an actor. At the age of fifteen, before I'd left school, I'd
got a scholarship to go to a drama school. I fucked up all my
academic work in the last three years of school, almost deliberately
actually, because I had this appalling confidence that I was going to
be a very successful Shakespearean actor. And because of this

ambition to go to drama school I had to spend a great deal of energy
fighting my mother. She thought actors were disgusting creatures:
rather poncey, and sexually ambiguous: and all that horrified her.
My brother used to put a heavy hand on me and say, 'You don't
want to do *that* for a living.' (I can truthfully say that my brother and
I really loathed each other.) I used to say, 'I'm *going* to do it – I
don't care what you say.'

I liked poetry. I started with Keats, Wordsworth, very much the
Romantic things, and I used to learn Shakespeare off by heart out
of sheer pleasure. I went to the sort of school where the English
master would encourage you to learn a poem a day. I did that for
years actually, even when I was an actor, so now I've got a huge
catalogue of poems in my head. We lived in the upstairs of a terraced
house in Battersea. The woman who lived downstairs used to take
the piss out of me; it was odd for a fifteen year old boy to be spouting
Shakespeare. I used to get sent up rotten, and I had a nickname
which was 'Bleedin' Macbeth'. I don't know where that interest came
from. My mother's side of the family were all plodding, country
people. They didn't have any interest in anything remotely literary
or artistic. I'm still looked on as the peculiar one in the family,
although when I got published it made a slight difference. But until
I got my name in the papers (and I was thirty then) they didn't take
me seriously. I was always asked, 'When are you going to get a
proper job?' My mother's stopped saying it now, partly because she's
so old. When I changed from acting to writing it was just one evil
that followed another, and this was an even more inexplicable one.
'Are you still writing that book?' People can't understand that you
seem to be happy to spend three years of your life writing the same
book. My family don't understand it; and so when you're in the
middle of something you sometimes begin to think, 'Christ! I'm
wasting my time – this is getting nowhere.'

There were two other boys in the school I went to with whom I
was extremely sympathetic. There was one boy there who was
amazingly well-read. I have never met anyone so intelligent. He
came from a broken home, and he was one of those manic readers
– he was never without a book. I would carry a book around, but
he was never without one, ever; and he was reading *Crime and
Punishment* and stuff like that at fourteen. I didn't get round to
reading that till I was in my twenties. And there was a Jewish boy:
one forgets the kind of casual anti-semitism that went on, even

amongst working-class people – it still persists. He'd somehow built
up a resistance to it. He was extremely musical and I used to go to
concerts with him.

I wasn't happy about my homosexuality. I'm not one of those
people who took to it like a duck to water. I felt immensely guilty
– for many years actually; society makes you feel guilty. I was
interested in sport. I played cricket and things at school, not terribly
well, but I wasn't a total aesthete locking myself off in an ivory tower
or anything. When I was in my teens I developed a passion for tennis
and went to Wimbledon every year. We didn't have tennis courts at
school. I would happily have played tennis had we had the facilities,
but it was considered a slightly upper-crust game. (And still is, which
is probably why we've never had any great tennis players in this
country.) I went on having friendships with girls – trying to get there.
And then, when I was in my twenties, I experienced a great moment
of truth. I'd thrown myself onto the bed with a woman, with me
simulating passion, and she said, 'You're not really interested in this,
are you?' And I said 'No.'

Having been gay in that time, it's odd to see how young gays now
behave and the comparative freedom they've got. (Though we're
entering a dark age again, I think, with Mrs T. The only good thing
about these recent revelations about 'agents provocateurs' is that it
happened to a Tory: it's coming into her own home as it were.) But
it's very odd to remember the kind of hatred that used to be
expressed. Kingsley Amis uses the word 'queers' in his new novel
(he also uses 'Jewboys'), and it brings back to you the moral attitudes
of the 50s. There was the difficulty of meeting people in those days
and all that. I don't want to sound self-pitying about it – I had a very
happy time in my twenties and thirties – but there are parents now,
you see them on television programmes, who seem to be quite
adjusted to the fact, whereas I couldn't tell my mother. She
obviously guessed eventually – she would have been absolutely pig-
ignorant if she hadn't. And anyway, when I was in my teens I
thinking that the magic day would come when I wasn't going to be
like this any more. I'd read about people who had crushes at school
and you think you're going to grow out of it. There is a theory that
gay people are adolescent in some way – but having met so many
heterosexuals who are retarded I don't feel any qualms about that
any more.

The theatre, of course, is a great refuge of homosexuals. But all

my ambition to become an actor faded as soon as I became one. It
was most peculiar. I went to drama school when I was sixteen, and
I lingered in the profession for about eight years. I started writing
plays because a lot of the stuff I was in was such crap. When you're
in television serials, actors often change the lines. You say, in
rehearsals, 'This is unspeakable – nobody can say this,' and you find
yourself re-writing it. And that's how I think it began. I wrote a play
when I was nineteen. George Devine at The Royal Court
encouraged me. Two years after I left drama school I got a big part
in a new play by Anne Jellicoe, called *The Sport of My Mad Mother*,
at the Royal Court, and that was quite exciting. After that it was
downhill all the way. I walked on at Stratford, and I had some very
good understudy parts, but although all the other people who were
understudying got the chance to go on, I never did. I didn't get big
parts – that was part of the disillusion. Also I saw actors at close
quarters: I saw their vanity; their lack of interest – I didn't enjoy
being stuck amongst them all day. Being at Stratford was the most
miserable year of my life. There were only two people in the entire
company who you could have a conversation with about books or
politics or anything. I was writing rather bad poems then; I've
destroyed all of them.

I wasn't as good an actor as I wanted to be. I wasn't getting to
play Shakespeare, and I was bored sitting around in Scouts' halls
waiting to say my ten lines. It suddenly didn't strike me as being
what I wanted to do. I did various telly things, and I was amazingly
miscast. I was in a television series of Shakespeare things called *The
Spread of the Eagle – the Roman Plays*, and I got a mention from
dear old Maurice Richardson who used to be the TV critic of *The
Observer*, and who was a wonderful wit . He said of my performance
as the soothsayer in *Anthony and Cleopatra* that I was 'the worst
soothsayer in living memory'; so then I thought, 'The time has
come!' But my very last performance was in a *Z Cars*. A very nice
man, now alas dead, knew I was out of work and rang up out of the
blue and said, 'You don't feel like playing a Liverpool thug, do you?'
and I said, 'Well, not terribly,' And he said, 'Well I can't get anyone
else at such short notice – will you do it?' So I did it, and I was
terrible, truly awful. For one thing, though I'm quite good at accents,
I couldn't get the Liverpool one; it just kept going – I ended up doing
Birmingham. I was taken to one side by one of the cast and given a
lecture on how to act, and my eyes glazed over, and I knew that

when this film was finished, that was it. And it was. That was the very last one; I never did it again. I did get asked a couple of times and I said no. I went and worked in Harrods as a shop assistant, and I started to write seriously.

I had a thirty-minute radio play put on. I joined a writer's group at the Royal Court. I went to a couple of sessions where we read out our stuff, and we were all massacring each other, and I didn't like it. I was a coward. I needed to do it alone and find my own confidence. Having been an actor I was then convinced I was going to be a playwright; but that was soon knocked out of me. The things that I was interested in were not the great dramatic moments, they were the things that people *didn't* say. I somehow avoided all the big dramatic scenes. I started *At the Jerusalem* as a play, and then my agent said, 'I think you really ought to write it as a novel.' It was wonderful advice. I just looked at what I'd been writing and I thought, 'She's dead right.' But it was through the theatre in fact that my first book got published. A director called Casper Wrede had been talking to Tom Maschler (who was then an editor at Cape; he's now the boss). Casper knew I was writing a novel and must have sung my praises because I suddenly got a letter asking me to send something in. I write in longhand, but I typed the first seventy pages and sent it. Two weeks later I got a letter saying, 'Finish this and we will publish it.' And they paid me to finish it – not very much money, but they paid me. This response from Maschler was the most wonderful thing that had ever happened to me. What I was doing with my life suddenly made some kind of sense. I was able to take this letter to Harrods' library where I was working and show it to the people I was working with: 'Look, I'm going to be published.' It doesn't happen like that very often.

I was attracted to drama because I liked 'being' someone else. That feeling was transferred from acting to writing. One of the things I like doing as a writer is trying to 'be' other people. I'm not an autobiographical writer, though I do use bits of my past life – everybody does. *At the Jerusalem* is all about old women. I was determined that the first thing I got into print wouldn't be autobiographical. I wanted to get inside the characters of these old women. I'm actually bringing the home back into this new novel I'm working on now in order to destroy it: I'm having it demolished. I'm attached to that novel because it was my first one. I also think I did get inside the characters of these women, and I hope I've made them as awful and as pleasant and all the various things, that people are. I didn't want to make Mrs Gadny a plaster saint surrounded by a lot of ghouls and demons, and I didn't want the home to be a nasty place. But old age is a terrible trap to write about because of all the sentimental pitfalls you can fall into. I wanted the book to be comic, and I did like those critics who said that the book was essentially a comedy with sad undertones. I think, had I written it the age I am now, I probably wouldn't have made it quite as naturalistic as I did then. I did enjoy writing the dialogue and I enjoyed playing about with conversation – people not hearing each other and all that.

The book I'm most fond of is the second one, *Trespasses*. It was much more painful to write than *At the Jerusalem*. It wasn't autobiographical, although it's got a first person narrative. It was experimental in a sense. It was written by a man going through a traumatic time in a home that he put himself in of his own volition, and he was trying to write himself out of his gloom; his wife has committed suicide and he is blaming himself for various things. It goes back and forth in time all the while. I didn't want to confuse the reader, but I wanted the reader to be constantly jogged into seeing what this man was trying to do. I started it, and abandoned it, and started again. I think the novel I'm writing now has some of the same obsessions in it. You have to write four or five books to realise what your obsessions are.

My third book was called *A Distant Likeness*, and this was again rather experimental. I pared it to the bone: in fact I think I pared it far too close to the bone at times. I was trying to get into the brain of a policeman – a species I don't understand, frankly. I wanted to imagine what it would be like to be a man on the murder squad. I'd met a policeman who'd come to quiz me about a car accident I'd witnessed, and I found him a fairly disturbing person. He confessed over a glass of whisky that he'd had a breakdown because he'd been on the vice squad. The things that he described seemed to me things that most people wouldn't wince at, but somehow a kind of rigid and unstoppable puritanism in his nature had made him horrified by these things. And he told me, 'Of course, it's only the special boys who're allowed on the murder squad.' And I said, 'What's special about them?' And he said, 'They're hard.' And he told me how some of them are thrown in at the deep end, and they're made to look at horribly mutilated bodies, and if they can stand to look at these sights then they're going to be on the murder squad. If you faint

away, obviously you're not. The book is a curiously chilly work, I
see now. I was unhappy while I was writing it because I was trying
to 'be' this unpleasant man. People who don't write novels don't
understand that you sometimes deliberately choose to 'live with'
people that you wouldn't cross the road to meet. There's a
monstrously unpleasant man in this new book – though I quite enjoy
writing him because I'm making him slightly comic. I think there are
comic lines in all my books. I'm very English in that sense: I believe
in a fair measure of laughter. I'm attached to *A Distant Likeness*
because of an old man in it, a recluse, the father of the murderer,
who's refusing to leave his home. I enjoyed 'being' him while I was
writing him.

The next book I wrote was *Peter Smart's Confessions*. This is the
closest I've ever been to autobiography, and it's the one book of
mine that I really dislike, even though it's had some success and
some people think it's funny. The running gag through that is a man
who's trying to kill himself and never succeeds. The idea came from
somebody I knew at drama school who was constantly trying to kill
himself and thinking up wonderfully impracticable ways to do it:
tying several ties together, making a noose, and then jumping from
a banister, and putting his back out for weeks so he was walking
around with sticks. I found that funny, and we used to say, 'Failed
again, Colin?' I used that as a starting point; and the book is about
a man who is a bad actor. There's a monstrous mother in it who one
or two think is a revenge on my own mother – but it wasn't. I came
to rather admire my mother in many ways. In a way, this woman is
caricatured; she never calls the boy by his name, she calls him 'you'
all the time, and she's a classic put-downer. There's a lot about acting
Shakespeare in it. There's a trendy production of *Hamlet* in which
Hamlet's misery is placed psychologically to congenital syphilis. In
the 60s particularly, there was this thing of finding out what
Shakespeare really meant in the plays, which led to some of the
wilder manifestations of Shakespearean direction. People outside
the theatre never know the madness that actors have to listen to from
certain directors. So I had this production of *Hamlet* with the hero
trying to play him as a victim of congenital syphilis and saying to the
director, 'How do you do it? Do you scratch yourself a lot?' A lot
of things in the book are based on my experiences: I was in dotty
productions of Shakespeare (just carrying spears and things) and so
on, but the book is too autobiographical for my taste. I don't like it

for that reason.

The next book was *Old Soldiers* which is one I'm very close to. I wrote it in about three months, having thought about it for three years. It began in very strange circumstances: I was in hospital (I had some sort of anaemic condition) and while I was lying there having blood put into me, an old man came over and started talking to me. He was talking about this person: 'he...' and I wondered who this 'he' was, and it suddenly dawned on me that he was talking about himself in the third person. I thought, 'This is most peculiar.' And then I got the idea of a man that is four different people (he started off as six and I cut it down). *Old Soldiers* is about two old men meeting in London and one of them is really four people: he's himself and three people he's chosen to impersonate. It's to do with this play-acting thing. That's something which runs through all my books: in every single one, I realise, there's somebody who's giving a performance of being himself or herself. I think this is a reflection of my love of Dickens, my favourite novelist. (I don't necessarily consider him the greatest, but he's the one who means most to me.) There are characters throughout his books who are giving a performance of something or other.

The last thing I wrote – which was commissioned – was *An English Madam*, a study of the brothel in Streatham run by Cynthia Payne. She and I got on terribly well. She liked the fact that I wasn't shocked by any of the sexual things that she talked about, and I didn't express any kind of loathing of the things that she has to cater for. In fact my attitude was one of bemusement more than anything. There were times when I used to sit listening to her when I thought, 'I might have invented you.' She is like a character from one of my books. She performs. She has to perform. A brothel is a place where people meet to put on a show. And I liked the idea of somebody catering for old men, and having an age limit. If you're forty you're considered very youthful, and you've got to prove that you're a decrepit forty before she lets you in. If you're forty and still very sexually active, she doesn't want you. She likes a place where the old men feel puffed out after a go upstairs, and come down and need a cup of bovril or poached eggs on toast to get them well again. All that, I found wonderfully funny. And I liked her. She's still a friend. I space out the intervals when I see her because she's so very exhausting. And she only talks about sex. She's not interested in anything else. It gets a bit wearing after about two hours listening to

somebody talking about nothing but fucking in its various forms. At
first it was wonderfully funny to hear about bank managers who like
being tied up and covered in mud. A couple of weeks ago a letter
came marked, 'Please forward to Miss Payne'. When I spoke to her
on the telephone I asked what was in the letter. She said, 'Oh, Paul,
I can't cater for this man.' I said, 'What does he want?' She said,
'He wants to be dressed up as a baby – and he's sixty-two.' He'd sent
her several photographs of himself dressed as a baby, in a pram,
holding a rattle. I said, 'Why don't you want to cater for his taste?'
and it dawned on me the moment I asked the question. I said, 'Does
he want his nappies changed?' And she said, 'He didn't say it, but
that's obviously what he wants.'

Her house was Dickensian in a way. It was like a time warp: these
old men going back to their childhoods. The girls were variously
dressed as maids and things; tweenies were favourite (undermaids
between stairs). And there were several men who liked dressing up
as women there. When one man, a terribly pompous and serious
BBC producer discovered I was writing the book, he said, 'This is
disgusting. We don't want this written about.' Cynthia said to me,
'What was he saying to you?' I told her he'd said it was disgusting.
She said, 'I'll show you a picture of him.' And she produced a picture
of the same man dressed as a tweeny, having 'her' bottom smacked
by a client acting the part of a butler. I thought, when I was writing
the book, I was going slightly barmy. One of the people in it is a
very nice man who likes doing the housework for Cynthia in the
nude. He said, in all seriousness, 'Paul won't be able to appreciate
me unless he sees me at work in the nude.' He wouldn't let me
interview him dressed because it wasn't the 'real' him; this was the
essential man. And so I followed him from room to room while he
was dusting and polishing, and he brought me tea and biscuits, and
every so often Cynthia would come in with a whip and she'd say,
'Don't cut them bleeding corners. Come on! What're you doing?'
And she'd wink at me and go out. And then we'd carry on with the
interview. Writing that book was an experience I wouldn't want to
repeat. I don't think I ever want to write again about anybody alive
because of the problems involved.

About five years ago I was commissioned to do a biography of
Henry Green which I've got to finish sometime; but there's so little
material I'm stalling for time. But as the years go by an interest in
him is developing, especially in America. I hope finally to produce

a book that will do him some kind of justice because I think he is
the most underrated English writer of the century. And he's one
who's had a great effect on me. I think three of his books are
masterpieces: *Loving, Living*; and *Caught*. John Updyke considers
him the greatest English novelist of his time. And so does Eudora
Welty. It's interesting that two very different American writers think
so highly of him. The reason they like him is because he disappears
from his books, and that's what I like about him: you can't place
him as a writer – it's only the characters who register with you. I like
those writers who somehow do a disappearing act; the lives of the
people they're writing about seem more important than they
themselves. You just cannot tell from one Green novel to another
what kind of man he is. He's not there. Nabokov was a great admirer
too. Nabokov wanted to meet him on one of the rare times he came
to London towards the end of his life. Green was by this time getting
on, and continually drunk (the tragedy is that he didn't write for the
last twelve years of his life – he just drank gin till it killed him), and
he took the line that Nabokov had published a filthy book: *Lolita*
(than which there is nothing less filthy). He wouldn't meet him,
which is a great pity. Green's real name was Yorke. He was one of
those unliterary writers – a kind I'm rather fond of. He was more
interested in football, and he liked going into pubs. He was an
aristocrat, but you'd never have known it. He liked sitting in the
public bar behind a newspaper, and he was slightly deaf. His
deafness got worse obviously towards the end of his life. I think that
was one of the things that made him such a strange writer: he liked
listening to conversations, and deaf people often get hold of the
wrong end of the stick, or they isolate certain phrases; and when you
read his dialogue you realise it's not naturalistic – it's just that one
bit removed, but it's more real because of that. It's the same thing
Dickens has – that slightly larger than life thing, which is something
that I like, something that I try to do.

I'm still in the thick of the new novel. It's been going on for ever.
I've been on it now for five years. It's called *Gabriel's Lament*. I
can't write unless I've got a title. I was amused to find that Muriel
Spark has the same problem. She says half the battle of writing a
book is getting the title. There's a long middle section set in
America. I got one of those bicentennial fellowships they gave in
1976 (five English artists went over to America and five Americans
came over here). I chose to go to the Mid-West. They ended up

sending me to Fargo, North Dakota, which is just on the border with
Minnesota. So I've made up a town in Minnesota which I've called
Sorg. It's the Norwegian for 'sorrow'. Some of the towns' names in
America are wonderfully strange. There are towns called
Intercourse, and Paradise. A local joke is that to get to Paradise you
go through Intercourse. And there is a town in Minnesota called
Climax. There is a famous newspaper headline (which may be
apocryphal) which goes: 'Intercourse woman dies in Climax.' So the
middle part of this book is set in Minnesota. There's a cast of
thousands. I've tended to write 'slim vols', but as the great David
Vine said about Jimmy Connors on one memorable occasion (one
of my favourite lines in a tennis commentary): 'Will Jimbo pull out
the big one?' I'm hoping to pull out the big one. It's a saga. It's one
of those books where I keep thinking I've got the end in sight, and
then I bring in more characters. There's nobody directly from my
past, but I've used my experience of working in shops: doing awful
jobs to earn next week's rent. This man does actually write a book.
He writes a book about itinerant preachers. In it this preacher I've
made up descends on London in 1870 and disappears, and dies in
the upstairs room of a workhouse which is later changed into a home
called 'The Jerusalem'. I'm bringing my career round in a full circle
(just in case I die this year). My central character works as a porter
in 'The Jerusalem', which also means that I'm bringing in, in a minor
way, some of the characters from the first novel, and showing them
from the young man's point of view (which is different from the way
I saw them in the novel). It's quite nice reviving them and then
killing them off again. It's a pretty ambitious book for me. With this
book I feel I've got the design in which to say everything I've been
trying to say for years. There've been pages when I feel, 'This is
absolutely right.' There are pages that it takes you forever to write:
days when you're trying to get somebody through a door, and all
that: but you suddenly get up one morning and start writing and you
do a paragraph and you think, 'Yes, that's something I haven't
managed to say before,' or, 'I've tried to say it but I've never quite
put it like that.' It's a wonderful feeling. It doesn't come very often,
but it's happening now with this book. I started actually writing this
book two years ago, but I was thinking about it and changing it and
everything for about three years before that. I got the idea in
America. It came to me one night in the summer, sitting in a friend's
house. They'd come to England, and I was living alone in their

house. The starting point was that I suddenly heard myself talking to my father. I wasn't drunk or anything.

I saw my dad the night before he died, and I knew he was dying because he was talking to my maternal grandmother – a woman he hated, and he was rowing with her in his sleep. I thought, 'This is very odd.' I'd heard that people talk wildly when they're dying, and that they often talk to people who have been dead or out of their lives for a long time. When he died I didn't cry or anything. I didn't feel anything, except a strange sense that he wasn't going to be there any more. And then, years later, it caught up with me and I felt a terrible sadness about it. I suppose I romanticised him because I knew so little about him. This book is turning that kind of loss on its head: it's about a different kind of loss.

I write for my own pleasure. But I like to think there's an ideal reader: somebody who will pick up the allusions that I'm putting in, who will understand all those nuances, and things like that. I don't think of an audience. The actress Edith Evans always maintained that only bad actors courted and wooed the audience. She studiously ignored the audience, which was why she was happy to play to one person. And Ivy Compton Burnett used to say that if she only had twenty readers who liked what she was doing she was happy. I like to feel that there are certain people who read me and who like what I write. Also you know that there are people that dislike your work. I like to know why they dislike it – it's good to know your enemies at times. There never has been a book that everybody thinks is wonderful; and the reasons why people think a book is wonderful or think it's awful are sometimes quite fascinating.

When I'm writing a novel I try and get something done every day, not always successfully. If a book is not making me happy I just abandon it. I write very slowly and I write in pencil, on the right-hand page only, leaving the left-hand side for afterthoughts, and I rub out a lot. I don't go through several drafts. The odd sentence will be rewritten when I type it out, but somehow, because of the snail-like pace at which I write, when I've rubbed out sufficiently, I've gone through the drafts. My books are very short, but they have taken a long time to write (except for *Old Soldiers* – but then I think I'd done all the work in my head first, so the mere writing of it was the least difficult thing. The difficult business was thinking it out, shaping it in my mind first). Some people go through several drafts. Some people write terribly quickly. Some people write a lot of

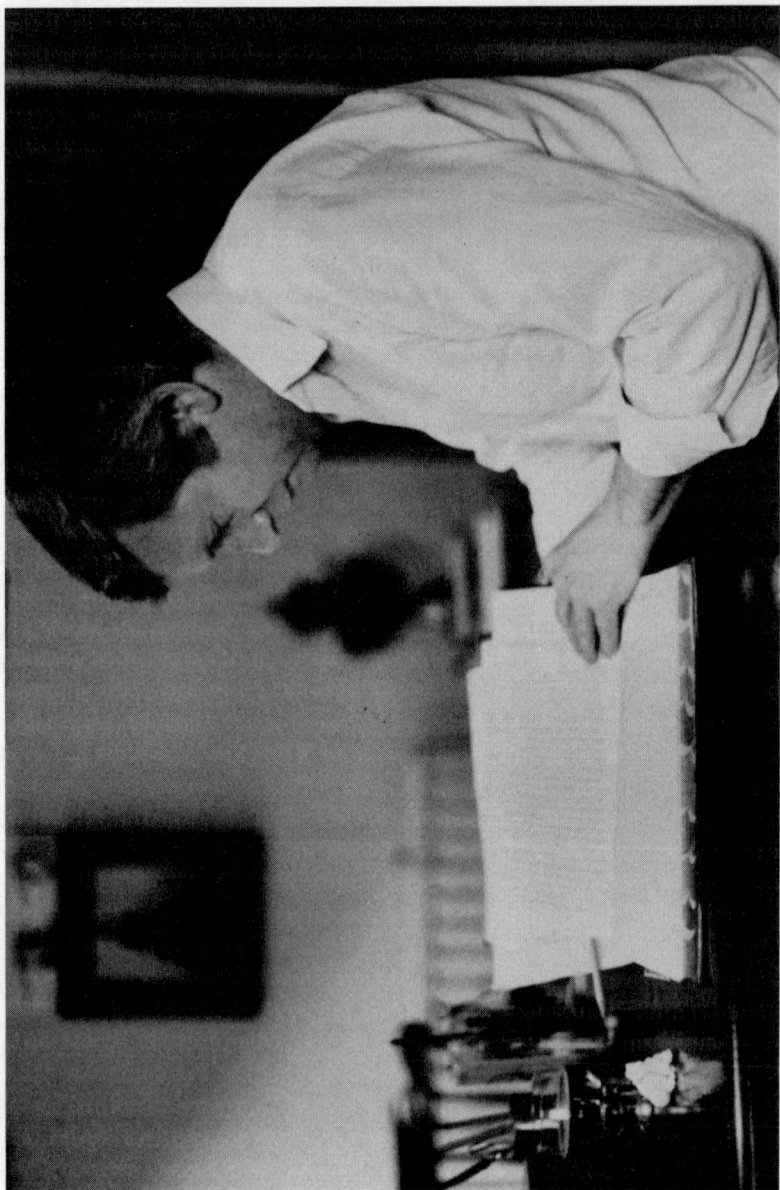

rubbish as a first draft, and then start all over again and reconstruct it. I wish I had that – I wish I could just sit down and bash it out straight away; but I can't. There are times when I get really desperate about it, when I think, 'Christ, if only I could speed it up a bit!' I'm writing quicker on this new novel: I'm sometimes doing a thousand words a day, which for me is a hell of a lot. Often you're stuck on the boring things like establishing where somebody is, why they're there, but all those things have got to be done. If you ignore them you're removing the structure that these people live in. Often, I find I look at pages I've really slaved over, worked at and worked at and worked at, just getting somebody into a room, just having them say, 'Hello,' or whatever, and I think, 'That reads as if it just fell on to the page.' And I know damn well it took a week to write. I think the problems are fascinating. I can't bear those writers who complain about the agony of writing – it's our chosen agony.

I don't want to groan on about publishers and agents. I've had all my books published by Cape and I've had a pretty fair relationship with them. I feel they could have advanced me a bit more at times, but I think everybody feels that. As far as agents are concerned, I had one really lousy one who shall be nameless, who did something really terrible to me for which he will never be forgiven: he turned down an offer from Italian television to make a film of *At the Jerusalem*. The book had just been translated into Italian and they wanted to do it terribly quickly. This was in 1970. I was as poor as a church mouse. I was living off my friend really, because I wasn't earning enough money. And the agent gaily told me later he'd turned down three thousand pounds because he didn't think it was enough. It was a bloody fortune!

I'm against what has happened to the Literature Department at the Arts Council. They've now got a piddling £25,000 to play with. I don't go along with this argument, which is part of Thatcherdom anyway, that writers should be able to support themselves. You read constantly of the sudden success of writers who never knew success in their own day. I do believe that some writers who are churning out book after book would probably be better if they did something else that paid the rent and then worked steadily at something that would bring out the best in them. The grant system *has* been abused. I do know of some people who have had money who shouldn't have had it. But it's a human thing. You've got to get the right people to make the right assessments, and sometimes they don't. One or two quite wealthy people have been given Arts Council grants. There was a woman writer on the telly who used her £5,000 bursary to re-do her kitchen. I thought that was pretty bloody shameless as she was living in a Georgian farmhouse. I don't agree with that sort of thing. But there are writers who only need a couple of grand to get them through to the end of a book. Some of the applicants are quite old, and it's rather sad actually.

I'm interested in music. I like certain jazz. There are certain vocalists I'm still quite fond of. I like blues singing. I like Billie Holiday very much. And I like going to certain concerts in the year – certain conductors. I think I've got an appreciative, catholic ear. I love opera. It seems to me to be one of the great democratic art forms. To go to the Rome Opera House, for instance, is one of the experiences of a lifetime. The audiences are ordinary people, people who work in factories and cafés and things, who go and listen to the music and react to the singers. And when there are bad notes you can't believe the insults that come from the audience. And there's none of this poncey thing of dressing up for classy revivals at Covent Garden: you can only afford to go there once a year when the stalls are thirty-five or forty quid. My days of standing are over, I'm afraid. When I was a kid you could stand in the Festival Hall for about five bob. So I heard great conductors. I heard Bruno Walter there, and Guido Cantelli, who was a kind of hero of mine, and the first concerts that Guilini gave, and Klemperer and people like that. I've always loved Verdi. The first time I heard Verdi's *Requiem* I was about seventeen, and I'd never heard anything like it. I go to that every year if there's a performance.

I got the Somerset Maugham Award for my first book, and you have to spend the money abroad so I decided to go to Italy. I was half in love with it long before I ever went there because of the language and the music. And then I went to Italy and saw Italian painting, and the landscape, and the people. Despite the Mafia, and the ghastly politics, the average Italian person is so nice. Even the thieves in Naples are chatting happily to you while they're picking your pockets. I think they're enchanting. And they pick people's pockets because they're dirt-poor, and always have been, and there's no hope there. It's another Italy in the south; but the people are wonderful. I've got a romantic love of the Italians.

I'm a socialist. I would never change. I don't know what kind of socialist I am. I do know that I will go to my grave being grateful for the Attlee government. It's now being said, even by Tory historians, that more was achieved in those six years than in any other period in this century. And the man who ruthlessly brought through all those great social changes was a man who'd gone through the full upper-class thing, and been trained to be a pillar of his class. What dismays me now is what is happening to all the things which I think we should be proud of, like the National Health Service, and our educational system. I hate Thatcher. I hate this government; I think it's loathsome. And I hate the new brand of Tory; I'm almost now sighing for the old aristocratic brand of Tory who at least acknowledged that the poor had to be respected: you didn't abuse them because you wanted their votes for one thing. That seems to me moderately more humane (though pretty shitty) than the sort of Tebbit theory which is, 'Get on your bike, and run over everybody around you, and get there!' I find that whole view obnoxious. I'm a passionate believer that there are people who have to be helped, and I don't see that it's wrong to be helped. The new thinking is that if you need help you're spineless and gutless; this is dangerous: it leads back to the 1930's.

Tennis I like. Just to watch. I haven't got an eye for a ball or anything like that. I just get frustrated. I can serve, and I get so excited that I've served properly that when the bloody ball is returned across the net I hit it all over the place. I'm hopeless. But I've got a great appreciation of it. I can sit and watch it for hours.

I've lived with David now for twenty years, and I've been a professional writer for seventeen. It hasn't been stable financially – I've had to do all sorts of things: more reviewing at certain periods than I ever wanted to do. I can't complain about that – thank God people offered me the work. On the other hand, reviewing is not a lucrative thing – you've got to do a hell of a lot of it to make ends meet; and if you do a hell of a lot of it you're not doing it well, and you're not getting your own work done. I started reviewing for newspapers after *At the Jerusalem* came out in 1967. I've reviewed for *The Observer* on and off ever since. When the radio programme, *Kaleidoscope*, started in 1972, a man I'd been in the theatre with, Ronald Harwood, asked me if I would review *Richard II* at Stratford. My immediate reaction was, 'No, no, no, I can't do it.' But David argued with me and said, 'Go on. Try it.' So I went up and reviewed it live over the telephone. I was as nervous as hell, but

I did it and they liked it. I went on to do more and I worked on that programme for several years, until I had a row with the boss. But it gave me a whole new career, which is broadcasting, which I really love doing. I suppose there's a residue of me that likes gabbing in public, and certainly my acting was a wonderful training for using the microphone. I knew instinctively to treat it as another person, to talk to it; and then it sounds natural. I've just done a programme on Passolini for the Beeb which meant going to Rome and talking to his friends. It gives me the opportunity to tell people who may not be aware of it that Passolini is a far greater poet than he is a film director. I enjoy, particularly, talking about neglected writers. I've done a lot of interviews with American writers, like Peter Taylor, and Eudora Welty, and a favourite of mine, a man called J. F. Powers, who writes wonderful short stories.

I do a lot of reading – and some of it for pleasure. I try and re-read favourite authors quite often. I read Dickens a lot. *Great Expectations* is my favourite, not because I think it's his greatest – *Little Dorrit* is a far greater book, and *Bleak House* probably, but it means a lot to me and I think it is the most perfect of his novels. I still find all those scenes at the end of the book heartbreaking and I've read it Christ knows how many times. Dickens is a hero. He really captures the comedy of London life. And as I get older I feel that people in his books who're dismissed as grotesques aren't really grotesques – I see people like that, like Chuffy in *Martin Chuzzlewit* who sits in his corner covered in dust. Lots of minor writers, like Pinter and Beckett, couldn't have existed without the things in Dickens which we now take for granted: the stupid conversations; the people conversing with themselves while they're pretending to talk to others; all that. Pinter has made a whole minor art form out of things that for Dickens were merely on the periphery of the story.

I read the metaphysical poets; George Herbert is my favourite. I love his poems because of their sheer beauty and their humanity. I love the one called *The Flower*. 'Grief melts away like snow in May, As if there was no such sad thing.' 'I once more smell the dew and rain, and relish versing.' – the delight in being able to write again after a period of awful misery. I think he was a wonderful man, and I feel that if he were alive now he probably wouldn't have a God. I feel the same about John Donne. I love the way they both argue with God. I think Donne is a very great poet too. The sheer thrillingness of the line: 'Batter my heart, three-personed God.' And that wonderful poem of Donne's, *Going to Bed*. 'Come, Madam, come, all rest my powers defy, Until I labour, I in labour lie.' And as he's undressing her: 'Oh, my America, my new-found land.'

I like Van Gogh's letters. I think they're marvellous. They're not just about painting, they're about life. He wasn't mad. He was taken up as a madman when it was fashionable to like the mad, about ten or twenty years ago. The circumstances of Van Gogh's life were deeply unfortunate, but the letters to his brother are a model of sanity. There's this sane voice going on all the time, and you just wonder what sort of terrible brainstorm happened to this marvellous man who saw things so clearly, and painted as if time was in his way. He was a great fan of Dickens. Dickens was his favourite writer.

Keats' letters are wonderful: the letters to Benjamin Bailey, and to his family. I prefer them to his poetry. That seems a silly thing to say – the poetry is marvellous, but the man in the letters is the man who caught the clap and lived, while the poems are all wonderfully ethereal and outside life in a way. The letters are about the man behind the poems. His prose has heart-stopping moments: things like, 'the holiness of the heart's affections.' How can anyone come out with a phrase like that in a letter – just off the top of his head?

I like Hazlitt. I love his sanity. I like his famous essay on death. He says in effect, why should I be unhappy about the fact that I'm not going to exist when it didn't bother me for centuries before I existed? I think that's a marvellous idea.

My favourite twentieth century book is a novel by Italo Svevo called, *Confessions of Zeno*. It starts off as a spoof on psychiatry and ends up as a great novel. It's about a man who's trying to give up smoking. It's one of those profound, comic books. There's an introduction by a psychiatrist who says that this is the work of a madman (but of course it's a staple joke that nobody's more mad than your shrink). The first chapter is called, 'My Last Cigarette'; and the book ends with him lighting up. It's full of marvellously human things: there are three girls in this rich family and he decides that he wants to marry the most beautiful one, the eldest, and she says, no, she's not interested; then he settles for the second one, and she tells him she's not interested – she's in love with somebody else; so he marries the third one who's terribly plain and dumpy, and he has the most wonderfully contented marriage because she allows him to have a mistress, and she doesn't nag him, so everything turns out perfectly for him. He's a fool, and he's got no talent, but he ends up

being very rich – money doesn't worry him and he's not anxious to
have it, so it comes to him. It's slightly autobiographical: his own life
was like that. I learned that, years later, when the one and only
biography of him appeared, by P. N. Furbank. He discovered that
all these things in the novel were true. Svevo wrote *Confessions of
Zeno* when he was in his sixties. He'd written two previous novels
which had gone unnoticed. There was a gap of twenty-five years
between his second novel and this final masterpiece. James Joyce
was teaching him English at the Berlitz school. Svevo, whose real
name was Eltore Schmitz, was a Jew, who thought in German and
wrote in Italian. He told Joyce he was writing something, and he
showed Joyce his two early novels. One of them, *Senilita*, which was
translated as *As a Man Grows Older*, is about a man who is
prematurely senile, and Joyce thought the last page was so beautiful
he learned it off by heart and would say it to people. And he said
to Svevo, 'You're a great writer.' And because Joyce had said that
to him (Joyce hadn't yet published *Ulysses*, but instinctively Svevo
knew this was a man who knew what he was talking about) he went
on and finished *Confessions of Zeno*. It's one of those books which
disappears and comes back. It will always come back because it's a
great novel. It was translated by a woman called Beryl de Zoete (the
mistress of Arthur Waley, the Chinese expert). Her translation is in
the most wonderful flowing English, unlike the Italian which is
rather lumpen because it's thought out in German – it's got a very
plodding German tread to it. It's a marvellous book, but the ultimate
joke is, the great Italian novel of this century reads better in a foreign
language.

* * *

Reading is a creative art. Looking at a television screen,
particularly if you're looking at a programme about wildlife, which
I think are the most marvellous things that television does, can be
extraordinarily educational. But what the picture can never do for
you, and what the word can, is allow you to work and exploit your
own imagination. It starts with the most simple thing: a boy or girl
reading *Treasure Island* for the first time will make their own picture
of Ben Gunn and Long John Silver, and they enter a world that has

been suggested to them. Words at their best, when they're used properly, don't actually spell it out in mind-boggling detail: they give you the chance to add something. The reader is having to work. The literature that survives is the one that allows the reader to enter into the spirit of the thing and use his or her own imagination to some extent. Even Dickens, who creates these memorable people, is conspiring with you as a reader to join in the joke. He wants you to feel the pleasure that he felt while he was writing them. I think that words are the most important thing we have. Words are abused, and changed, and slaughtered, and used as a cover-up, and the reading of good literature has never been more important than now. When you listen to certain American politicians talking gobbledegook, and then you read the great American prose stylists like Thoreau and Emmerson, you realise what a terrible pass we've come to. We now cannot understand the English language any more, whereas some of the most vivid and wonderful writing has come out of America in the last hundred years. I just re-read, for the first time in twenty years, *Moby Dick*. I read it on a train going up to Inverness and I was sitting there actually gasping at certain phrases. I think words are the greatest thing we have, they're the most common thing we have too. Words are all around us, we can't get through the day without using them. The person I'm most grateful to, for everything, is my English master. I think children who are deprived of literature are severely deprived.

London, May 1984.

NIGEL GRAY'S COMMENT.

As well as being a much-praised novelist, Paul Bailey is one of this country's few contemporary fiction reviewers of note. Confident and outgoing, with a mischievous sense of fun, he is someone with whom you very quickly feel at ease. One of his qualities (sadly rare in the English character) is a good-humoured tolerance of the quirkiness of his fellows.

I met Paul only a few months before I interviewed him. I'd been making a paltry living as a writer for some years. My wife's mother had once warned her, 'If you marry that man, you'll end up thin and ragged.' We were desperately trying to prove her wrong. I decided the thing to do would be to get a job teaching Creative Writing in an American university. Thinking that a Master of Arts degree in Creative Writing would be my ticket to ride, I was making weekly visits over a six months period to the University of East Anglia. Malcolm Bradbury led the writing workshops to begin with, until he popped over to the United States; Angela Carter stepped into his shoes for a while, until she went off to a fellowship in Australia; and then Paul took over. Paul has extremely keen critical judgement, and consequently was not liked by a majority of the students.

I subsequently visited Paul a couple of times at his home in London and met his partner, David. David was already ill then, between stays in hospital, but still very full of life and fun. I liked him instantly. Paul had to continue his work on *Gabriel's Lament* while nursing David at home, or visiting him in hospital. David died on March 26th 1986. It would be crass of me to try to suggest the trauma Paul suffered. I have shared my life with my wife, Yasmin, for ten years, only half the time David was with Paul. I can only try to imagine life without her, but I find it unimaginable – I fear it more than amputation of a limb. But somehow, after David's death, the book was completed – Paul more or less locked himself in the house and finished the last fifty pages in a frenzy of writing. It was published in the September of that year to critical acclaim, and was short-listed for the Booker Prize. It is essentially a comic book, although quite sad, and even harrowing towards the end – perhaps an apt memorial to David.

A woman who is mentioned on the penultimate page of *Gabriel's Lament* takes up the narration of Paul's next novel, *Esther's Mission*. Gabriel himself makes a further appearance, but is now seen through the eyes of another.

I talked to Paul recently about the effect on him of David's death. The most terrible thing, he said, was the kind of freedom it gave – a freedom he didn't personally want. Grief expresses itself often in purely physical ways – ghastly stomach pains, and vomiting attacks.

He tries not to think in terms of anniversaries, but it's hard. Christmas, for some reason, is difficult. Last year he made a conscious effort to get through Christmas – only to collapse at New Year.

To be positive, he said, it had given him insight into whole areas of feeling which he'd only guessed at before (like physical courage – something which David had in abundance).

Paul is disturbed by this government's growing anti-homosexual vindictiveness. It is something which he sees as one more sinister aspect of Thatcherdom. The Tories have created a greedy society whose purpose is to help people with money make more. The only thing to hope for is a further, more drastic, stock market crash. Losing money, he believes, would be the only thing Thatcher's fans could understand.

Although he is not a prolific writer, Paul's work has earned great respect. His first novel, published in 1967, brought him honours from the Arts council of Great Britain and The Author's Club, as well as the Somerset Maugham Travel Award; he was the recipient of the E. M. Forster Award in 1974, and won the George Orwell Memorial Prize in 1978 for his essay, 'The Limitations of Despair.'

Paul Bailey was born in Battersea, London, on February 16th 1937.

Paul Bailey's Book Choice:

Great Expectations	*Loving* Henry Green
Charles Dickens	*Caught* Henry Green
Little Dorrit Charles Dickens	The Poems of George Herbert
Bleak House Charles Dickens	The Poems of John Donne
Confessions of Zeno	Van Gogh's Letters
Italo Svevo	Keats' Letters
Moby-Dick Herman Melville	The Essays of William Hazlit
Living Henry Green	

Books by Paul Bailey:

At the Jerusalem	*Old Soldiers*
Trespasses	*An English Madam*
A Distant Likeness	*Gabriel's Lament*
Peter Smart's Confessions	

Chapter Three

JOHN BERGER

My childhood is something I haven't altogether come to terms with yet. If I think of my childhood, I think of my mother, who is now nearly ninety-two, and whom I see once or twice a year. That's the only reason I go to England. And I try to make her laugh – and she does laugh. And I think of my father, who died six years ago, quite peacefully in his bed one night. And when I say that, I think of the enigma of history. Because maybe the only thing I know really well about my father is his experience of the First World War, which happened before I was born, but which I believe marked his life indelibly. He was an infantry officer on the Western Front from October 1914 until the end of the war. The number of infantry officers who survived four years on that front was tiny. He survived – and I'm sure he was a very brave soldier – and he was haunted for the rest of his life by what he'd seen in those trenches. He would have nightmares often, and I would hear him screaming, and the next morning he would tell me he had been dreaming about the Western Front, and so I would ask him more. And all this when I was very young, which is perhaps why it's the only thing I know for certain about him, because it's the only thing he talked to me about very, very, directly. And then, in his eighties, he died one night so peacefully in his bed at home. I wrote a small essay about drawing him in his coffin – the last drawing I made of him. What I wrote there in those few thousand words seems to me to be true. For the rest – I don't know.

By the age of seven I was already, most of the time, not at home, but sent to a series of boarding schools. And although I believe that those schools, and my being sent to them, probably had a very, very deep effect on me, I don't have much to say about them. I don't have much to say about them because, in a sense, it's all been said. Maybe the schools I was sent to were rather special: they were centres for educating the children of army officers, police superintendents, clergymen. They were exactly what you would

expcct them to be. If you want to know about them you can read
Musil in *Young Torless*; you can see Lindsay Anderson's film *If*
(although the reality was much harsher than what they show in that
film). I've often asked myself why I haven't written about that
experience. But what the British ruling-class did to its own children
doesn't seem to me to be very important on a world scale, even
though, in fact, it destroyed most of those children.

I ran away when I was sixteen, which was the end of my formal
education. The people who know me best tell me that, as human
beings go, I'm not a very neurotic one. So how I managed to survive,
and how I got out, I don't know. I suppose, from an early age I was
– not physically, but spiritually, if you wish – alone; and the reality
which was around me was up pretty close. There wasn't much
mediation between the reality that surrounded me, the reality I was
experiencing and living, and my perception of it; the mediation that
most children have through parents or elder brothers. To tell the
truth, up to the age of sixteen I can't at this moment recall anybody
who meant anything very much to me (except for two women who
were much, much older than me, and who were far away from me
really: one was the younger sister of a schoolmistress at a tiny school
I went to before I was sent to these institutions; and the other was
a woman who lived a few houses away from where I lived when I
was about fourteen.)

I find, even retrospectively, that what happened to me remains
mysterious to me. Despite the fact that I can be quite analytical; and
I can be quite analytical about myself; and I think I have quite good
psychological understanding about other people; and I *can* have
about myself; what strikes me most is what is mysterious and what
escapes explanation. The old-fashioned word for that is 'destiny' –
a word that I give more and more value to. I think that every life
has its own destiny. The word is now so little used that it perhaps
almost immediately leads to a misunderstanding: that when one talks
about destiny one is saying that choice has no part to play; that
destiny suggests a rather passive attitude. That is not what I mean
at all. I don't see it like that. On the contrary, I see it as active. But
there is always a part that is mysterious in a destiny, and it is perhaps
something which the outsider (that's to say, somebody who is –
supposing they're interested – watching, or considering this destiny
from outside) can perhaps see better than the one who is within.
That's why you have story-tellers – in the the beginning those story-

tellers, starting with Homer, were the narrators of destinies.

From the age of nine I wrote a lot of letters to my parents and to other people whom I knew, but from whom, for one reason or another, I was often separated. And the writing of these letters, that's to say, the recounting of experience, was important to me. I felt a need to recount my experiences to somebody who was absent – to put it on paper was the only way of talking about it. And then, almost imperceptibly to me, these letters became, sometimes, poems; perhaps then not sent as a letter. But, at that time anyway, the writing of a poem wasn't so very different from the writing of a letter. (Except that, perhaps, the letter was always addressed very specifically to somebody, and the poem perhaps to nobody whom I'd yet had the luck to meet or to know, but whom I hoped to know.) And then also those letters sometimes became stories, which were no longer necessarily relating what had actually happened, but were relating the speculations of my imagination as a consequence of what had happened.

I read a great deal from the age of eight. I think at the beginning I was reading what you would expect, but quickly a wider range of reading matter. At the age of ten I was certainly reading, avidly, Dickens. And quite quickly afterwards I was reading Hardy. But I was also reading Hugh Walpole. And I was reading poetry, particularly contemporary poetry. I was in some ways very precocious, although I didn't understand a great deal of what I read. By twelve or thirteen I was reading Auden, T. S. Eliot; by the time I was fourteen I was reading Ezra Pound and Rilke. I was encouraged by nobody – I was reading completely independently. The more traditional books, for example Dickens and Hardy, were in the school library. When I was not at school, there were very good public libraries where, with two tickets, one could get out ten books a week for nothing. There were books at home, but nothing much.

I liked Herbert Read as a poet, especially his poems indirectly inspired by the First World War. Also his theoretical anarchist writings. Later, I also became interested in his writings about art. I remember I sent him some poems I'd written, and, perhaps not to my surprise then, but to my surprise in retrospect, he replied, quite encouragingly, and also quite critically, pointing out all kinds of weaknesses and making suggestions. And this was very, very important to me. His letter of reply, I used to carry in my pocket – it was a kind of identity card. (Afterwards, I actually came to know

Herbert Read and we had terrible battles. First of all, before I knew him, we found ourselves in total political opposition, especially about modern art. But then later, we became friends, and I reminded him of what he had done for me when I was fourteen. I went to stay with him in Yorkshire: his younger children were at school, and there was a kind of circle which completed itself.) But looking forward when I was fifteen, I didn't picture a future for myself as a writer, although the act of writing was important to me. It was the only way I had of trying to make some sense of what I could see, and what I was experiencing, and what I saw others experiencing.

When I left school the war was on – I knew that within three years I would be in the army. I went to an art school – The Central Art School in London. One reason I went there was completely opportunistic – I could get a small scholarship which was just enough money to enable me to survive. I was also quite interested in drawing and painting, and I think I had talent. So I spent two years in that art school, drawing mostly, particularly in life classes, but painting as well. That experience of drawing, I've also written about. At the age of sixteen I was already in love, and living with a woman who was two years older than me, in a tiny, tiny room, with a tap two landings down and a gas stove on the landing below. Then I was called up.

By my background and schooling I was what the army called 'officer material'. It was expected that after initial training I would agree to become an officer for the infantry, but that I refused. I refused for two reasons. Maybe first, because I'd seen how that class was educated. Many, many of the kids who went to the schools I was at became professional army officers, and I wanted nothing more to do with that world or that class. It isn't that I hated them. Maybe I hated a lot of what they did, but I didn't actually hate them. But it seemed to me that they were so far from reality as I perceived it that they were almost mad. That's not very well expressed because they were not mad at all. But it was impossible for me to take that distance from reality which for them was normal. Therefore, had I stayed, it is perhaps I who would have become mad. To put it in very intellectual terms, their alienation alienated me. I felt profoundly alienated, even though I could be at ease with them, could talk with them, share their sense of humour, enter for a limited period into their fantasies, admire their qualities (because under certain circumstances they had qualities). But it was not for me to be a part of that world, any more than it has ever been since. My break with the milieu of that class occurred then, and was final.

And the second reason is that in those early months of training I found myself, for the first time in my life, with what in the army are called, 'other ranks': that's to say, young, working-class men, who had spent the first eighteen years of their lives very differently from me, but whose company I preferred – not for any ideological reason, or not primarily for that; not because politically I wanted to identify with 'the struggle of the working-class' (because my political consciousness, in a formulated way, really occurred later), but because I preferred the way they related to one another, and sometimes to me. How they considered me, I really don't know. My small gift for writing was at least useful because, sometimes, they would ask me to write letters for them to their girlfriends or to their parents. They would tell me more or less what they wanted to say, and I would write. These were kids who had been at school before the war. A quite significant minority of them had difficulty in writing, and some were illiterate. So I remained in a training barracks with a rank of lance-corporal. New recruits continually came in, but there was a staff who stayed there, of which of course the very lowest rank was lance-corporal. I remained there, in Northern Ireland, not far from Belfast, until the war ended. Quite a few of my contemporaries with whom I was recruited who did become officers were killed in France after D-Day. So in a certain way I was lucky.

Under the 1945 Labour government, every ex-soldier whose education had been interrupted had the possibility of a government grant to continue his education for two or three years. I fell into that category and I went back to art school for three years. So I was independent, and though we didn't have much money, we had enough to live on. During that period I went on drawing and painting. But being in the army during the war, and the experience before the army of the bombardment of London – all that didn't lead to one being a quiet, obedient student. So, in fact, I, and lot of others with me, did more or less what we liked. A lot of the time I wasn't in the art school at all. I began going a great, great deal to the cinema, and I saw an enormous number of films. That was a kind of education in itself.

During this time I was becoming more and more politicised. I was

reading a great deal. I was meeting people. And I found myself
closer and closer to the Communist Party. It's difficult now for
people who didn't live in that period to understand. It was the
beginning of the Cold War, before the Soviet Union had nuclear
parity, a time when one of the options openly and frequently talked
about was a preventative war using atomic weapons against the
Soviet Union. At least twenty million people in the Soviet Union
had lost their lives in the war, not to mention the other losses before
the war due to collectivisation and the purges. It was the Soviet
Union which had actually broken the back, at Stalingrad, of the
German Nazi army; and it was now, potentially, being threatened
by a nuclear war launched from Washington. This idea was
supported by many intellectuals in Britain as well as in America in
the name of their freedom; and we felt the threat was real. It seemed
to me then, as to many other people, that it was necessary to take
sides – a third position wasn't possible. I was not aware of the extent
of the Gulag, or the scale of what, in my opinion, was the most
terrible part of internal Soviet history: the collectivisation of the land
(because that meant not only the uprooting and death of millions
directly, but also indirectly because of the consequences of the
famine which was the natural result). But I think that even with the
knowledge that we now have of the dimensions of that catastrophe
and of those crimes, I would still take the same position as I did then.

As soon as the Soviet Union achieved parity, the situation
changed. The situation changed objectively because that very fact of
parity made Western policy decision-makers hesitate, and it changed
subjectively because the world was no longer polarised into just two,
one of which was weaker and one of which was stronger.

And so, I became increasingly involved in political activities,
especially in the peace movement, which at that time was more or
less a front movement for the communist parties. I had no illusions
about that. It didn't make the cause any less important or any less
justified. We were also perfectly well aware of the front movements
organised by the West, particularly by the Americans. We were
convinced that the magazine *Encounter*, was financed by the CIA.
We were right. That is now admitted and forgotten almost, whereas
the idea that the communist movement had its much more
transparent and not very disguised front organisations is still talked
about. So I spoke at meetings. I wrote articles for the Left press and
the communist press. People assumed that I was a Party member. It

would be interesting to know how accurate the official files were, and whether in those files I was marked as a Party member. In fact I wasn't. But of course I never denied it when I was accused of being so. I wasn't, because I had one reservation. I would like to be able to say that that reservation was that I had read Victor Serge, or that I supported Orwell's *Homage to Catalonia*. But it wouldn't be true. My reservation was much smaller. But perhaps although it was smaller, it was more honest, because it was something of which I really did have first-hand experience: that was the official Party line about the arts – about literature, about painting, about music. This, I could not accept in its intolerance, in its small-mindedness, in its crass link between the power of art and political power. Therefore, despite the fact that a great deal of persuasion and pressure was directed towards me to join the Party, and although I retained very good relationships with the Party, and even with people on the Central Committee, it was a step I refused to take.

I was also, from quite early on in this period, writing about art, architecture, urban development. I was earning my living, such as it was, by teaching in the evenings in the Worker's Educational Association, and by writing journalism for *Tribune* when (and before) Michael Foot was editor, and for *The New Statesman*.

The very first book I wrote has never been published in England, although it was written in English. It was a study of the Italian painter Renato Guttoso, which was commissioned by a publisher in Dresden in East Germany. The writing of that little book was quite important to me. First of all, because it was the first book I ever wrote, and I discovered I could write more than eight pages. Secondly, because the money that I earned could not be transferred to Western Europe: the only way of benefiting from it was to go to East Germany. I went on several occasions and spent quite a lot of time there. That led to a number of journeys to other Eastern European countries, and all these journeys were invaluable to me. I began to learn something about how people lived in those countries. It was a colossal immunisation against the propaganda clichés about life in Eastern Europe (which haven't changed much in forty years). I don't mean that what was happening in Eastern Europe measured up to the ideals of the Communist Manifesto. On the contrary, I was very much aware of how very far they often were from that, and how catastrophically they were sometimes opposed to that. But what I began to learn was something different. And oddly enough it wasn't about the present – that's to say, about the present then. It was more about the past: about what people had suffered and experienced, particularly during the war, but also before the war, say from 1933, from the advent of fascism onwards; and about the scale of these experiences; and the way people who had survived had come to terms with them, and despite everything had made some sense of their lives; and about the way these experiences had effected relationships between people. I began to learn about another history of our time in comparison with which the British experience was relatively privileged, and its visions different – I'm tempted to say, narrower. I began to discover something of the history of middle Europe. I also began to discover something of the Slav temperament, of which so much nonsense is written and talked, but which exists nevertheless. All that might not have happened if this first book hadn't been commissioned by Dresden.

But in order that what I've just said doesn't appear too rosy, I'll say something about the man who commissioned the book from me, and with whom I became friends. His father had been a German communist who was killed by the Nazis. He himself had been an apprentice plumber (he was too young to have been in the German army). After the war the new Communist Government gave him the opportunity of further education. He was among the first generation, in East Germany, of communist intellectuals. He studied art history at university and then, still quite young, became one of the chief editors in the most important art publishing house in East Germany. He was a man with an extraordinary knowledge of philosophy and art history, whose whole life story and opportunities were intimately connected with that of the German Communist Party. He tried in those years to run that part of the publishing house for which he was responsible, in as open and intelligent a way as possible, opposed to the dogmatism of the official Party line. For example, he published a remarkable book on the Soviet designer, Lissitzky; he published a book, which at that epoch was extraordinary in Eastern Europe, on Picasso. He was under constant, constant pressure and threats; and he was finally thrown out of his job. He went back to work as a plumber – the same trade he'd begun at fourteen before his further education. In a certain sense he was lucky: the record of what happened to so-called 'enemies of the people' (that's to say, those considered to be political opponents or those with independence) in

East Germany was in fact better than in some other countries. There
were very few who were sent to the Soviet Union or Siberia; there
were relatively few executions; there was imprisonment sometimes,
and civil control (people losing their jobs – but losing a job meant
losing an apartment, I don't want to minimise what they suffered);
but they weren't liquidated. Had he been a Czech he would have
been dead. Had he been a Russian, I suspect he would already have
been dead or in prison before I met him.

My second book was my first novel, *A Painter of our Time*. For a
long while I'd had fiction in mind. In the intervening period the
largest part of my energy was spent as an art critic: seeing and writing
about dozens of exhibitions every week. But I always knew that I
was not going to go on doing that for too long. Criticism, in that
sense – art criticism, literary criticism, theatre criticism – should be
a temporary affair. If you spend your life doing it, very quickly you
will degenerate as a critic. There is always a danger in that activity
of becoming a parasite. That's to put it negatively. To put it
positively: if you're a good critic you lend your imagination to the
imagination of others – that's to say, to the imagination of the artist
under consideration and the imagination of a possible public. You
are a kind of interpreter between these two, using your own
imagination. But if you go on doing it for very long, either your own
imagination dries up, or it revolts. Either you become an automatic
and superficial and boring critic, or you become bitter, which is one
way your imagination goes into revolt; bitter because it isn't natural
for an imagination to be always using itself for other imaginations.
It seems to me evident that the best critics have always been part-
time critics; either part-time over a long period, or intense critics for
a short period. So I always knew that I was not going to go on doing
it indefinitely; and I knew that fiction was something I wanted to see
if I could do. In *A Painter of our Time*, I see now, I sort of sum up
my experiences of the art world: of painters' studios; of art dealers;
of the strange relationship between painting and life, art and politics;
that world in which I'd been immersed for the previous ten years.
Without that experience I couldn't have written that book. And in
a way, that book, although I didn't think about it in those terms
then, was a kind of adieu to that world which I'd lived in intensely
and which I've never lived in like that since. At the same time, you
can see in that book already, this experience of life in Eastern
Europe – in the case of that book, in Hungary. It is only this year

that it has been translated into Hungarian, but nearly thirty years
ago copies of the book in English got to Budapest, and I had two
completely separate letters from Hungarians saying that they had
read the book and that they would very much like to know where
the paintings of Janos were to be found in London. That is to say
that this diary of his, which I had invented, and which talks a great
deal about his experiences and memory of Budapest, were
convincing enough to persuade Hungarians that they were real
diaries and that therefore the paintings existed. So perhaps I had
learnt a little on those journeys.

That book was important to me for another reason. It was, after
all, the first novel I'd written, the first book of mine published in
Britain, and when it came out it was massacred by the critics. For
example, Spender, writing, I think, in *The Sunday Times*, said 'This
book, which smells of the innocent blood of the concentration
camps, could have been written by only one other person, and that
is Goebbels as a young man.' The publishers, Secker and Warburg
(who were also the distributors of *Encounter*, withdrew the book
from the bookshops, so that the book was actually still-born. It was
published, but unavailable. Seckers were put under pressure by the
Committee for Cultural Freedom of which Spender was a member.
That was an important experience for me because it made me tough.
It taught me that publishers are not saviours, and critics are not
conveyors, necessarily, of real literary judgements. When one writes
one's first book one is very vulnerable. If I became tough it was as
a result of having to live with, and overcome that experience. It was
nothing compared to what can happen to writers in other places of
course, but still, it meant from then onwards I didn't have any naïve
illusions about what having a book published signifies. Also, it has
given me a different perspective about the lifetime of a book – which
doesn't necessarily depend on the way it is judged initially. Ten years
later it was republished as a Penguin. Retrospectively I am, in a way,
grateful for that experience.

Soon after that (but not because of that), I left Britain and came
to live on the Continent; and I knew that it was definitively. It was
the end of a period in my life. Ten years, more or less, from '49 to
'59, had been years of extremely engaged, militant political, and
artistic political activity (including Aldermaston and all of that first
nuclear disarmament campaign). And during those ten years the
telephone was ceaseless – not because I was important, but because

there was so much to be done: so much to be organised: so many
committees; so many groups; so many meetings; so many pamphlets.
For ten years I'd lived that life. But then I wrote that book. And
perhaps, perhaps I could write others. I wasn't certain. But I wanted
to try. People asked me why I left Britain. Perhaps the simplest way
of putting it is to say that I felt more at home on the Continent – but
that doesn't say very much. I could give all kinds of complicated
explanations – but let's just say, that's how it lived me (rather than
that's how I lived it).

The next novel I wrote was *The Foot of Clive*. It's a book that
began with a real story which at the time was very well-known. There
was a London criminal who had shot a policeman when threatened
with arrest, and there were many witnesses. He escaped, but finally,
after a search of days or weeks, the police found him in a hotel
bedroom in, I think, Notting Hill. It was at night. He was asleep in
bed. They got into the hotel, they came into his room, and they beat
him up – to such a degree that before his trial he had to be taken to
hospital. The situation was a very special one because the death
penalty was still functioning, so this man was going to be patched
up, cured, tried, and then, for certain, hung. There was no question
about his innocence or guilt; and for such a crime there was no
question of reprieve – everybody knew that. He was taken to the
general ward of a London hospital, and there, he was treated for
eight days, I think, and then taken to prison and eventually tried.
This story struck me very deeply, and it was on the basis of this that
I wrote the novel. In the novel, in the general ward of a London
hospital, there are a group of patients (all male obviously), and then
this criminal is brought in. Screens are put round his bed, but
everybody knows who he is. Those eight people, who come from
very different social milieux, are living and sleeping in the same
room, and being treated by the same nurses and doctors, as this man,
who they've never seen, but who is behind the screens, who is being
patched up in order to be tried, in order to be hung. So what
happens, not to the man behind the screens so much, but to those
eight men around him? How do they live those eight days? Or to
put it another way, what can we observe of the class and social and
human relations of a group of people when the light of death is put
upon them. Of course, in a sense, in a hospital, death is always fairly
present, but in this case it is a very special, naked and brutal light.

So how does that community seem under that light?

I left Britain when I was thirty-three. But I'd lived most of my life there, and there were things about Britain that demanded to be written. And perhaps, now I was no longer there, I could see more clearly. *The Foot of Clive* is a kind of microcosm of British society, and the two principal characters are working-class. In *Corker's Freedom*, I wanted to write about a very British variety of what, in sociological terms or political terms, is called the petit bourgeoisie. It's a book about a middle-aged man who runs a seedy little employment agency in South London. He finds jobs for people and takes their first month's wages. But at the same time, this man, like us all, has his dreams, his fantasies, his ideals of happiness, his cowardices, his courage; and I wanted to try, whilst not at all disguising his prejudices and so on, to nevertheless show the potential of such a man had he lived differently. So the portrait of him is sympathetic. It's the funniest book I've written. There is, for example, a section describing a lantern lecture he gives in a church hall which I think is a very comic scene.

I wrote the Picasso book next. That's maybe another encouraging example for other writers: when that book came out in Britain it was patronised, dismissed, treated as something aberrant, and vulgar, and prejudiced, and politically dogmatic, and spiteful towards Picasso (which is far from the truth). And now, Picasso is dead, and twenty years or more have passed, and the book continues to be sold and used – I don't think it has dated very much. People name it as one of the very few books about Picasso that is worth reading. It came from the closest study of Picasso's paintings, and of his life; and it came from trying to understand what is Spain: and from trying to understand what is old age (because Picasso was still alive and a lot of it is about him as an old man). I just applied myself to looking and listening as it were, and put it on to the page. So if I say it's a valid book, I don't say it out of vanity. That validity owes a great deal to so many other things than myself. But it is an example of how, when a book *is* valid, time works for it. (Also, of course, time can later destroy it – in twenty years nobody may read it any more.)

Next came *A Fortunate Man*. At one time I had lived on the England/Wales border, not far from Monmouth. After I left Britain I used to go to visit a friend there who was a doctor, and that made me think that it would be worth trying to write a book which was honest and not idealising, but which paid a kind of homage to what a really good doctor was. So the idea began like that. I was already friends with Jean Mohr, who is a marvellous photographer, and we decided that, because it was based upon someone living, it was a book that would lend itself to text and photographs. And so Jean and I began this quite long collaboration that we now have, of trying to use texts and photographs in a creative way together.

The methods that we used in *A Fortunate Man*, were pushed much further in *A Seventh Man*. In making those books, particularly in making *A Seventh Man*, we discovered something, I think, about the way that texts and photograph, when put together, affect each other, and allow a different or new approach to a subject. And we discovered that the text, given the presence of the pictures, can change: that is to say, that at some moments it can be highly reasoned, analytical; at other moments it can be narrative, like fiction; at other moments it can be poetic and in the form of a poem; at other moments it can be historical and political. All these approaches and disciplines, which usually are kept absolutely separate, and exist under separate covers (by separate writers often), can in fact be brought together in that very energetic way, given the existence of the pictures. I wish other photographers and writers would look more closely at what we did in order to push it further. I think that we indicated a road, as it were. Perhaps we didn't get very far along it, but that road is now open. In that sense, those books have had a certain influence, but I think that there is still more to be done along that road by others.

The one social milieu in Britain that I hadn't written about was the aristocracy. In *G*, I wanted, amongst other things, to write about that. And the first part of *G* does that. But that of course wasn't the origin of the book. My grandfather, who came from Trieste, to some degree determined my choice of Trieste as one of the principal places in *G* (although the character has nothing to do with my grandfather). Equally, my closeness in feeling to that part of my heart which is Slav is reflected in *G*, because, of all the characters, the one I like best as a person is the Slav girl, Nusa. I think it took me five years to write *G*, working almost all the time. I never believed I would be able to finish it. Of all the books I've ever written it was the one that drove me nearest to a form of madness. *G* is formally more experimental, more broken, more diverse, than previous fiction that I wrote. After that, I wanted to return to the simplest form of story-telling, which is what I'm still trying to do. But the way that people have reacted to *G*, in letters and so on, suggests to me that it isn't that inaccessible. People who are far from being literary intellectuals, in all kinds of countries, have read the book, and have written to me, and their responses do not suggest that it is a highbrow cult object. I think its differences to my other novels are more apparent than real. In *G*, I was trying to arrive at a vision that was global: which put history; private lives; subjectivity; objectivity; real events; fantasies; the total enigma of sexual passion; economic history; all this together. And when you try to put all that together, with this global ambition (achieved or unachieved), maybe that demands a certain complexity of method. Having put it together once, maybe one can then return, with the experience of that still within one, to writing more simply. Now, for example, in more recent fiction, what is unsaid, what is between the lines, between sentences, contains (hopefully) some of the kind of complexity and vibration which in *G* had to be spelt out more explicitly. And at the same time, I think one would see in earlier fiction preoccupations (even in the very first novel) which are developed in *G*. And another thing I would say, is that in English fiction (with some obvious exceptions, like Sterne), the combination of fiction and philosophical speculation, or historical speculation, is something which is rather foreign, and is therefore seen as rather inaccessible and difficult. Much to my surprise in a way (but I think it confirms this), *G* was a bestseller in Hungary. I believe more copies have been sold in Hungary, which is a tiny country, than in Britain, and I think this is precisely because of their very different literary tradition.

The subject determines the style and the way of narrating – or should determine those things – much more than one tends to believe. After I'd written *G*, I said to myself, 'Well, as a juggler you're really not doing so bad. You can keep eight balls in the air. You've learnt something.' And then for many reasons, I wanted to write about peasants; and for the first year I didn't realise that, in fact, I had to completely re-learn to narrate. If you're writing about peasants, you can't write in the same way as if you're writing about people who live in cities: the middle-class, or even workers. Every story is such a strange amalgam of the subjectivity of reader, character, and writer, that those white spaces between the things chosen to be said, imply so much; those white spaces change completely according to whether you're writing about a young person or an old, a peasant or a steeplejack. And I realised that in

order that the lifetime of a peasant can enter the story of a peasant, you need a different kind of syntax: a different way of telling a story; a different way of beginning; a different way of ending; a different form of sequence – everything is different. And so I had to re-learn. I think, by the end of the book, I had learned something. Although now that I'm writing the second volume of that trilogy, I realise that I'd learned less than I thought. I'm having great difficulty in writing these new stories because even what is in *Pig Earth* is not yet precise or good enough.

I've lived here amongst peasants for nearly eleven years now. *Pig Earth* was the result of the first seven or eight years, and in it there is perhaps a certain sense of discovery of a community and how that community works, lives, makes sense of its life, makes sense of death. What interests me now is not so much the recording or telling of that community, but that (as I see it, maybe I'm wrong) there are certain stories which recur and recur in the history of world literature, which in Europe, at this moment in the twentieth century, can only be told with the kind of resonance and depth which is necessary to them, if the protagonists are peasants.

Writing film scripts is different from writing novels because film-making is a more collaborative activity, a less lonely activity. It's also different because the word as such, counts for less in the film. (I make a big distinction here between the theatre and the cinema.) Screenplay writing requires as much working and reworking, but it's of a different kind: in film, it is in terms of narrative economy and of narrative tension. Ever since those days when I spent so much time in the cinema (instead of being in art school), I would have loved to have been a film director, where this odd combination of the visual and the verbal has perhaps its most direct expression. A long time ago I decided I wouldn't or I couldn't, because all the hassle of getting the means and the money seemed too much for me. And maybe I wrote novels, in some ways, as a way round that; I think my novels are very filmic. *G*, particularly, is very filmic in some ways.

Recently, I wrote a play, in collaboration with Nella Bielski, and that I found absolutely fascinating. Since then I've written another play, and I think that I would like to write more for the theatre. The peculiar disciplines of the theatre interest me very much indeed. My reservation is the very limited public who (in Western Europe) go to the theatre; limited, not in numbers but in social background.

Mostly it is a middle-class form. But it needn't necessarily be that.

I don't think of myself, even now, as a 'professional' writer. That may sound a bit absurd because I've written quite a lot of books, and anyway, I earn my living by writing. In any file on me I'd be labelled as a professional writer. (Or, as the journalists never cease to say, a 'Marxist art critic' – but that nevertheless implies that I'm a professional writer). Why do I say I'm not a professional writer? First of all because I never have the sense of having mastered a skill. And it seems to me that I am now further from achieving that kind of confidence that a professional writer has, than I ever was. Secondly, because it always seems to me very problematic whether I will ever manage the writing of another book. OK, I can now look back upon the fourteen or fifteen books I've written and say, 'Look, you always felt that – you'll manage this one too.' But somewhere inside me I'm not convinced. And then maybe also because professionalism implies a certain kind of consistency and continuity, and in a way I think that I don't have that. I'm always trying to do something different. That's to say, I'm always putting myself into the position of a novice, even by the choice of what I want to write about (or not even what I want to write about but what possesses me and compels me to write about it). After spending years writing about art, then writing novels about urban people (of which I suppose *G* is the culmination), ten years ago I started trying to write about peasants, where all that experience couldn't prevent me from being a beginner again. And so even now, looking back, I don't have the sense of a profession or of a career as a writer. I write with such difficulty. Despite what people might think, I have no verbal facility. I don't think or feel things in terms of words. I'm obliged to work on each book so much, making so many versions, rewriting almost every page many times: rejecting, correcting, reducing, sharpening. When a book is finished finally, the gap between my intention (the intention can be questioned) and what is there, is, at least in my eyes, not very great. This is not because I've succeeded, but simply because I can't do any better.

The other reason I don't consider myself a professional is that, unless it's a question of writing an article with a dateline, the immediate tasks imposed by life, whatever they are, material or emotional or whatever, always have a priority. I say to myself, 'Well, I'll do that, and when that's done, I will write.' It's not virtue on my part: it's because, when I'm aware of the need of something or somebody immediately around me, I cannot lose myself in the act of writing as is necessary. For myself, I cannot accept this idea that one sacrifices daily life – those people around one who are close to one, whom one loves, or even whom one doesn't love but to whom for one reason or another one has a sense of obligation – for the sake of a book, for the sake of literature, for the sake of writing. That's not to say that when I was writing *G* for example, I wasn't bloody-minded and impossible to live with. And it's not something I prescribe.

What interests me politically, as a person and as a writer, are those truths possessed by those without power, to which those with power are more or less blind. That's to say, those who possess power are more or less blind to certain ongoing truths. Those without power know very well certain truths, and they are blind to others. There is a kind of division of the residence of truths. And it seems to me that it is in the truths possessed by the dispossessed that there are more clues to the enigma of life itself. But I want to emphasise that I'm not saying that all power corrupts, or that I am opposed to all power. What I am saying is not a political programme. It is simply a definition of what interests me and engages me personally.

When one is talking about world politics. I think enemy number one of mankind is the United States. About that I haven't changed, I'm afraid (but I don't think the United states has changed either), for forty years. For me, that is the first political truth about the world today. It is a very strange enemy number one, made up of idealism, and a terrible criminal innocence (by which I mean a kind of naivety in relation to reality, which nobody has the right to have) that is life-destroying.

* * *

Victor Serge's, *The Case of Comrade Tulayev*, seems to me to be a very great historical novel. It is about the early years of the Russian revolution – that revolution which has changed, for good and sometimes for bad, the history of the world. I think that Serge saw, and understood, in extremely intimate, personalised, human terms, that enormous upheaval.

Another book about Russia, *Life and Destiny*, by Vassily Grossman, is similar in some respects. It is about the year 1942. It ranges from the German concentration camps, through the battle of Stalingrad, to the labour camps in Siberia. And he says, whilst recounting these cataclysmic events, that there are certain moments when, suddenly little breaths of goodness unexpectedly and inexplicably appear in people; and we only realise how precious these moments are when they are seen against such backgrounds. It is these moments, when this breath appears, which explain something about the secret of life.

Frantz Fanon's theoretical book, *The Wretched of the Earth*, although written twenty-five or more years ago, is still a book which allows one to understand a great deal about what is happening today, particularly about the relationship between the third world and the first and second worlds. Re-reading it recently, I was as impressed by it as I was the first time I read it.

Twenty Years A-Growing, by Maurice O'Sullivan, is a marvellous book. It describes the impact of the modern world upon a world that had hardly changed for centuries (and all this within this century, within five hundred miles of London, off the West coast of Ireland). It is a book that shows in every word how it is when people believe that their lives are a story – that the life we live is a story, somewhere, somehow, being told. And this belief has an extraordinary effect upon story telling. It takes us back to the very source of why stories are told and why people need them. The whole of this book is infused by that collusion between lives and stories which antecedes literature, before that division has occurred which opens up between literature and life.

Yashar Kemal's *Memed my Hawk* is a novel which has many qualities, but above all, it is an extremely human, gentle book about hatred.

I love the poetry of Neruda. When I read his poetry I hear a voice which talks about the world, rather like the voice of a very great actor. That's to say, a voice which seems to be contained in a bubble, which comes from the mouth speaking it intact towards you, and which far, far, surpasses all the usual limitations and parochialisms of poetry.

The poetry of the Turkish poet, Nazim Hikmet, is in some ways similar to Neruda's, but with all the difference between the climates of South America and Turkey.

A third poet I admire (who's still alive) is a Syrian called Adonis. He is, for me, among the very greatest lyric poets. The whole evolution of contemporary Arabic poetry is very interesting. Adonis was one of a number of very gifted poets writing in Arabic who where associated with a publishing centre in Beirut. I read his poetry in French because no collections of his have been translated into English. *The Book of Migration* is absolutely fantastic. Adonis is a love poet essentially, although he's very political, and greatly influenced, as are all Arab poets, by a Koranic tradition. I can think of no other contemporary who writes love poems as well as he does, and yet he's practically unknown in the English-speaking world.

A writer who suffers from being obligatory on so many syllabuses is Dickens. If you read *The Old Curiosity Shop* and *Our Mutual Friend* you can see the complete journey that Dickens made, and the way he becomes more and more possessed by what he sees around him, and more and more the agonised mouthpiece of his society.

At a completely different level, the two fiction writers who most influenced me were Proust and Hemingway. I first read them when I was quite young: Proust in my late teens, Hemingway earlier. (One has to be quite young to be influenced.) I admire Proust because of the way he whispers into the ear of language itself. He uses language as if all language, when consciously used, is like a prayer; I admire him because of his determination to save moments from neglect and forgetfulness. And although the world of Proust is not a world that I feel close to, the qualities of his writing completely transcend that world. It seems to me that the relationship between Proust and the language that he chooses is the same (although in Proust it is in a very literary and sophisticated form) as that of everybody when they need to put into words feelings, or suffering, or hope. That's to say, when children talk to themselves in bed, or old people mutter to themselves in the street, their relationship to language is perhaps not so different from Proust's (even though the language will be different).

Hemingway's relationship to language demands the same precision as somebody using a tool; somebody who has mastered a trade or technique, or a practical or active skill. In Hemingway there is action, not only because he describes action and his narratives are fast-moving, but there is action within the writing itself. These two poles – that's to say, the recording of things remembered, and the immediate active presence of things done – had an enormous influence on me.

* * *

I frequently use the term, 'story-telling'. It doesn't cover all literature, but it does cover a large part of it. But story-telling, of course, has other forms apart from the book: oral story-telling; the theatre; the cinema; television; even, at a certain level, sacred ritual. Without story-telling, I think, Man wouldn't be Man. The need to tell stories and to listen to stories is absolutely intrinsic to human consciousness. Human consciousness is always asking questions of origin, 'How did it begin?' and that immediately implies that you have to invent a beginning and a story. Human consciousness is aware of the passage of time, of things being swept away and our need to preserve them from being swept away. Hence again, stories. The first faculty of human consciousness in its imaginative form is the ability to empathise, to place oneself in the position of the other. You see that capacity in all very young children when they are playing; and they have it until it's knocked out of them. It seems to me that the faculty of imagination actually begins with that potential of being able to put oneself in somebody else's skin, and to feel the experiences of somebody else even though they're not our own, and from that comes, once again, the need to tell and listen to stories. And, perhaps finally, there is, in the structure of our consciousness, the need to give form, to arrange experience. It's the same impulse that we use in making a home. But don't misunderstand me – it is something one can see just as well in a nomad's tent or in a one-roomed tenement as in a large house (sometimes even more strongly). When I say 'home' I'm not thinking of *House and Garden*, but that shelter within which one is temporarily protected from the devastating winds of time and history and destiny. In a home, however chaotic it may be, things have a place, and that place has been chosen, and to some degree the objects have been chosen (for necessity or other reasons). And it seems to me that stories are exactly like that. They are a habitation. And if they have a form which is imbued with life, then they offer shelter.

Haute-Savoie, France, June 1984.

NIGEL GRAY'S COMMENT.

John Berger is a strong man, strong in every sense: physically, intellectually, spiritually, morally (though his morality is not a conventional one). He is a man who inspires trust, affection, respect. He is unarguably one of the most original and talented writers of his generation. Perhaps, given his insight in the field of visual art as well as the perception and understanding of his writing, it is apt to say that he is a man of vision.

His novel, *G*, earned him the Booker Prize. He has also been awarded the George Orwell Memorial Prize, and his script for the film *Jonah Who Will Be 25 in The Year 2000* won the New York Critics Prize.

My relationship with John got off to a faltering start. In the early '70s when I was editing a literary magazine, I wrote to him asking if he had anything we might use. He submitted a poem (maybe more than one, I don't remember). In any event, despite my great admiration for much of his work, I didn't like whatever it was he sent and rejected it. Many lesser writers have never forgiven me for similar crimes.

I have known John for ten years now, and during the chats and discussions and arguments we have had, I have been continually impressed by his considerable intelligence and his deep humanity. One of my most valued memories is of sitting in the large summer afternoon kitchen of his old farmhouse in France, among the debris of a fine meal of produce grown by John's wife Beverley in their kitchen garden, having been invited to listen to and comment on an unfinished story which was causing John problems.

Once in Europa, the second volume of the trilogy *Into Their Labours*, (of which *Pig Earth* was the first), was published in the United States (though not in Britain) in '87. John is pleased with it, feeling it to be freer than *Pig Earth*. It comprises five stories which are all love stories of one kind or another, and deals with the transformation of village life. The final part, *Old Wives Tale of a City*, which will be completed by the end of '88, is a kind of novel, told by an old woman who has never left the village, about the city

– all cities. John has found that to write about the metropolis he has to write quite differently to the way he has written about village life. It has been necessary to absorb the city atmosphere much more and consequently he is spending more time in Paris. But at least the novel is coming much quicker than the earlier books – which after having lived with the project for fifteen years is something of a relief.

John has also collaborated with the Russian-born writer Nella Bielski on two plays. *Question of Geography* is set in Magadan, the port for the Gulag, in the summer of '52 – the year before Stalin died. It deals with the way seven or eight people who have been in the camps, but who are on temporary release, unable to return to 'the Continent', living under the continuous threat of re-arrest, attempt to create a sense of their lives. The second is a play, only just finished, about Goya.

After *Into Their Labours*, John says he will be glad to write no fiction for a long, long time. He plans to write a book about Spanish painting, and to continue to collaborate on plays. He wants to stop having to invent things on his own. 'It's much more fun,' he says, 'to invent things together.'

John finds political developments since '84 personally distressing, as though the years he lived most intensely (from the age of twenty to fifty) had been wiped out. The axioms by which people lived then have become as dust. And that, he finds quite hard. But of course it has all happened before. We are faced with a long period of resistance, he says, in which we must keep our nerve.

John Berger was born in London on November 5th 1926.

John Berger's Book Choice:

The Case of Comrade Tulayev
  Victor Serge
Life and Destiny
  Vassily Grossman
The Wretched of the Earth
  Frantz Fanon
Twenty Years A-Growing
  Maurice O'Sullivan
Memed my Hawk
  Yashar Kemal
Collected Poems Pablo Neruda

Collected Poems Nazim Hikmet
The Book of Migration Adonis
The Old Curiosity Shop
  Charles Dickens
Our Mutual Friend
  Charles Dickens
Remembrance of Things Past
  Marcel Proust
Farewell to Arms
  Ernest Hemingway

Books by John Berger:

A Painter of our Time
Permanent Red
The Foot of Clive
Corker's Freedom
The Success and Failure of
  Picasso
A Fortunate Man
  (with Jean Mohr)
Art and Revolution
The Moment of Cubism and
  other essays
The Look of Things

G
Ways of Seeing
A Seventh Man (with Jean Mohr)
Pig Earth
About Looking
Another Way of Telling
  (with Jean Mohr)
And Our Faces, My Heart, Brief as
  Photos
The White Bird
Once in Europa

0

Film scripts:

Salamander
The Middle of the World

Jonah Who Will Be 25 In The Year
2000

Plays:

Question of Geography
(with Nella Bielski)

Francisco Goya's Last Portrait
(with Nella Bielski)

Chapter Four

MALCOLM BRADBURY

I started writing very early. I was a somewhat weakly child: I was born with a heart condition which meant I couldn't play games or join in most activities, and that left me on my own a good deal. The result was that I turned to books as a prop, or alternative world, and I became a great reader. From around the age of seven or eight I was spending a lot of my time in the local public libraries, and like lots of writers – Borges, for example – I've always been fascinated by libraries and the wonderful labyrinthine world of stories they open up for the imagination. I suppose it's very appropriate that I married a librarian, and met her across a library desk when I was doing a thesis and chasing up footnotes. Of course all this is a passion that's shared by a lot of writers and academics, and even before you start to write you're drawn to the place where books are kept, and what's inside them, the great storehouse of ideas and dreams.

My parents were mildly bookish too. My father was not highly educated, because he had to leave school at 15 and become a booking clerk – that word again – on the railway. But he was conscious of what he'd missed, and put a great value on education. And he educated himself a good deal through books, learning shorthand and technical subjects, but also reading a lot of history books and factual books of all kinds, though rather less fiction. But he belonged to libraries: he was a typical user of the old Boots Lending Library, the old private libraries where you paid, I think, threepence a week or threepence a book to borrow, and he belonged to the Mechanics Institute Library in Nottingham, and he took me in there to read the newspapers and magazines. He was very hardworking and determined, and he was interested in things like design. Later he joined the station-designing and then the advertising side of railways, and after railway nationalization he became an advertising man who was responsible for selling the kind of posters you see on railway stations and buses. I think he wanted me to go into something of this kind, design or advertising, and I was good at art and worked for a time in an advertising agency in Nottingham over the summers. I can't quite say he encouraged me to be a writer, an ambition which I really did have very early on, from about fourteen or fifteen, perhaps because he didn't think it was a career, more a hobby. But he always showed an interest and increasingly a pride in what I went on to do.

My mother read quite a bit too, and still does. They're both still alive, in their eighties. And although I can't say she influenced the sort of things I wrote, she certainly encouraged me in the sensitivity which is part of the repertoire. That had to do with the fact that if you're what used to be called 'a delicate child,' and that was the phrase applied to me, you tend to get treated 'delicately', and play that role. I was attached to my mother and found her a tower of strength, especially during the war when my father was moved around a lot on his job. She came from a Sheffield family, a railway family. Her father was an engine driver and there were several unmarried sisters who also worked on the railway, as typists, like my mother. That was how my mother and father met.

I was born there, in Sheffield, but we then moved to London, when I was still a a baby of one or two. We lived out in Metroland, in Rayner's Lane, but it's a period of my life about which I remember very little, except the start of the war and various raids, on Northolt and so on. I was seven when the war started, and we rather strangely moved up to Sheffield to get away from the London Bombing, and also because my father's job changed. But of course Sheffield was a major target and that was a terrible and miserable period, seeing the city come down, the shops and factories falling. The schools went onto a shift system and moved about the city. Around this time I was sent a good deal to my father's homeplace, Macclesfield in Cheshire, which I found miserable because these journeys on the train – you wore a little parcel-label with your name on it so the guard could put you off – were separations. As a result, I think I made less than I should of the world of Macclesfield as it was then, an old silk town with a fine moorland countryside, and above all a late nineteenth century industrial community still going strong. I think about it now as a kind of lost material as well as a powerful and interesting family past. My grandmother started work in the silk-mills around the age of seven or eight, under the most primitive and Dickensian working conditions. My grandfather was a Methodist lay preacher and a builder's foreman, working on great houses. He was a man of great strength and honesty, a friend and adviser to a lot of people, with a great severity, or so it seemed to me, severity of the moral Methodist kind, very against the evils of drink and so on, but with an enormous feeling of responsibility for others.

During the war we moved to Nottingham, and lived in West Bridgford, a residential suburb that was called 'Bread and Lard Island' because it was the posh bit across the river, near the cricket ground, that Nottingham people struggled perhaps a bit too hard to get to. I went to infant school and then, as the war ended, became one of the first of the Butler Education Act kids. I got a free grammar school place, something my parents couldn't probably have afforded for me otherwise, and I felt pushed hard to get a good education. My father felt I was getting what he had missed, and he was severe but encouraging. Then came the question of university, something my father knew little about, and had some mild suspicions of. It's the sort of story written up in Richard Hoggart's *The Uses of Literacy*, where the opening doors of the university became, for the Scholarship Boy, the opportunity for a kind of advancement from the lower middle-class background. So my father wasn't sure whether I was wasting time and avoiding getting a job, or going on to valuable education that would improve my chances of doing so. As far as he was concerned, getting a good job was the crucial moment in everyone's life. I've spent my life in universities ever since, to my father's perfect satisfaction, though he probably has little idea still of what the academic life is really like, even after reading my novels. But a good education was about getting on and gaining in self-understanding. And when I went to university I found myself part of a very highly motivated and competitive generation of my own kind. We were the new meritocrats.

Inevitably English was my subject through school and into university. As a child, what I'd read mostly were the classic boys' authors: Henty; Rider Haggard; John Masefield. John Steinbeck was another, and I notice a lot of people who come to university are still Steinbeck readers, which is interesting, since he's never had much of an academic reputation. But there was some magical appeal there – strong themes and strong narrative – that still clicks on somewhat when I pick up his work. Maybe the definition of a children's classic is a book that stays as a secret pleasure. The other striking thing about Steinbeck was that he was for me one of those writers who radiated a sense of massive experience. He'd been a hobo, bumming around, he was busy, physical, romantic, all the kinds of thing that in the end as a writer I have not been. My idea of a writer now is far less someone who has been and done things, but someone who has read and thought and felt. And the writer who really meant most to me – it was natural enough if you came from Nottingham – was D. H. Lawrence, the self-searching and self-educating Lawrence, with his drama of soul and his drama of feeling, which was closer to the sort of person I was.

Lawrence was actually first published in a local paper, the *Nottinghamshire Guardian*, so I set out to follow his footsteps by writing stories and sending them to that paper from about the age of fourteen or fifteen. And I had several stories and pieces published there, or in the morning or evening associated papers. My literary ambitions were very catholic – I wanted to be a writer, any kind of writer – and one thing I was greatly interested in was writing for the radio. That was the great time of the family round the radio for the big comedy shows, and my heroes were people like Peter Sellers, and Bernard Braden, and Frank Muir and Denis Norden. I started sending scripts to the BBC Variety Script Unit and got some encouragement, and bits of them were used. And the other great destination was *Punch*, which I started sending things to very early. There was a famous folklore that said you submitted to *Punch* for about 10 years before they took anything, so I was delighted to be accepted by them just around the time I started at university. My main interest was comedy, light or heavy. And my ambitions were to finance serious comedy – the novel, the form I've always put highest – by writing lighter forms. For some reason not fully clear to me, I've always thought the novel the fundamental and serious form of expression, the life-exploring and truth-telling form. So the big secret ambition was my novel, and from an early age I felt it was in the novel I would most fully explore myself, the form, and what I wished to say.

I went on to read English at Leicester, which was then a university college awarding an external degree of the University of London. I didn't go far away from home partly because of the heart condition, which affected my life quite a lot until I had open heart surgery when I was twenty-seven (up to that point the operation didn't really exist in this country – I was once almost done in the USA, but the costs were terrifying). Almost as soon as I got to Leicester I began my first novel, *Eating People Is Wrong*, and though it didn't come out until seven or eight years later, it was very much a book of someone going into the university wonderland for the first time. I had something of a crisis about whether as a writer I ought to be studying literature academically. By this time I'd published a bit and a writer was what I knew I was. I was afraid of being taught the rules of tedium and tediousness, the weighty canonical past of writing rather than its nature and value in the present. I think all good writers are good readers, and they can never elude the tradition. On the other hand they must be given a sense of the contemporary, of the living issues of writing, which are aesthetic and philosophical and involve a sense of the future as well as of the past. What helped attach me to literary study was in fact the changing reputation of Lawrence. I'd come to him really through Nottingham, because he was writing about the landscape I knew, social and physical. But his reputation was on the upsurge, largely because of F. R. Leavis, for whom he was the great twentieth century novelist. There was the coincidence then of a writer for whom I had a great personal attachment gaining recognition as a modern classic, and Leavis related him to the past as part of a vital creative tradition of British fiction. I've had various rude things to say about Leavis since, partly because in opening some important doors he shut some others of great significance. But it was Leavis and his 'Great Tradition' that made *Beowulf* and *Sir Gawain and the Green Knight* and the somewhat benighted, philologically based sub-Oxford syllabus we did, bearable.

Maybe it's worth saying a bit about literary education in British universities and their relation to contemporary writing, since it's something I care about a lot. Leicester was an outlying college of the University of London and it was teaching a syllabus that was rather at the end of its days. Half the work was in language, which meant not linguistics but Anglo-Saxon and Middle English, and that was to provide the stamina, the All-Bran of the course. It was all very Nordic and philological, and it really belonged in a nineteenth century thought system which made literary study into a form of nationalism and provincialism. The people who taught me, spread my interests beyond the syllabus, though, and I was able to work in literary criticism and above all American literature, which was an optional paper. I started reading the post-war American writers like Bellow, Salinger and Updike and I found them genuinely contemporary, post-war, and cosmopolitan in a way I did not find most of the British writing I read. I was also reading Sartre, Camus,

Thomas Mann and various continental moderns, and these led me
out of the limitations that annoyed me, as did some marvellous
teachers like Philip Collins and Arthur Humphreys. I made my peace
with the course and the university system. I put in a great final burst,
got a fortunate First, and everything changed. I'd already got myself
a job in advertising, working for Kodak. But with the First there was
a scholarship to do research at London University, so I withdrew
from the job and became a long term research student. And very
happily I've stayed in university life ever since. The other great
influence was Leavis and his missionary passion about literature.
Leavis had his faults, but he did believe in the critical and creative
act, that good literature and thinking about literature transformed
human culture. It was a moral force, and that idea influenced me
powerfully, won my agreement. Lawrence has a famous phrase that
Leavis regularly quoted, about the novelist being more important
than the philosopher, the priest or the saint because he imaginatively
reaches for the heart of the moral truths of experience. I had that
impassioned moral fervour – it helped me, I suppose, get my First –
and it had to do with the commitment and sense of value that I think
goes equally into the writing of literature and the good study of it.
Literary study isn't, despite modern theory, an abstract activity, and
what makes a good student is what makes a good writer: a sense of
the fundamental human value of the entire activity.

I suppose you might call all this a provincial quarrel with
provincialism, which I think was what was happening in the culture
then, and which fed that burst of new activity that changed the novel
and gave it a post-war spirit. In 1950 William Cooper published
Scenes from Provincial Life, which naturally caught my attention,
since it was set right where I was, in Leicester. There were other
related books, like *Lucky Jim* – that, in a sense, was set in Leicester
too, because Philip Larkin (whose novels were also important to me)
was librarian at Leicester then, and Amis came over a lot and drew
on it for material. I was encouraged that the kind of world I lived in
was available as a literary landscape, and *Eating People Is Wrong*
was in a way a reflection on that, and a general reaction for me to
the 50's, because as I kept writing it that became its subject.

I have to talk about liberalism, which was the humanistic spirit of
mind in which I felt myself to lie (Forster and Orwell were other
influences). I'd reacted to some degree against my religious
background in favour of humanism, and I'd reacted against politics

in favour of the literary imagination. The 50's was the troubled time when the ethos of liberalism changed from its 1930's form. My central character in the novel is someone who has been left-wing in the 1930's, in the Auden-Spender spirit; been through the phase of political clarity and concern; then, in the 1950's, found himself seeing politics as a dangerous and totalitarianizing illusion, and discovered the centrality of literature and personal relations. This was the liberal imagination in the Lionel Trilling sense: that what makes literature valuable is its sense of contradiction and ambiguity, its struggling discovery of moral realism. Literature, great writing, therefore takes situations which the mind might interpret politically, philosophically, religiously, but it explores them in their felt and pragmatic reality, through the life dramas of individuals, the conflict of personal and social existence. Intractability and difficulty are the real stuff of literature. My book was a comedy about someone of that belief who finds the intractability multiplying to the point where he cannot cope with it; so I began a kind of exploration of the ironies of modern liberalism, a theme I've stayed with since and one I believe to be of fundamental concern.

It was a hard book to write because I set myself a task which I now feel was odd: writing, as a 20 year old student, about a 40 year old teacher who I wanted to understand from the inside. It was a difficult act of impersonation or imaginative transfer, and since I'm now well past 40 and am a university teacher I'm pretty impressed with the way I did it, considering how little I knew. I'm interested in the need to do it, which obviously has something to do with speculative identification with my own growing up. The context of the book now dates very clearly, but the 1950's was the period when many of our modern attitudes of mind, and the conflicts inside them, began. I now see it as a strong foundation stone from which to start building. It's nice, for me, that I like it a good deal, though in some ways it's perhaps my lightest novel, very youthful but with skills in it I'm awfully pleased to see I'd developed in my early twenties. The books afterward go away from it in a variety of ways, so I suppose I'm right about it being a kind of foundation stone rather than a youthful toy.

In some ways it was inevitable that the next book would be about the United States, because it was an enormous intellectual influence on the period and certainly on me, and having briefly been there as an undergraduate I wanted to go back and study there. I was a research student in London for two years working on Anglo-American modernism, and then in 1955 I went to the States, to Indiana University, to teach composition and be a graduate student in literary theory and American literature. There were a lot of reasons why this Anglo-American artistic and intellectual connection was growing at the time, and why a lot of us became Midatlantic men or women. But two things were particularly important and got reflected in my next book, *Stepping Westward*. One was that the States was immensely freeing after the rather chilly and repressive atmosphere of austerity Britain in the post-war, end-of-Empire, closing-in years. The other more disturbing thing was that it was also the period of uneasy and frightening Cold War, and the unpleasantness of McCarthyism. So in one sense America was fun, splendid, rich, open, and freeing, and in another sense there was something frightening, the intolerance and anti-intellectualism of the Cold War world. And that's what *Stepping Westward* is all about. It's about somebody, again a British liberal, who's a writer, and who goes to America and has a sense of being tempted by these extraordinary freedoms and excitements. But at the same time realises that behind at least one version of this freedom there is a demand for allegiance; the Loyalty Oath is the main thing on which the plot turns. (When I went to America I had to sign a loyalty oath promising that I wouldn't overthrow the American Government by force.)

America did hook me very powerfully – much of my academic life since has been in the field of American literature and American Studies, and much of what I've written about as a critic has been American. I did get enormous excitement out of going systematically into American literature, which is what I was doing in the States. So another thing the book, to me, is about is the relationship between an English writer and American writing. The writers who really stirred me up were Bellow and Malamud and Mailer and Salinger. I wanted to write a book which somehow opened my style, my perception, to their ways of seeing and working. And it was in some ways a counter to other books I'd enjoyed but wanted to quarrel with. One was Evelyn Waugh's *The Loved One*, which is a very funny but wicked parody of America. The other was Kingsley Amis's *One Fat Englishman*, which is about this clever, if unpleasant, English snob who goes to vulgar America and puts down Americans. I wanted to turn the story round, and have America give something and mean something to the characters, so in that sense I've always described it to myself as a Henry James in reverse. There was a 'vaunted scene' at the other end to which there has to be a real response. For James, Europe is the 'vaunted scene', and many of James's novels consist of bringing an American character onto the stage of Europe and portraying an initiation: a change of nature; a change of understanding; a learning to see. That is what I was trying to do, the other way round.

I did think, around this time, of staying in America. I was offered a job at Yale and was very tempted to take it. I was being published a lot in American magazines, *The New Yorker* and so on, and *Eating People is Wrong* came out in the States. I could see a career largely focussed, let's say around the *New Yorker*. It's a great cosmopolitan magazine, it loves finished and artistic writing, and I suppose I saw myself as potentially a sort of British Updike. It seems in retrospect an interesting moment because if I had done that I'm sure I would have been a very different kind of writer, because the relationship of the serious writer to the market is different in America. I'd had my heart operation, I was getting married, I'd got a first book out, I had a good agent there. But mainly because I was marrying a English girl who didn't know the States, I took perhaps the safer course. I've stayed in touch with the United States and I go there often, but it was a very decisive choice. It shaped me in the direction of being a British writer, and since I value the cosmopolitanism of literature I've often wondered about the alternative. And after that there was some loss of contact with the American part of my audience, so that it's only lately that my books – although they've appeared in hardback there – have started to come out in paperback. The importance of that to me is that I feel a special affinity with American writing, as I've said, and as I've tried to elaborate in a critical book on the modern American novel.

I actually began *The History Man* in the States. It was going to be a novel set in an American university in the late 60s, and then was switched to being set in a British university in 1972. I'd started it with a number of ideas which didn't quite get fulfilled or rather had to be converted into another currency. I happen to be a very, very slow writer, and in order to try to speed myself up I invented the idea of a novel that would take place over a period of three months which would be the three months over which I was writing it. So it started at the beginning of a term, it would finish at the end of that same term. It would in a sense be a diary novel, or a novel which had a highly foregrounded actuality to it. I started the book in 67, so there was a version of it where *I* start work on October 1st 1967, and *the book* starts on October 1st 1967. I couldn't write as fast as I was hoping, so, let's say I get to the end of chapter three and already the clock has run out. So next year,' 68, I start again on October 1st, thinking, 'Well, I've got three chapters to help me, so I'll make it this time,' and I get to the end of chapter four and the clock runs out. And so on. And each time I did a new version I wanted to be terribly honest to the year, so I'd be careful about what was in Biba, what was in the boutiques, what the designs of Habitat spoons were that year, what was in the newspapers. And so it went on, until I decided to fix it in 1972 because by 1972 I could see that the material I was dealing with was already on the wane. This novel about a 'revolutionary' was being moved into a period when the 'revolution' was dying. Over '73 and '74 I reworked it a couple of times more (I revise obsessively) and it was submitted in '74 and appeared in '75.

I see it as a break away from what I'd done before. *Eating People is Wrong* and *Stepping Westward* are good-humoured, gentle, genial comedies with sympathetic characters, and the reader is supposed to be tempted in and engaged by the comedy. I saw them as being in the tradition of books like *Tom Jones* – the good-humoured, traditional comic novel. But *The History Man* was intended as a totally ironic book. I wanted to use the ironic voice. I wanted to stand back and separate myself from the experience, from the material, partly for technical reasons. I felt that it was too easy to persuade the reader into the text by a kind of genial, comic realism, and I wanted the reader to be more aware of the text. I wanted the fictionality of the book to be present as something that had to be seen and understood. The book is very deliberately laid out: nearly all the paragraphs are the same length, and these long blocks of print are deliberately made rather hostile on the page. And the central character is decidedly not sympathetic, though I hope not totally unsympathetic either – in other words a complicated central character. And in some ways there is a great deal of suppression; I'm trying not to give out all the story, in order to make people think as they read the book, 'What is missing? What do I need to understand to get through this?' Above all, there is a great deal of suppression of the story of Howard's wife, Barbara (who is in a sense

the central character for me: there's a hidden central character as it
were), so by the time you've put the book down you realise that
something terrible has been happening to Barbara all the way
through. Also there was this question of topicality and the way in
which the realism is used. I suppose most novelists use realism as a
kind of supportive documentation to make people feel that this is a
probable world and to provoke recognition. I want a kind of hyper-
realism, and excessive realism. I want the reader to feel they're being
told almost too much. In a way it is over shot, the camera is too
insistent, as if something else is missing; and what is missing is the
consciousness, or the interior life, or the psychological life, of the
central character. Everything is seen through his eyes, but they're
flat eyes, they're camera eyes, they're not the eyes of full
consciousness. It was a period when I was asking myself all sorts of
questions about the nature of realism and quarrelling with the
realistic tradition of British fiction from the 50's onwards.

That continued with *Rates of Exchange* really. In that case I
became interested in the way in which we transact paper fictions,
and the whole question of how we seek to give value to written pieces
of script, and to guarantee them as true in some fashion of other.
This particularly engaged me in relation to monetarism and the
whole social argument that's going on at the moment about whether
money is so true that it compels us to believe that certain forms of
political activity, certain forms of political conduct, certain directions
for the nation, and for the world, are possible. I'm growing more
and more interested in the way in which the fictions of others (in the
case of *The History Man* it was the sociologists, in the case of *Rates
of Exchange*, the economists) are administered as interpretations of
human experience. I now think the novelist is a person who creates
fictions in the consciousness that they are fictions and therefore
needs to apply fictional self-knowledge to everybody else's fictions,
to the fictions that run and control society – the plots of others. I
see the novel as a great form of scepticism and of quarrel with other
people's truths. It's a great agnostic form. In that sense it still has a
moral function undoubtedly, but the nature of the moral activity is
different from that which Leavis believed it to be.

I think, as I've said, that one factor that is stable in all this is that
I've always regarded myself as a liberal. By liberalism I suppose I
mean certain things which are really rather nineteenth century. In
terms of the question of how an individual relates to society and what

claims society has over an individual- in the self and society equation the self counts very substantially. I'm a liberal in the sense therefore of quarrelling initially with religious totalitarian world views. I'm an atheist, and that was very important to me when I was younger since my parents were Christian. (It no longer seems all that important because I no longer think religion is all that powerful.) I believe persons and personal relationships are far more important than large scale Christian definitions of moral law and so on: 'The ten suggestions rather than the ten commandments,' to quote Chris Bigsby. In political terms I'm against any form of totalitarian expression. McCarthyism made me aware of the danger of totalitarianism of the Right. And I think there are enormous and necessary anxieties that we should be having about the way Mrs Thatcher is going at this moment. Freedom of thought, it seems to me, is so subtly rooted in culture, so easily taken away, and so absolutely essential, that it is a very delicate plant. Being a liberal has led me at various points into intellectual quarrels with the Left and the Right. In the late 60s / early 70s, it was with a certain kind of radical Left. What my main dispute was about was the strong behaviourism and anti-individualism that was coming into sociology, and I felt that something had to be defended. There was a kind of dogmatism and violence that was coming through in the radical imagination that I wanted to quarrel with. But equally, I feel passionately about, and quarrel with, the way in which the Right has moved and its de-personalisation and reification. These are the sorts of things that anger me, and I think this present government is guilty of many forms of that.

I briefly mentioned Forster, but E. M. Forster was a writer who meant a great deal to me. He put great emphasis on personal relations as the one thing that we really have. But there is something curious about writing passionately about personal relations and not actually having any because you're sitting at a typewriter all day. Writing does exclude other people. You don't consciously use it as that necessarily, but in the end there is certainly a paradox if you are trying to imaginatively bring people alive and you are deadening your relationships all round you; and even a hypocrisy: you are asserting one thing and then being unable to perform it. I think there is something frightening about this obsessive drive to write. I certainly have it, and I have it in an almost uncontrollable way. If I'm not writing I'm miserable. And certainly that's one of the things that made me want to stop teaching full-time. I felt I wasn't working enough and that I needed this act of being in front of the typewriter more. The thing about living with a book is of course you are living with it *all* the time: even when you are not writing you are working it over in some fashion; when you are sitting down at dinner or whatever, it's still there, and you're still fussing about it; you go silent on people and they don't really know why, and it is because this book is nagging away at you and you're afraid that if you get too involved in something else you'll lose it; you don't want to go out at the weekend because you are interrupting the set of feelings and habits that you need to keep the book going. I think the fact that I've not been a full-time writer has been of benefit to my family, and to me too. I think the solitude of writing is probably the hardest thing to manage. If one didn't have an institution to belong to, in my case a university, where would one get intellectual stimulation? Friendship? Things to do which arise by surprise and involve all sorts of obligations? Where would one keep in touch? How would one know the difference between 1983 and 1984? I think you can get lost in literary solitude, and I think I'd be tempted to do that if I didn't have a job other than writing.

Most serious writers say they write for themselves, but that's not entirely true. I think if I have a model audience it's probably essentially a graduate audience. It's an audience that is interested in intellectual issues to some degree. Until *The History Man* was done on television my audience matched the one I thought I had – then suddenly I found that the audience was becoming quite different. There is no doubt that *Rates of Exchange* has reached a broader audience than any book I've ever done before (you can tell this from letters that you get and so on), and so my sense of my audience is changing. It's also been changed by writing for television. The model of expression that I was using is breaking up in all sorts of ways – and very profitably. I think that's very creative – I want this multiplication and variation of the audience to make me write differently, to put me under test, to give me challenges. I'd like to say that I meet those challenges while still remaining a serious writer.

I think I was very lucky in the way *The History Man* was done on television. It was cleverly done. The script was shown to me and I discussed it with Christopher Hampton who wrote it. There is no such thing as an ironic camera, and since the book had been written from the standpoint of irony it was very hard to match that. But the problems themselves were fascinating because they are instructive about the creative mechanisms that one uses to compose books. This produced a situation with *Rates of Exchange* (I had some indication that it would be done as a television series) where I was able while writing it to think about that, and it effects the book. I was actually able to suppress part of the story in the novel to save it for the other version, in other words to play on the fact that the television version is different from the novel version – to actually conceive of that difference as part of the drama of writing. Another thing was that I see myself writing in a different dramatic relation to my characters from the early books. One element in that difference is that instead of inventing characters who exist only in words you are inventing characters who are going to be given flesh and whose psychological sequence has to be dramatic – that is to say, they have to be performance parts. I feel I've learned a lot about the management of the dramatic content of the novel from that experience; and also about the way in which writers invent characters. I think probably when you first start writing most characters are very close to surrogations for parts of yourself. It was very hard for me to write about a forty year old professor while I was a twenty year old student, but none the less that professor was probably derived by my trying to think what I would be like if I were forty years old and a professor. But there's another way of thinking about characters in fiction, which is that you're not trying to surrogate for yourself – you are trying to create dramatic performance roles for other figures. They must have something to do with the theatre of your mind, they are necessarily a part of your subjective theatre, but they can be conceived quite differently. I found that very useful indeed in changing my writing, and I think in the end writing becomes boring unless you have dramas that make it change.

For a period of about ten years I was very taken by the need for fictionalism; that is to say it seemed to me that the most important writers for my generation were people like Borges, Nabokov, Calvino; writers who were very, very insistent of the fictionality of their novels, and this was a way of getting out of the imprisonment of naïve realism. I think we've asked so many questions about the nature of this fictionality that we are now in a position to come back to realism and express it in new forms. I never took up the fully fictionist position that there is no such thing as realism, or it is absurd to attempt realism in novels. I believe that the nature of the novel's

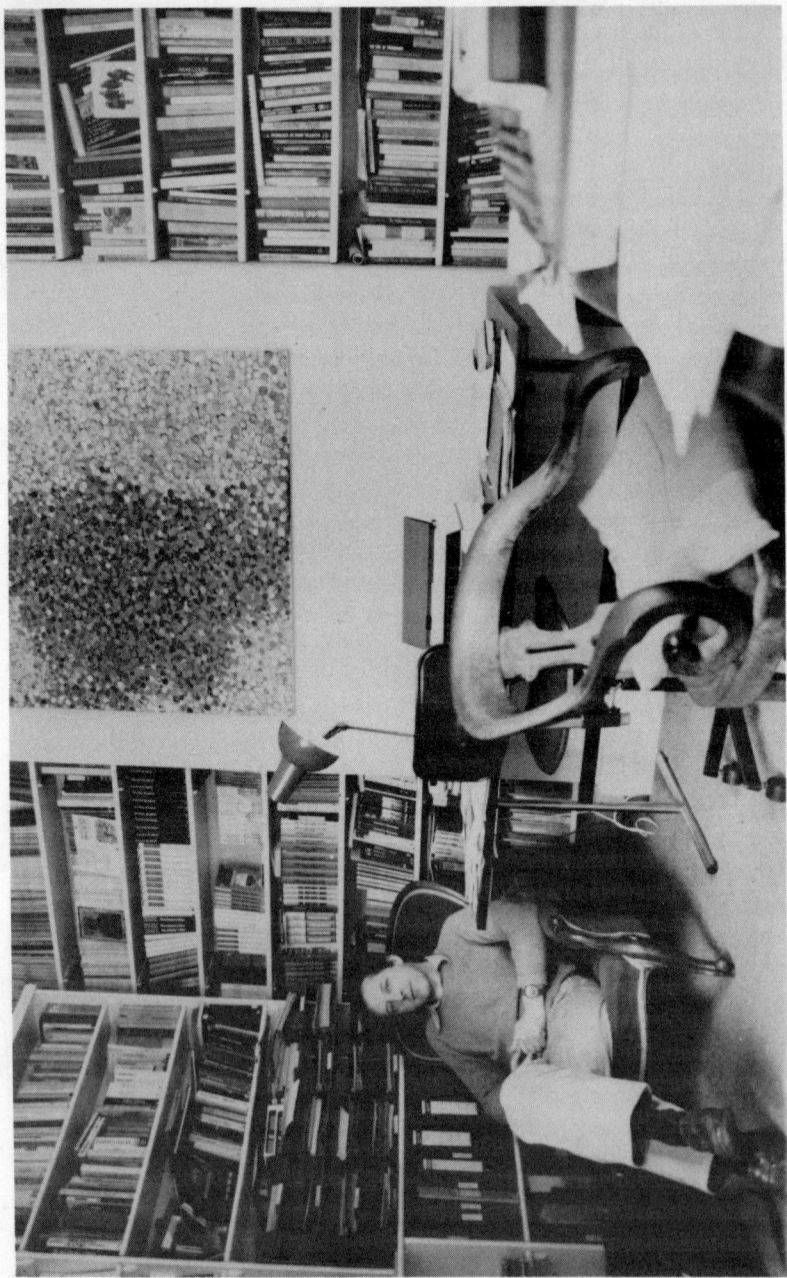

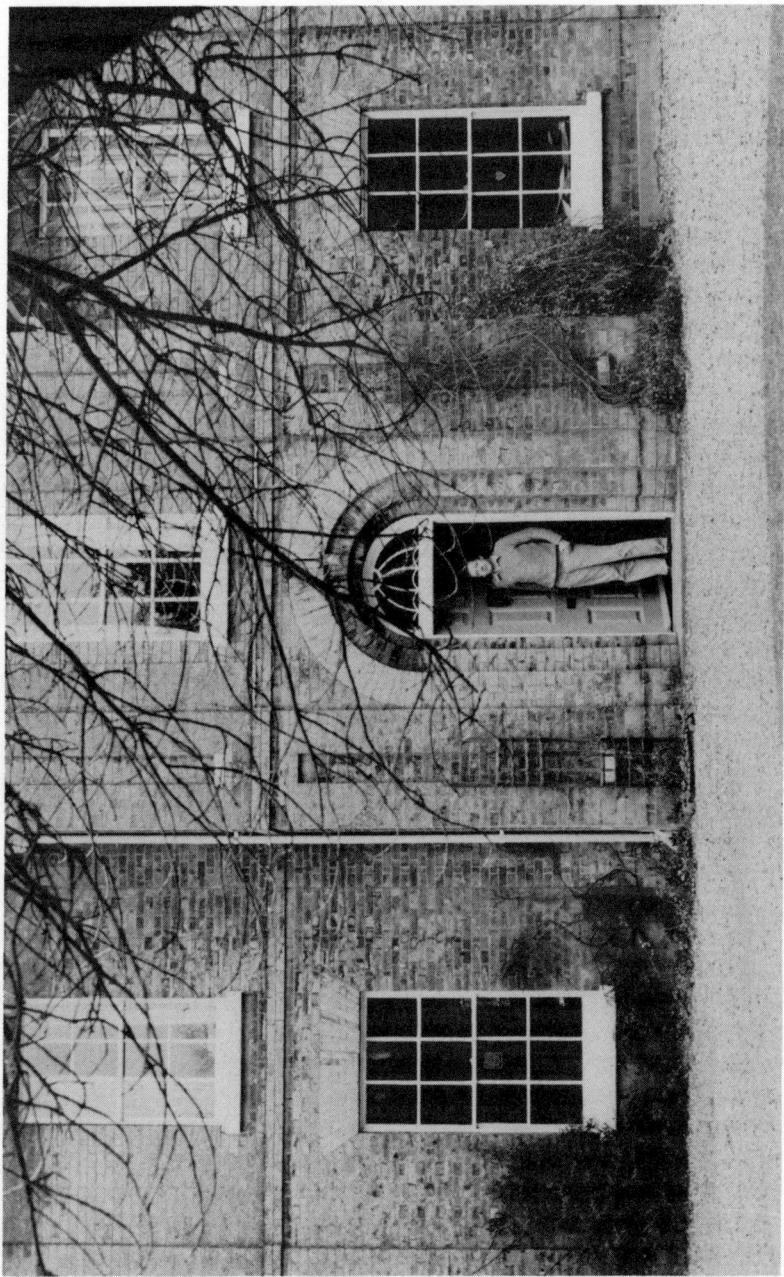

enquiry is that it must keep testing both its own fictionality and its own capacity to seem realistic. The result is that at the moment I'm moving back a bit in my immediate writing towards the realistic again, but certainly in very different ways to the ways that I was writing in the 50's. In the 50's, realism seemed to have an awful lot to do with familiarisation by provincialisation. You told stories about homely people – everyday stories about country life or town life or whatever, and there was a communal folksiness about an awful lot of the fiction. I think that's been pushed to the side by the complexity of modern relationships and modern fictions – the fictions that have come along since, so that now, what realism must be, is something built on different concepts about the real from the ones that were around in the 50's.

I still think the novel is the most serious of all the forms – more serious than writing for television for example – and part of the reason for that is that you control it. It's not a collaborative affair – it's a personal affair. Those are your words and they are expressed directly to the reader: whereas working for television is working in a collaborative situation where you can't personalise it too much. If you seek to personalise it in the way you do with the novel then you are shutting out relationships to many original and splendid people; and one of the nice things about working for television in Britain is that there are original and splendid people involved in it, and it's exactly in finding a good director or a very good cast that the lessons come: you learn, and the thing grows as a piece of creation by those means and that's the excitement of it. There's also the financial reward. I take a very, very long time over novels, anything up to ten years, and you can't write for television on that timescale. You probably get more money from the television thing that you've taken three to six months over than the novel that you've taken ten years over, so in practical terms for me it's very good to have some things that I do quickly. And I think it's very good to work to deadlines and be forced to speed up. Also I have something in me (it was there from about the age of sixteen) which says, 'I want to be professional about this.' I take a certain pride in the professional aspects so that if someone asks me to do something which I think of as difficult, I'm very drawn to it to see whether I've got the professional skill to do it. I like to learn that professional skill. For example, I've never written a stage play – I would love to find out whether I can write a stage play and to see just what the limits of my skill there are. So there's that on the one hand – then there's this much more impassioned aspect of writing which I tend to associate with novels. I do tend to see my novels as compartmentalised away from the other things (despite what I was saying about part of the exchange of *Rates of Exchange* being with the television version). But in the end I would want people to read the novel rather than just watch the television version and say that'll do.

I work on a typewriter, and when I start a book I always start in the belief that that first imprint on the paper is *it* – that I'm actually writing the final draft. I know it's not true. It's a device – but I need to tell myself that. In fact it can be anything up to fifty drafts before it gets there – in some parts of the book anyway, particularly the first chapter. I think there were about fifty first chapters of *The History Man*. I keep rewriting in a local way, that is to say, you write something one day; you come down the next morning and look at it; go over it; and then type it again. So there's little revisions; and then there's massive revisions where maybe you say, 'No, this doesn't belong in this part of the book – it belongs in the last chapter, not the first,' or whatever. So there's that kind of reworking. Then there's another kind of reworking: although rhythm is not what is conventionally looked for in prose, I do have a very strong sense of prose rhythm, and so I keep on working the thing over the way you work if you're writing a lyric poem – you know there's a duff word somewhere in the sentence, you don't quite know which word it is, so you've got to keep going at the line until it cracks. In the end, what I'm doing much of the time is rewriting, and I find that obsessively fascinating. I really like doing it.

One of the things that fascinates me is how you get a book. Where does a book come from? What makes you start one? That's the hardest for me. If you are taking that amount of time over a book it means it's got to be a pretty substantial idea. So I take about a year to work out a book before I even write a line (apart from making notes in notebooks and so on and drawing little charts), so there's a very long period when the book is coming although you're not actually writing it.

I think PLR has been absolutely necessary and very important, as an act of justice really. It's extraordinary how badly most writers live given the amount of trade that goes on in their name. If you just look at the evidence from the Society of Authors about the pathetically small sums that some people of real quality and value earn, then the whole thing seems to me at times even tragic. The trouble is that publishing is a very successful, commercial activity (publishers make a lot of money and bookshops seem to do all right and so on) and it's very hard to persuade anybody that writers need help. There are very few writers' bursaries and so on, and now they're talking about abolishing the Literature Department in the Arts Council. The thing that I believe is important is to actually give writers money to write. Much, much more could be done about this. There have been all sorts of attempts to give writers money for readings, or lecture tours, or sitting in supermarkets and talking about their work, but actually just sitting down to write, which is the hardest thing of all to finance, is not properly supported. I suppose I feel this particularly passionately about that kind of writing which you might call small press: poetry, short-stories, and so on. And I do believe that these forms are crucial.

I think there has to be quite a lot of evidence on the ground before you do give people money. I go to a writer's colony in the States. They seem to me to understand what it is that people need: a bedroom, a studio; a month or so where you can write intensively without interruption; a kind of monastic atmosphere during the day (when nobody's supposed to interrupt anybody else). This applies as much to Philip Roth or Saul Bellow as it does to beginners. So you form a group of people, some of whom are well-known, some of whom are virtually unknown, who are stimulating and affecting each other. You're not simply giving people money – you're giving them stimulation and creative opportunity, and very often, somebody with whom a risk has been taken turns out a better writer than they might have been had they not gone there. That can work in America because there is a kind of structural generosity which is partly to do with the fact that this is money from corporations and so on that otherwise would have gone to the tax man. Unfortunately our laws don't allow for that use of money. We seem to be moving into an age when everybody says commercial sponsorship is the answer, but commercial sponsorship is not going to do anything like that. They're taking commercial sponsorship out of their advertising budget and they want a T-shirt or something. If you put writers in a room nobody sees their T-shirt, so they're more likely to sponsor an opera or a sporting event than they are to sponsor somebody to go away and write. British tax law is notoriously hard on writers, to the point where many of them won't live in the country any more. That seems to me to be unfortunate. I do think there are ways of looking at what happens in the writing of books which are never really understood by tax people (there was a period when I used to be able to get my typewriter allowed against tax by calling it an agricultural implement) like spreading the profits from a book over the period which you've actually taken to write the book. If it does take you ten years to write the book you ought to be able to spread the rewards over ten years, but taxation all comes at once, and in that sense it's inequitable. I think writers should pay tax like everybody else, but there is the question of unevennesses and inequities within the working of the system. But my irritation finally has to do with the low value we still place on serious artists, and the refusal to take them seriously. The recent treatment of literature by the Arts Council is a classic example. A country should find a way to support and assist its serious writers.

I'm a passionate believer in teaching creative writing. There is an enormous value in thinking of teaching creative writing in the sense that other professional skills can be taught. You expect to teach people to dance or to act and I think there is a way in which you can and should teach people to write. I don't think this means you can simply take a literary innocent and turn them into a literary sophisticate by some one-year course. I think an awful lot of what goes into making a writer is first of all personal and not even exchangeable in discussion. Secondly there has to be an enormous amount of motivation, and probably the good writer is someone who is deeply, deeply motivated to write; you can have literary skills, but without that motivation you just won't get anywhere. I also think that a lot of creative writing courses are a waste of time, particularly in the States where an awful lot of it is crude exercise setting: 'Do a character,' 'Go and write a sketch,' and so on: and where there is an attempt to teach 'the rules of writing'. I think good writing doesn't have rules of that kind. What I think can best be done is to take somebody with talent, with aspiration and will, and spend time with them when they're working on a major project that they perhaps would have done anyway. I think a collectivity of people in a workshop situation is a good thing: working together, talking regularly about writing, taking the business of writing seriously. That solitariness of writing is one of its problems, and in Britain, where there is very little public literary debate, very little talk about the aesthetics of form and so on, it's very easy for writers never to get

challenged technically and never to challenge themselves technically
and never to ask themselves crucial questions; and so a lot of writers
in Britain don't seem to me to have œuevres, they don't develop,
they don't grow. I think a creative writing course can play some part
in giving the ambition to grow, giving one a sense of long-term
literary purpose, as well as help with the production of one particular
book.

At the moment I'm between books, and that's a peculiarly
indecisive stage. I want to start as soon as I can on another novel,
and I want in the end to have gone as far with the novel form as I
can. In other words, I see myself in the middle of a journey through
the writing of fiction – a journey which in a way starts with a rather
simple view, and has grown more and more complicated. It starts
with a kind of realistic and rather provincial vision of the novel, but
I want now to become a more international writer, that is, to see
more globally; to enlarge the issues; to enlarge my sense of
experience; to step away from that youthful provincialism with which
I think most writers start, into something of scope and scale. But
quite how that goes, what the next step is, is something I'm still
thinking very hard about, and I haven't come to any clear answers
yet.

* * *

The two of Lawrence's novels which meant most to me are *Sons and
Lovers* and *Women in Love* because of their moral urgency, their
kind of priestly passion. His profound seriousness about what he was
doing, and his concern to take this through into a form of fiction
which presses on the unconscious, or which reaches the unconscious,
is very important. *Sons and Lovers* and *Women in Love* were either
side of a dividing line which he saw in his life: after *Sons and Lovers*
he wanted to take the novel into a new shape, into a new form. *Sons
and Lovers* is the last of the good, old, formal ones as it were, and
Women in Love is the new method – it's a kind of abstract novel, or
post-character novel. Lawrence was also an extraordinary short-
story writer. I like those stories, like *The Fox*, that are particularly
concerned with nature, or the relationship between the human being
and the natural world (which includes things like *St Mawr*).

Forster was very important, particularly *A Passage to India*, which I think is a very great novel. Evelyn Waugh I regard as a much more important novelist than perhaps it's conventional to assume, on the grounds that he is a great absurdist. It's not the nostalgic, sentimental Waugh of *Brideshead*, but the Waugh of *Black Mischief*, and *Decline and Fall*, and *Handful of Dust*, that I admire.

Bellow's early books are remarkably good, in particular *The Victim*, which was his second novel. Again, it's a liberal book about moral responsibility, about how one person is responsible for another, and it's that quality, and the Russianised depth that he gets down to, that I like about it. With Malamud the point would be similar. I'm not sure now what I regard as his best book, but in some ways it might be the stories in *The Magic Barrel*. Again, there is this enormous sense of the moral weight of the existence of others that I like about his work. With Mailer, it's extremely hard to explain why one liked him so much. I must admit that going back to him I don't get the same pleasure that I used, and the book I think is his best is actually not a novel at all but *Armies of the Night*, about the march on the Pentagon.

I admire all of Borges stories, particularly *Labyrinths*; and Calvino for things like *Invisible Cities*; and Nabokov for *Ada or Ardor*; for their exploration of the fictionality of fiction. I think Borges is the great metaphysician of this; there is an intellectual truth and intensity about his way of exploring these issues. In Nabokov it's much gamier, it's a kind of play rather than a clearly stated truth. With Calvino it's even more playful – it's pure play.

Tristram Shandy is extraordinarily modern, but at the same time, for me, it's the beginning of the novel: somehow in the things that are in that book he sensed all the novel of the future might do. Sterne sits there and says, 'What is the opportunity here?' and already he's beginning to doubt all the essential principles. 'A book – what is a book? And how can we play with that? What does it mean to start a story? Most stories start with the birth of a hero; why don't I start with the conception of the hero? What's the difference between a novel and any story in prose?' There were lots of stories in prose before. And he turns to advantage, or at least to scepticism, almost everything that is available in the potential repertoire of the form.

Another writer of great importance to me is Beckett, particularly for *Murphy*. It does seem to me that Beckett poses many of the questions that have to be faced up to by a writer in the later twentieth

century who has taken modernism seriously, who thinks that Joyce
and Proust matter and that steps have to be taken beyond there. I
think Beckett is a great focus of those questions, and he has stepped
from being apparently a very light and playful writer to a writer of
enormous dignity.

I greatly value Marquez. I think *One Hundred Years of Solitude*
is an extraordinary novel in that it crosses the novel as a European
form with a kind of magicality and fantasy that has been very rare
in the European novel. It goes through a sort of sea change so that
the elements of the strange and fantastic, which on the whole are
tricky presences in fiction, acquire an absolutely rhythmic and
necessary place in the novel. One doesn't expect the novel to have
that kind of give. It's very hard not to feel that he's actually changed
things.

* * *

I think that literature has within it an extraordinary range of
perceptions about human nature and human value which are
absolutely necessary in the store-house of human self-knowledge.
We learn what we are as human beings from all sorts of information
sources, but to reach inside, to reach the social and historical depth,
I think literature plays a great part. And what distresses me in a lot
of criticism is that it is never talked about like this any more. So
much criticism is either about symbol-hunting, or the nature of the
language as a form of textual presentation, and a curious dead hand
is laid over all that importance. I think the other importance (which
isn't true of all literature, but is increasingly true) of its role in our
kind of society is its scepticism and its refusal to be taken in by
prevailing fictions. I think literature is a form of agnostic knowledge.
And a very important one.

Norwich, March 1984

NIGEL GRAY'S COMMENT.

The creation of literature, and the deconstruction of it for purposes of analysis and study, appear to be conflicting activities; yet Malcolm Bradbury is able to wear the gown of renowned academic and the mantle of respected novelist with equal style. He is a quiet, good-natured man who probably has difficulty in saying no to any of the many demands made on his time and for his attention.

As I mentioned when writing about Paul Bailey, I had gone to the University of East Anglia to get an M.A. in Creative Writing in the hope that it would open a door into creative writing teaching in an American university. (I got the M.A., but not the job in the States – my wife avoids her mother on days when she looks particularly thin and ragged.) I never got to know Malcolm Bradbury socially, but during the weekly writing workshop I came to like and respect him. I sometimes felt he was too nice – that he could not bring himself to say hard truths that needed to be said. But then, if he had had that toughness in his nature, he probably would have said no when I asked him for the interview.

Since 1984 he has been extremely prolific. *Cuts: A Very Short Novel*, in fact a novella, is about a Thatcherite Britain in which the word 'cut' becomes the most common noun and the most regular verb, and the book reveals the author's dismay at contemporary materialism and instrumentalism. But it's also about cuts in another sense, as an artistic or technical term in television, which is where the book is set.

Quite a lot of Malcolm Bradbury's life has been set in television during the past few years. He adapted two novels of Tom Sharpe for television as series, and is now engaged in three more series, one a particularly important homage: an adaption of William Cooper's *Scenes from Provincial Life*. He's also been involved in a major series on the Modern movement, and has written the book to go with the series: *The Modern World; Ten Great Writers*.

His somewhat difficult balance of writer and critic has to some extent been extended or purged by writing a book on a non-existent French structuralist called Henri Mensonge.

Not a bad tally for someone who writes painfully slowly. In all, he has completed six books and four television series in the last two or three years. This reflects several things: his part-time teaching contract; his word processor; his sense that time is getting on and that there were so many books he meant to write and never did; and a period of uncertainty in publishing which has caused him to delay starting another full-length novel. He prefers to wait until the dust, caused by the take-overs and the square dance of editors, settles. And in the meantime television keeps making offers he can't refuse.

His new novel, when it comes, will be about the 1990s – the era after glasnost, the new materialism, the collapse of Lib-Labism, the decline of postmodernism and structuralism, indeed all those things that suggest that as we move toward the turn of the century there will be a great new accounting as the world map of politics changes.

Malcolm Bradbury has been much honoured for his academic work. His novel, *The History Man*, received the Royal Society of Literature's Heinemann Award, and he is a fellow of the Royal Society of Literature.

Malcolm Bradbury was born in Sheffield on September 7th 1932.

Malcolm Bradbury's Book-Choice:

Sons and Lovers
  D. H. Lawrence
Women in Love
  D. H. Lawrence
The Collected Short Stories
  D. H. Lawrence
A Passage to India
  E. M. Forster
Black Mischief Evelyn Waugh
Decline and Fall Evelyn Waugh
Handful of Dust Evelyn Waugh
The Victim Saul Bellow

The Magic Barrel
  Bernard Malamud
Armies of the Night Norman Mailer
Labyrinths Jorge Luis Borges
Invisible Cities Italo Calvino
Ada or Ardor Vladimir Nabokov
*The Life and Opinions of Tristram
  Shandy* Laurence Sterne
Murphy Samuel Beckett
One Hundred Years of Solitude
  Gabriel Garcia Marquez

Books by Malcolm Bradbury:

Fiction:

Eating People is wrong
Stepping Westward
The History Man

Rates of Exchange
Cuts: A Very Short Novel

Humour:

*All Dressed Up and
  Nowhere to Go*
*Who Do You Think You are?:
  Stories and Parodies*

Mensonge
Why Come to Slaka?
Unsent Letters

Criticism:

Evelyn Waugh
What is a Novel?
The Social Context of Modern
   English Literature
Possibilities: Essays on the
   State of the Novel
The Modern American Novel

Saul Bellow
The Expatriate Tradition in
   American Literature
No, Not Bloomsbury
The Modern World;
   Ten Great Writers

Television series:

Blott on the Landscape
Porterhouse Blue

Imaginary Friends
Scenes from Provincial Life

Chapter Five
DICK DAVIES

I knew that my grandmother was somehow different from us, but I never realised that she was Italian until my late teens. I can see that it was very difficult for my mother. She was in her late teens, early twenties, during the war, when England was at war with Italy. Her mother was never interned or anything like that, but she always had a very strong Italian accent and it was a source of embarrassment for my mother. My mother never learnt Italian for instance, which seems to me the obvious thing to do if you've got an Italian mother, and she's never been to Italy. I don't think she ever got over being part-Italian and it was, as it were, hidden from me.

So part of me is Italian. Another part of me is Irish. The Irish part I only took on board fairly recently, although I was vaguely aware of it. So I've got this funny sense that what I thought I was is not what I am. And where I thought I came from is not where I come from. I feel that I am much more various than I thought. In fact, I feel that the parts of me that I'm interested in are those alien, various parts, and I want to take them on board and to celebrate variousness. It seems to me an awful thing when people talk about Britain as a multi-racial society (even people who are 'on the side of it') as if we're making the best of a bad job. It seems to me the best thing that has ever happened to England – that there are so many different races living here; and always have been. It's something that should be encouraged, not discouraged. It should be a source of hope.

I think the most important thing about my background in terms of coming to write is that we moved around a great deal when I was a kid. At one time I added up that I'd been to thirteen different schools. This gave me a feeling of not belonging to any particular community, and also of being rather fearful of the new communities I came into. I was always having to go to a new school, and being afraid of doing so. Because of this I became both fascinated by, and afraid of what was different or alien or strange. I decided, when I was about ten or eleven, that the way to deal with this fear was to meet it head on; to try to enjoy what was different. For example I used to try to take on the accent of the new place – although that didn't work. But I used to try to merge myself into these communities. When I was young the most important thing was being accepted by other pupils. But more and more it became important to be accepted by the teachers. The way to do that, I found, was to know more than the other kids, and so I became a very studious child, and I did try to be a teacher's pet as I got older. I think that was pretty obnoxious from the point of view of other kids.

It seemed a very dislocated, upset childhood. There was a sense that things weren't permanent. This forced me in on myself. When we went to a new place I didn't have anybody to play with so I'd just sit at home and read. I think I lived, from about the age of eight or nine till after I left university, in a kind of fantasy world of what I read.

There was quite a lot of books in our house. I was lucky in that way. Both my parents read quite a lot. There was a short time when my mother read poetry to me, and I realise that it was very important to her in a rather obscure way: not because of the poetry, but because of what the poetry was about. She used to read me poems, and she seemed to be getting an immense emotional charge out of them. There was a poem by Longfellow called, *The Slave*. In its own terms it's a good poem, although it's easy to laugh at it because it's so over the top. It's a kind of lament about an African Prince, dying on a slave plantation in the Caribbean, looking back at his home across the ocean. It's written in very rhetorical, colourful language, but it was written with some intensity, and clearly my mother identified with it. She had had a rather unhappy childhood. All the poems she read were about people who had been maltreated or had had a bad deal out of life. I can remember my mother crying, actually, reading these poems to me. In a way, because my mother was somebody who had quite a busy life, those moments when she read me the poems were very important to me. They seemed to upset her; on the other hand they seemed to comfort her. It was a kind of emotional focus for me. So I was attracted to poetry from very early on, often without understanding it.

I never read children's novels. I don't know why. I'm not saying I was a particularly precocious child, but I wanted novels about grown-ups and I wanted novels about grown-ups who did fabulous, impressive things. I liked Scott very much as a kid. Scott is a writer

I can't read now. I liked Dickens. I liked big novels you could lose yourself in – both Scott and Dickens wrote novels like that; and novels that created a whole world that was quite different to the world I lived in but which had recognisable characters; and novels in which there was a strong romantic action. A novel of Scott's I particularly liked is *The Talisman*. The setting is Palestine. It's only now that it occurs to me that that fitted in to my feeling about going to a new place where you've got to be accepted and you've got to fight. The hero of *The Talisman* goes to the Holy Land on the Crusades fighting the Arabs. On the other hand he's got to fit into the society he finds himself in. I wasn't conscious of it as a kid, but I think I identified with that. Perhaps that started me off with my thing about the Middle East. Anyway it was probably the first time the Middle east impinged on my consciousness.

From fourteen to seventeen I was at one school. I had two English masters there who were both very good, and they devoted a lot of time to me and guided my reading. I read D. H. Lawrence and James Joyce; I went on with Dickens; and I read modern poetry. I never quite took to the poetry in the way my English masters obviously expected me to. The poems that they held up for my admiration, which they obviously admired very much, were poems I never really liked as much as I said I liked them in my essays. I still in fact liked the kind of poetry I'd read as a younger kid. I like poetry that comes out of a strong individual situation, although often it'll be quite an obscure situation, but in which I can identify with the emotional cause of the poem. A poem like *The Waste Land*, for example, which has such distant and diverse roots, is not a poem that means anything very much to me and it never has done, although that was the kind of poetry you were supposed to admire when I was an adolescent: poetry that opened out and commented on society as a whole and drew in mythical elements and that kind of thing. I like poetry to be focussed and to come from an individual consciousness. *The Waste Land* obviously does, but it's trying to speak for a society)

There's a very good remark by, I think, Raymond Chandler. He said he began writing because he couldn't find exactly the kind of novels that he wanted to read and so he thought he'd write them. I think it's the reason most people start writing. They think the thing they feel about reality hasn't quite been said. That's why I began writing. Also I realised that I was going to have to make my way in the world. As soon as we stopped moving, when I was in my teens,

I got hungry for change, so I wanted a job that would take me to different places. I realised that there weren't many things that I was any good at. I might be good at writing, and a writer it seemed to me could go anywhere. I thought I might be a journalist for a while, but journalists have to report external events, and the thing that's always moved me finally is internal events, what happens in people's minds, their emotional reactions to things. That's not what journalists write about usually, so I quickly gave up the idea of being a journalist. Writing seemed to be a way of getting through life while staying in my head as it were, which is what I wanted to do.

Why poetry rather than prose, I don't know. It's something to do with the rhythm of poetry, which is a concise, economical way of conveying emotion. In a poem you can stay pretty well internal, handling thoughts and wishes and fears and that kind of thing, and the external setting can be got rid of or got past quite quickly.

At school I wrote short stories and poems. I knew that the poems were more important to me than the stories although none of them were very good. Then I went up to university to read English. I don't think I did much writing in the first year, but by the second year I'd started to put all my energy into it. I was lucky in that I got from a comprehensive school to Cambridge and I was very well taught there. On the other hand I felt very out of place, and my feeling of going into environments where I didn't belong was very accentuated. My second year was a bit of a write-off. I had a nervous breakdown and spent a lot of time in mental hospital. As soon as I left university I went to another society completely. Partly, I think, I was running away from England because I felt I couldn't fit in in England, but partly I felt I'd got to go out and meet it. I went to Greece, and then to Italy, and then America for a while, and then Iran for a long while.

I never doubted that I wanted to be a writer, although for about nine years almost nothing I'd written was published. Nobody was interested. I never doubted that I could be a writer. I just felt it hasn't happened yet. In my early twenties I wrote a good deal of poetry; and I wrote the usual autobiographical novel and quite a lot of short-stories which I've destroyed. The novel, I never sent anywhere because I realised it was no good. I sent some short stories about, but they were all rejected. I had about two poems a year published. *The Spectator* took some, *The Listener, The Critical Quarterly*, magazines like that. I don't know why but I didn't know about the little magazines like *Agenda* and *Stand* and *Outposts*, which are obvious places to start sending stuff to. I didn't even know about the Eric Gregory Award, which every young poet knows about now. Part of the reason was that as soon as I left university I left England. Also, because I had the breakdown, my early twenties, to be honest, are a blur to me. Whilst I was in hospital I had ECT, and one of the things that ECT does is to mess up your memory. Then I had some poems in an anthology published by Faber. That was in 1972, six years after I'd left university. That was really the first public acceptance I'd had. By then I was twenty-seven.

I don't think of myself as a particularly erudite person, but on the other hand a lot of my time and imagination has been taken up with reading. People often say to me, 'Your poems are obscure and I can't understand them'. That depresses me because I always try to make a poem as clear as I can. But often it will come out of something that I've read, or experienced abroad, so the origin of it is obscure, but I try to present it fairly plainly in the poem if I can. All the experiences I had after university were sort of alien experiences, especially in the Middle East. They weren't experiences that English people could immediately relate to, so that was a problem. I tried to solve it by writing about being a stranger, or about not fitting in, or about travelling. Life is a journey. It's a cliché, but it's true. It's a metaphor I feel very strongly. Even if you're in one place you're travelling. A lot of my poetry is about that.

I am drawn to writers who are obviously conscious of the writers before them. I'm like that myself. I can't write without being aware of what's been written before. Many people think that that's parasitic, that it weakens what you write, that it vitiates it. I think it can give a kind of depth and strength. The disastrous thing that can come from it is that your poetry is only of interest to people who have had a particular standard of education. That's inevitable but regrettable. It's not something that I rejoice in at all. I dislike poetry very much that is deliberately hermetic. I don't see the point of writing what you know other people are not going to be able to pick up on. That just seems to me to be talking to yourself. The kind of writing that particularly moves me is when one tradition comes up against another. A lot of writers I especially admire are writers who write about a mix of traditions or a mix of cultures; the plight of people who are between cultures or who have to go from one culture to another.

There's a quote in a poem by A. E. Houseman that I remember

reading as an adolescent, and feeling, 'That's exactly right – that's what I feel about the world.' It's nothing very special but it's always been my private little motto as it were.

'I, a stranger and afraid,
In a world I never made.'

Those two lines are very much what I feel about things. That Man, in general, is a stranger in the world, and because he's a stranger, he's afraid. And all the evil in the world, I feel, comes out of that fear, out of that inability to trust. I feel very strongly that Man is alone, and alien. It seems to me a truth (never mind that my own experiences have conditioned me to see it as a truth) that Man isn't like the rest of the world; he isn't like the plants and the animals and the rocks and all that – he's different in some way, and he doesn't seem to fit in. And he doesn't seem to fit in with his own kind. And although his overlaid reaction may be lots of other things: false happiness; aggression; cruelty; turning in on yourself; the fundamental reaction is fear. I feel that, very strongly, and I think my writing comes out of that sense of being a stranger and afraid in a world we don't really understand. The most moving moments for me in literature are when Man can overcome this; when he can make some contact and feel in touch with the reality that accepts him; when he can give something to it and receive something from it; when it's not just a kind of blank cold wall of rejection. That feeling is very important to what I write and to everything I've done since I left university, like wanting to live in other cultures; wanting to overcome the sense of strangeness; wanting to learn other languages; wanting to read the literatures of cultures that are quite different from my own, and to translate them.

People often feel that translation is a kind of second best, that you do it when you haven't got anything going for yourself, but for me it's not that. I get a great sense of personal communion out of translation: of reaching across the vast differences of language and culture and religion to a real human contact.

I am aware that my own poetry is very private. This is something I don't know what to do about to be honest. I would like my poetry to be much more public, and I have tried to write in much more easy-going, obviously accessible modes. But I think that the way I've been conditioned; the kind of literature that I've read; the kind of people that I grew up admiring and still admire; the kind of minds I'm attracted to; means that I am stuck with this private kind of poetry. One of the kinds of literature that I find very difficult to take, in fact, is literature that tries to cut out the individual mind; that tries to speak to the mass. I can admire it in the abstract and I can see why people want to write it. But the literature that appeals to me, that moves me, and is the only kind of literature that I can honestly try to write, is literature that tries to speak from one individual to another. To a large number of people as individuals, but not to a large number of people as representative of a nation or class. That kind of thing seems to me to be setting up barriers rather than breaking them down. It is the individual mind talking to the individual mind that I care about, but I can see the dangers of that. It leads to hermeticism; into thinking that there are only a few minds in the world that are interesting; into all sorts of terrible snobberies and complacencies. I just hope my poetry isn't like that. I don't want it to be and it upsets me when I realise that some people think it is. On the other hand many people have told me that it does get across. One thing that's particularly heartened me is that people from quite different cultures have been able to latch on to my poetry and to see something valuable in it. That I have got across some kind of cultural divide in that way pleases me very much.

If I look back on my first book there are about ten poems in it that I'm really ashamed of, about ten poems I'm really quite pleased with, and the rest I feel fairly indifferent about. It's not a book I feel marvellous about. Neither is it a book that has any particular shape. A couple of reviewers professed to find a shape in it, which was very nice of them, but I think they were seeing a shape that wasn't really there. It's just poems that were written over ten years. The thing that spurred me to put it together was the Faber anthology contract. I had to offer them my first book. I hadn't thought about a book until then, but I put one together and sent it off, and they rejected it almost immediately. They said the poems were too literary, which is what I was afraid of. Then I sent it to other publishers.

The second book is much more shaped. It was written over a shorter period. I like the poems more. It is much more about something than the first book. All the things I've talked about are, elusively, in the first book, but I can see them very strongly in the second. The first book was published in '75 when I was in Iran. The second book was published in 1980. I was back in England by then.

Although it's four years ago now, the book seems to me very recent. A lot of poets bring out a book every eighteen months or two years. I don't know how they do it. I wish they wouldn't actually. It seems to me that most people don't have that much to say about reality. You shouldn't take up people's time with saying trivial things. Every little chance thought that goes through your head isn't worthy of recording on paper. I can't get on with poems that are just the jotting down of bits and pieces of daily life. For me, poems should come when you have something special and particular to say. I don't write very much – perhaps six or seven poems a year that I keep. Perhaps double that that I actually write, and treble that that I start. I want a poem to sum up and encapsulate experience. Thom Gunn said that every time he finished a poem he felt he hadn't got anything more to say. I feel that too. You finish a poem and you feel, 'Well, that's where I am at the moment. God knows what the next poem can be about'. Usually they're about the same things because a person's view of the world tends to be limited and he can't get beyond its limits. I write the same three or four poems again and again; but reality needs to present itself in a slightly different way. It's a complicated relationship between sameness and difference. There's a quote of Marcus Aurelius that Seferis uses in one of his poems: 'If you want more, dig deeper in the same place'. I think you have to. You *can* go out of your own feelings of the world, but you can't write well if you do.

I find form very difficult to talk about. I write in fairly traditional forms, and the older I've got the more precise they've become. One could see this as *rigor mortis* setting in, as I'm sure lots of people do. I try and loosen the forms occasionally but in general I choose to go along with them. I think it goes back to my childhood in a way. The poems I read as a young child were poems with a very strong rhythm and it was the rhythm that moved me. Also, at the end of the poem (when the form works well) you have a sense of something complete and finished, and the last rhyme will be like a great smashing chord at the end of a symphony. A poem written in a more open form never gives that sense of finality; that sense of arriving at a truth. (Of course it can give exactly the opposite sense when the form doesn't work well – a sense that you're manipulating truth in order to fit it into a straightjacket.) Also, you can indicate subtly, but much more exactly than in an open form, what is emotionally happening in a poem. You can speed it up; you can slow it down; you can show where the emphases are; by the rhythm or by the rhyme. It seems to me a much more finely tuned way of writing. In the best poems you feel that this could only be said in that form, though I must admit that that's a very rare feeling. But a poem is written line by line, and you've got to fit the lines and all that. There is a satisfaction in achieving that. I think it might be a musical thing. Music is something I've always loved very much, but I had no musical training whatever as a child. I have no technical knowledge and I can't play anything. I think if I'd grown up in a completely different environment I might have been a composer. It's a sense of getting the key right; the harmony right; getting the counterpoint right and all that. And that is very satisfying because it seems to correspond to the truth about things. I don't want to suggest it's satisfying in the sense of doing a crossword puzzle, although that can enter into it. There are poets with whom I feel the form is a game, an end in itself, and they've lost sight of the content. There is another, perhaps more profound, reason for writing in form. I can't remember who said this, but I read it somewhere: 'Writers who write in open forms tend to be writers who trust the world, and writers who write in closed forms are writers who tend to be afraid of the world.' The form is a kind of castle. I don't want to push this side of it too much. I don't want to present an image of myself as terrified of the world. I don't think I am. But that sense that reality is unknowable and potentially threatening is a sense that an awful lot of modern poets have. You can see it in their poetry. The form seems to be a kind of defence. It's not keeping people away; it's making yourself safe; like having a room instead of living in the open. It's also making your ideas clear to yourself, and giving them more force.

There's a lot of free verse I like very much, although I must say that poems I really like, the poems I go back to most, are formally structured poems. There is a problem about what you do with poems in translation. Often they're in free verse although in the original they were formally structured. For some reason I can get along with translations in free verse more than original poems in free verse. You give the writer the benefit of the doubt as it were.

I've done two long books apart from the books of poetry. One was a critical book, and one was a translation I did with Afkham, my wife. The critical work was about Yvor Winters, a poet I particularly admire, and who very strongly influenced me. When I was doing the critical work I knew that I would do a thousand words every day. The translation was more fluid. I would work on the basic problem of just getting the meaning right, but the versification was more haphazard. I would try to do the versification in office hours but I found I could never do it in the afternoon. I found I had to be fresh and do it fairly early in the morning. The versification often in fact depended on what I suppose people would call inspiration. Some days I would be able to do twenty or thirty lines fairly quickly and I'd be pleased with it, and some days I'd just be stuck on four lines and I'd get nowhere.

For my own poetry, it's been my experience that if I chase a poem too hard I never get a good poem out of it. I find what I think most poets find, that a poem has to come from a much deeper stratum of your consciousness. Some people say that the poem presents itself to them. It's never been quite like that for me. What usually happens is that I have an idea and I just leave it in the back of my head. Sometimes the idea will stay for ages. For example, I had an idea for a poem when I was in Cochin in '74, but I did nothing about it because I knew that if I pounced on it I would write a wretched, moralistic, crude poem. In fact I forgot about it. I don't know whether my subconscious had been working at it or not, but it lay fallow. I came back to England in October '78, and my wife and I bought the house we're now living in in December. We'd been in the house two weeks. The Cochin poem is about getting married and about a mixture of cultures – it's a kind of celebration of those two things. This was the first house we'd bought so the marriage was sort of confirmed and that took me back to when we were first married. Also we were in a new country again: a completely new country for my wife, and (I hadn't lived in England since 1970) in a sense a new country for me. England changed a lot in the seventies – all its values seemed to be very different, and it seemed to me a shabbier, sadder place than when I left. So that's what sparked that poem; and I wrote it in two days.

In writing a poem, the idea is the easy thing. I've had many ideas that I thought would make lovely poems that didn't turn into anything. The story of Theseus going into the maze to kill the Minotaur seems to me a good way of describing a poem. You've got to find a way in, and then you get to the mystery, and grapple with it. Either it destroys you, and then you haven't got a poem, or you get hold of it (I don't want to say you kill it) and you control it. What you've got to find is the way into the maze. For me its a phrase; two or three words which seem to lead me into the idea. To an outsider it might seem a trivial phrase; not a phrase that has any profound meaning. And it's not something you can search for. It's got to come. Once that's come you can start searching, using that phrase as a kind of touchstone. Do the new things that you make fit that? Do they go with it? Are they right for that atmosphere? Often you find a way in, but it's a false way and you don't reach your next goal.

At the moment I'm getting together my next book of poems which I think will come out in '85. It's almost there, I think. That's not something you can work on, although it's in my head. You have to wait for the poems to come as it were. A few more poems and there'll be enough for a book. I think it'll be an advance on the last book in that it'll be more focussed; and I'm more pleased with the poems. It's always the most recent poems you feel best about. Thank goodness. When you start feeling that your early poems were your good ones you've had it. The most galling thing for a writer is when people come up and say, 'I don't think you've ever surpassed your early work.'

I've just finished, with my wife, a translation of a long Persian poem by Attar, called *The Conference of the Birds*, which is coming out in '84. It has a very strong sense of man being a stranger in the world. Also it gives a panorama of a society which is both very different from ours and very similar. It's extraordinary how similar: the same kinds of people; the same attitudes of bullying or kindness or whatever. There's a human constant. I think it's a very good poem. It seems to me to be a poem that describes the world in a way that it hasn't been described quite in Western literature, but which we can respond to and see as valid and true despite its Islamic dress. In fact the Islamic dress is very lightly worn. It's almost a transparent veil. You can see the body underneath, as it were. (Perhaps not surprisingly, Attar was condemned as a heretic.)

What I'm spending most of my day doing at the moment is reading Persian. I'd like to prepare for another translation in two or three years time. I think the next one is going to be a treatment of the *Alexander the Great* myth by Nezami. He sees Alexander as, not just a person who charges across Asia and conquers things, but a person who looks for the meaning of life, who has a kind of responsibility towards the mystery of life. That sounds very portentous, but that's one of the things that attracts me about Asian literature. There's a sense that life is not something we can take for granted. In your progress through life; your relationships with other people; your

activity in the world, socially and politically; you must have a sense
of responsibility to this inexplicable thing which your life is. If you
don't, you're doing the dirt on it; trivialising it. That attracts me very
much and I'd like to bring that over into a Western language if I
could.

I have written prose. And I keep coming back to prose. I feel more
at home in the world as I've got older, and better equipped to do it.
I have got some short stories together which perhaps I'll put into a
book later. They're on the same themes as the poems, but the themes
are treated in a more specific way; they're located in a particular
context. The stories are mostly about the Middle East. None of them
has been published in England, although a couple were published in
Iran in translation. I wrote a play which was about coming back to
England and my disappointment with it, but I couldn't see how to
do the last act properly and in the end I gave up on it. I think it was
very sentimental, but I liked writing it. I also wrote a libretto for a
children's opera which was performed, and I liked doing that.
Whether opera libretto or play I don't know, but I'm attracted to the
idea of theatre. I have a novel in my head – which I'm going to write
in my forties. I think it will be a big thing for me – some years work,
and I'm bringing myself up to that. But that's a long way ahead.

Almost no poets live by the royalties they get on the poems they
publish. I certainly couldn't. Until 1978 I lived as a teacher. Then I
came back from Iran with the specific intention of writing a book on
Yvor Winters. I'd saved a bit of money to carry me over and the Arts
Council gave me £1,000. We'd intended to go back to Iran, but in the
meanwhile the revolution happened and we couldn't. I decided to try
to make a go of it by becoming involved in the poetry world, which
it is possible to live off although quite precariously. So since '78, and
intensively since '80, I've done a great many reviews for various
magazines; I've become a contributing editor of *PN Review*; I've
done a fair number of poetry readings; I've had two Writer-in-
Residence jobs. It's all stuff that is peripheral to poetry rather than
the poetry itself. (Out of my actual poetry I've probably made less
than a thousand pounds in my life.) A lot of people who live off their
writing have to be instinctively frugal, or they have to be managed
by someone who is. We live far below what is officially the poverty
line, but I don't feel poor. That's because my wife is extremely good
at making money go a long way. Also, we bought our house outright.
It's only a small house, but there's no mortgage and no rent, and

that's a great help.

Agents are not interested in poets (unless they've made the big time, like Ted Hughes or someone like that). I think in my early twenties I must have sent poems out a great deal. But you feel rejected when your poems are rejected. You feel that it's you who's been rejected and it's hurtful. Now, I feel rather conservative about sending things out. I only send things when there's a high probability of them being accepted: I send to magazines that have accepted stuff by me before, or where I think the literary editor is sympathetic to me. I very rarely send to a place out of the blue because it's so galling when the stuff comes back. The contract I had for the critical book seemed to me pretty wretched (no advance and no royalties until 500 copies had been sold), but other people have said that academic publishers always give that kind of contract. I've been told that the Penguin contract is OK for a translation. I don't feel hard done by by publishers – I've been writing for a long while but I've only been trying to live as a writer for the past four or five years, so, although I'm thirty-eight, I still think of myself as beginning. I'm still grateful for whatever comes along. So far we've been able to survive, but each year you think, 'What are we going to live off next year?'

When I was at university I joined the university Labour Party. The last Home Secretary to sign a warrant for someone to be hanged in England, Henry Brooke, came to give a speech to the university Conservative Association. We decided to go along and picket the hall. The police formed a cordon. Brooke arrived and was hustled down this alleyway. At one point the cordon broke and the crowd was around Brooke and I was very close to him. I was shouting with everyone else. Brooke wasn't hurt at all but it was clear that he was absolutely terrified. He was a little man, not a very prepossessing man to look at, and very afraid. You know the phrase, 'He shat himself with fear'. You could see that he might literally do that. The police got him through, and we were locked out. But afterwards Henry Brooke's face haunted me. I had no time for what he'd done. He's not remembered for anything else. He seemed to me a nothing Home Secretary; a very ordinary man, very much a product of his class, not somebody I would normally have any feeling about except that he and I would have nothing in common. But I saw him very afraid like that, and it affected me very strongly. It gave me a great suspicion of crowd action. When I've written poems that could be called political they're always about individuals who're surrounded

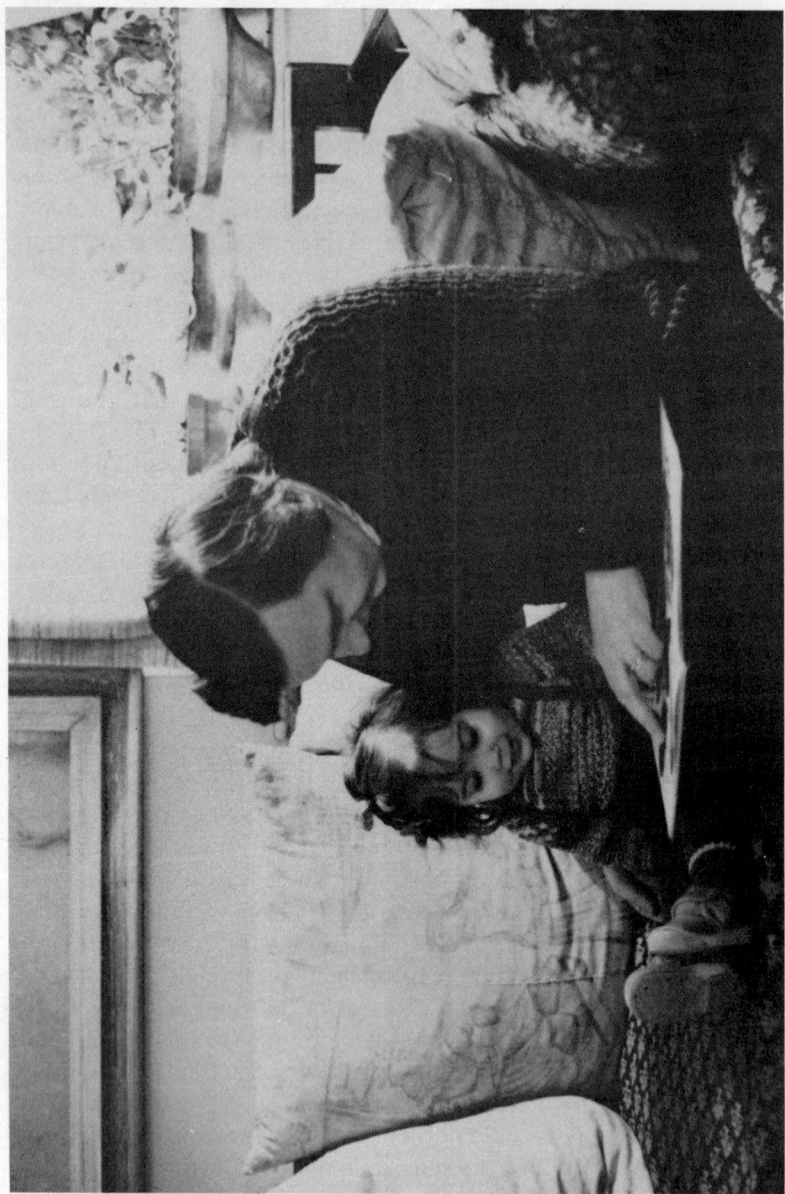

by people who hate them. For me finally, when the crunch comes, what that particular person's beliefs are doesn't matter. It's the sense of being a trapped rat that I sympathise with (and that I've written about in one or two poems), even if that person *is* a rat, in fact, as perhaps one could say Henry Brooke was.

I was in Greece at the time of the Colonel's coup. English friends of mine were deported. I didn't have to leave, and I found out afterwards it was because my employer had paid a bribe to the local police. I left fairly soon after that anyway. I'd intended to stay in Greece for another year. The coup happened in April, and I left at the end of my contract which was the end of June. I could not believe how afraid people were after the coup. All these stories started coming out about the Civil War. My best friend in Greece was the only male from his family who had survived – he was a baby and had been hidden. All the other men had been killed. And what was awful was that some of them had been killed by the Communists and some of them had been killed by the Fascists. I saw the fear that the people had of this new government. To me it was unbelievable. It was a very repressive and unpleasant government, and it certainly has a terrible record on torture, but in a provincial place in the first two months after the coup the signs of it weren't very noticeable. Nevertheless, everybody was afraid, very cowed. That had a strong effect on me. I think what it did confirm in me was the feeling that the state can really do what it wants with the individual. Our sense that we can direct or change or choose the state is an illusion. The grocer we went to sided with the coup. We stopped going to him. We thought we'd make that little protest and we went to another grocer. But he sought us out and said, 'Why don't you come to our grocery any more? Is it because we support the colonels?' I was stupid enough to say yes. I could see he was a very nice man, a decent man, but he was quite prepared to say, 'Yes, the Communists should be locked up. And if a few of them are tortured, well, the police have got to get the information.' I could see that this decent man could very easily go down the path of becoming the criminal accomplice of a brutal state. And if he could, then most people could, and, I felt, I could.

When we were kids, the films were all about the war. I got interested in the war and interested in Nazism, and I felt certain that if I'd been in Germany as an adolescent in the 1930s and everybody around me joined the Hitler Youth, then I would join the Hitler Youth. I'm not saying that I'm a fascist or a potential fascist or anything. I'm just saying that you can see that most people will go along with the mob, whatever the mob is doing. It takes an awful lot of guts and understanding and sheer basic cussedness and bravery to say, 'No, I won't!' And I thought, I don't have that. In Greece, half the people were terrified, and half the people were drifting along with it because it was convenient and it kept their life going.

In Iran, one of the families we knew best was mixed up in politics. One of the brothers was in prison for quite a while. The other brother, who was my close friend, was in prison for a little while and then out and then in again. He was somebody who was broken by the state. He'd been cowed into signing something. He hadn't betrayed anybody: he had that self-respect. But he knew that he had signed away his beliefs – that what he believed in, he'd renounced. And he was afraid. When he came out he wouldn't take part in political activity although he sympathised. The other brother who was in for a long time was appallingly treated and very badly tortured. I saw what happened to him. He was somebody I liked very much. But he became a different person. He became a robot for the revolution. When he came out he was prepared to kill; to see people who were innocent killed. We had an argument about a bank clerk who got killed. I said that killing that man didn't justify the end. He said it didn't matter if the innocent got killed because it would bring a better world. I was revolted by that, although I liked him personally and I could see why he'd become like that.

Those experiences: the little thing with Henry Brooke; the fear that I saw in people in Greece; the sense of how evil it is to collaborate with evil; the repression that there was in Iran; and the terrible repression that there has been afterwards as a kind of explosive reaction; all this has made me very suspicious of mass politics. I feel that people in England don't know what they're talking about when they talk about repression and the brutality of the state and that kind of thing. When I line up with liberal, left-wing causes, it's with a sense that the people I'm with don't know really what's involved. Maybe that's arrogant of me but I do feel that. You don't know what you're unleashing when a mob gets going. Obviously when people who were in charge of the prisons were shot you sent up a cheer. But that kind of thing is never controlled. I don't think there's ever been a revolution where it's only the guilty ones who die. It always extends. And the other thing about revolutions, as far as I can see, is that a revolution is

necessarily a physical and bloody and violent thing, and it is physical
and bloody and violent people who come to the top.

My writing tries to defend the individual. I try to defend the
decencies – which is what goes during Nazi Germany or Khomeini's
revolution. Obviously anybody will try to defend those. But it seems
to me they must be rooted in personal, psychological commitment
rather than commitment to a group ideology. A group ideology can
always override the personal thing. Once you say, 'This person is
expendable,' you've had it. Once you say, 'This innocent person can
suffer for the rest of us,' there's no end to it. It turns into terror. My
writing is political in that it asks for tolerance. It asks people to
understand other ways of living, and to recognise that variety is a
good thing and not a threat. The only political activity I do now is
write letters for prisoners for Amnesty International, because it is
for an individual – it's one person you can save.

* * *

The two modern poets who have influenced me most from a
technical point of view are Yvor Winters and Thom Gunn. Winters
was a kind of humane liberal. He was very perspicacious about the
kind of flirtation with Fascism that went on among a lot of writers
in the 1930s. He never indulged in it himself, and he very quickly
diagnosed it and he knew it for what it was. He got Pound and Eliot's
number very early on. His coolness and sanity preserved him from
a commitment to what finally is a barbarism, and it seems to me his
technique, which some people see as being very classical and cold,
is evidence of the habit of mind that preserved him. He also had this
sense of Man as being a stranger and afraid. Fear is a kind of basic
emotion behind most of his poems, and I was attracted to them for
that reason too.

Gunn inherited Winters' technique – a cool, classical, precise way
of writing, with no emotional fuss or self-indulgence. Gunn's mind
is very far away from where my mind is, but it's his technique I
admire, and my technique is learned from his. Obviously from other
people too, but he is a clear influence on my poetry. He's fairly
concerned also with solitary people who stand out against what's
around them. In his early poems it's a kind of amoral thing: he's just

interested in the idea of one man being different from the rest, and saying, 'Up yours!' to respectability, and that's maybe very adolescent. In the later poems it becomes a more moral thing. For me his great poem is *Misanthropos*. It is a sequence of poems about the survivor of a terrible war, presumably a nuclear war. It's the Gunn theme of the solitary man making out in the world by himself, but at the end he meets other people and he has to make this human contact. That poem appeals to me tremendously. It's a sort of myth for our time: a survivor who has to make contact with others.

Cavafy is one of my favourite poets. He was a Greek who lived in Egypt. He's the poet of the man who is involved in different cultures, and doesn't know where he belongs, and is trying to preserve his state of independence and his humanity at the same time. Cavafy is steeped in history and that appeals to me. He's very good at seeing how the cultures of the past were just like the cultures of the present. He can write a poem which is set in the fourth century in Alexandria, and it's like reading a poem about somebody who's living in Mayfair now. The analogies are beautifully and quietly done.

I like Baudelaire's poetry very much. There's a lot of fake Gothicism you have to get past, but the great thing is the way he never lies. He's trying to preserve his sense of human contact, but he is not going to give in to the prejudices of those around him. He has absolute honesty before the experiences of his life, and he can put this across in measured, precise and telling verse which never falters or crumbles.

I suppose my favourite poet is Dante. He's the first poet in the West that I can think of who was utterly tolerant. He saw that it was good that human life was various. He is so sympathetic to different ways of living. Also he has this sense, that I was talking about in connection with Attar, of responsibility before the mystery of life. He's concerned to see what it is to live in the world. And Dante's religion is one which anybody can respond to. It's not a religion which is excluding; it's a religion which is a sense that life is valuable, serious – mystical, if you like.

I very much admire Giuseppe Di Lampedusa's *The Leopard*. It's a novel about an aristocracy – a mode of life very different from one that I've ever had or been able to identify with. On the other hand, it's got a sense of a society at a crisis point; old values disappearing; new values emerging. The character at the centre of it is a

magnificent portrait of somebody who has understood life but who
feels impotent to act. He feels that he knows what life is like but that
his knowledge is no good to him, and that all he can do is watch. I
suppose that many modern 'intellectuals' feel that. To say that you
know what life is like is the most hopeless arrogance. Nobody finally
does. But you feel you have some insight but that you can't apply
this insight in the public world; that the state is not amenable to the
values of the individual. When the individual gets caught up in the
state and becomes part of the apparatus of the state he seems to
renounce his humanity and decency. And it's only in small pockets
of the world that that doesn't happen, by chance and for a short
time. That's what appals me about England: that people don't realise
that the colonels could be here. They think there's something
magical in the English character that will preserve them from it. It's
not true.

E. M. Forster was at King's when I was an undergraduate there.
He was the grand old man of the college, and though I had very little
contact with him, his influence was very strong, and I realised after
I'd left Cambridge that his way of looking at things had permeated
very deeply into me without my realising it. Whilst I was there I felt
I was in revolt against the values of the college. When I left I realised
I'd absorbed them. His great novel is *A Passage to India*. His view
of Asia is seen by many people as a rather sentimental view perhaps,
but it seems to me a valid one. Reading that novel is one of the
reasons I went to Asia, and it is one of the books that changed my
life. It changed the way I felt about the possibility of getting on with
what was foreign and strange. Forster welcomed strangeness, and so
it became something I could approach positively. The book also gave
me an insight. I'd always thought of strangers meeting as equals,
which is very naïve. It's never an equal relationship, and Forster
shows that. He shows the ways people try to get round that, and how
you can try to make human contact despite that.

Another novel I liked very much is *The Tale of Genji* by Lady
Murasaki. It is an immensely long novel written in the eleventh
century in Japan. It is a picture of court life – a completely different
life from any that I could conceive of living, and yet it gives this very
strong sense of common humanity. Despite this completely strange
setting you recognise all the fears and hopes and shyness and
aggression and everything by which people live. It's a novel you have
to persevere with, but eventually you get sucked in. It's a great world

you can live in, and you feel at the end of it that you know more about what it is to be a human being than you did at the beginning. One of my favourite writers is Chekhov because of his marvellous humanity. There's a wonderful poignance in his plays and his stories. He had a marvellous way of getting across the hidden wishes and griefs and hopes of people. He can be very moving in a trivial domestic setting, and he is able to show that in that setting, lives can be wrecked and people can live in despair. Or he can write about something that is really awful, like the story of the sane man who gets locked up in a madhouse because he complains about the way the madhouse is run (which seems like a prophetic story about what's happened in Russia).

Montaigne is my favourite non-fiction writer. He's a very strong writer. His essays seem to me to be about the most honest essays you could read. He's very perspicacious about people's motives and about greed and selfishness and vanity and that kind of thing. He recognises it in himself and he doesn't deny it, but he fights it too. He has a marvellous sense of honour which is not based on being respectable, but on the necessity to be decent in all circumstances. He's the best companion you could have in your mind. If you're in a crisis and you say to yourself; 'What would Montaigne do?' (if you get the answer right) I think you're going to act properly. He's a moral guide, but he's not a moralising guide.

* * *

It's very saddening that literature now at universities tends to be treated as a kind of game for the reader, rather than trying to understand what the writer was telling you. (As a writer, obviously I'm going to be on the side of the writers.) People write because they want to get across a set of values to other people. To trivialise literature seems to me to be doing the dirt on it. The best literature is the nearest we get in the ordinary world to the sacred. It is a person's view of life, and a person's values, and they are given because the world, for most of the time, is a fearsome, barbarous place. Literature is a light that keeps that barbarity back for a while, and inspires people to move against it.

Aylsham, Norfolk, November 1983

NIGEL GRAY'S COMMENT.

Dick Davis is a warm and compassionate person, although at the same time he has a slightly frosty reserve. It is as if the Irish-Italian half of him has remained separate from, and in subordination to, his Englishness. He is quiet and gentle; never playful or boisterous. One imagines that his childhood must have been stifled in a blanket of lower middle-class respectability; that he was always staid. Middle-age probably suits him better than youth.

It is odd to think that if we had known each other as schoolboys we would probably have loathed each other – him the school swat, me the yobbo dunce. And yet, when we met, speaking for myself anyway, I felt an immediate warmth and fondness for him – I suppose it was rather like meeting a long-lost brother.

Dick came to Northampton as Writer-in-Residence in the local college. Until a year or two earlier I had been Writer-in-Residence in Northampton's new development area, and so I went to visit him to welcome him to the town (a town incidentally that neither of us liked). Dick's Iranian wife, Afkham, was very unhappy here too. We introduced her to Golnar, also Iranian, the wife of an Irish friend, and Golnar and my wife, Yasmin, who is Sudanese, were the only friends Afkham had during a rather miserable nine months.

The following year, when Dick and I were both desperately poor, I saw an advert in *The Guardian* for a two-year Writing Fellowship at the Newcastle and Durham universities. I sent off for details, and then took the application form over to Dick. I told him that from the list of past holders of the fellowship it was clear to me that he was just the sort of writer they were looking for. Dick remained unconvinced, but I persuaded him to apply, and he got the fellowship. And from there he went to teach poetry at the University of California in Santa Barbara, where his Englishness stands him in very good stead. And appropriately enough he's set up home in a house on Cambridge Drive.

In his poetry he is a master craftsman. Love poems are perhaps the most difficult of all poems to write well – *Memories of Cochin* is a love poem both to his wife and to the people of the world, written with exceptional skill. To my mind it is one of the most beautiful poems in the English language. It is included in his collection, *Seeing the World*, which received the Royal Society of Literature's 1980 Heinemann Award. He was elected a fellow of the Royal Society of Literature in 1981.

Dick Davis was born in Portsmouth on April 18th 1945.

Dick Davis's Book-Choice:

The Collected Poems of   *The Collected Plays* Chekhov
  Yvor Winters   *The Complete Stories* Chekhov
Selected Poems Thom Gunn   *Collected Essays* Montaigne
The Complete Poems of Cavafy *A Passage to India* E. M. Forster
  Les Fleurs du Mal Baudelaire *The Tale of Genji* Lady Murasaki
The Divine Comedy Dante
The Leopard
  Giuseppe Di Lampedusa

Books by Dick Davis:

Poems:

In The Distance   *The Covenant*
Seeing the World

Criticism:

Wisdom and Wilderness; the Achievement of Yvor Winters

Translations:

The Conference of the Birds by Farid udDin Attar
  (with Afkham Darbandi)
The Little Virtues by Natalia Ginzberg

Chapter Six
JOHN FOWLES

I think now, when I look back, that I was probably lucky because I was brought up in an environment which didn't encourage art. This will sound reactionary, but I believe creating a sympathetic artistic environment for children is a fairly sure way of guaranteeing they will not become artists – or artists of any value. My parents were middle-class. My father worked in the City of London, where my grandfather had started a flourishing tobacco business. He imported Havana cigars and sold expensive briar pipes, and the firm had two or three shops in London. It went on all through my childhood till it was wound up in the Second World War. But my father never wanted to be in the tobacco trade at all. He was going to be a solicitor, but when he came back from the 1914-1918 war he had to take charge of his twice-married father's numerous family and so take on the family business. (He had a horrid war, which deeply scarred his life: he survived three years in the trenches, and was wounded, but had to go back.)

He did have a certain artistic streak in him: he liked Beethoven, and German lyric verse, and things like that, but he wasn't creative in any literary sense. Curiously, I did discover later in life that he had written a novel about the First World War; so, obviously, it was a latent talent in him. He had tried to get his novel published. The reader was a novelist called Philip Gibbs, and one of Gibbs's novels, rather ominously, does suggest that he had my father's novel in mind. It wasn't very good, and it was a painful thing to have to tell him that nobody would publish it.

I think my mother was an excellent mother, but she's not artistic in any creative sense. My ancestors were humble country people. I've never traced my family tree, perhaps rather oddly, because as curator of the local museum here I quite often have to help other people trace theirs. On my mother's side they were preachers and small farmers in the extreme west of Cornwall. On my father's side they were, I suspect, Somersetshire peasants. My great-grandfather was clerk to an attorney, so he had risen slightly, but it was my grandfather who rose as a business man.

I think all artists are probably made in their first two or three years. I take a neo-Freudian view on this. The theory I more or less accept is one called 'Symbolic Loss and Repair'. In very simple terms, as an infant you're wounded or deprived in some way you can't understand, but so deeply that you have to spend the rest of your life repairing it by painting pictures or writing or whatever it is. I find the theory fits in with other known facts, like the obsessive nature of writing, which is very mysterious. Perhaps I am aware of it more than some others because I have been successful. Why do novelists always have to go back and start again? I've suggested that Thomas Hardy's endings are always tragic because they give a sense of incompleteness – an excuse to keep him writing. He was the first writer to begin to see through this repetitive obsession, which is one reason I find him fascinating. He wrote a very bad novel called *The Well-Beloved*. It's the one book of his that every writer must read, although from a literary point of view it's quite arguably his worst. From the point of view of the psychology of a writer it's one of the most revealing. It's a very distressed novel; you feel he's really writing it with a kind of hatred and contempt for himself.

The theorists think that the wound must be an infancy experience, but with me it was also caused by the fact that as a child I didn't at all like Leigh-on-Sea and the life we lived there. I knew something was missing in that world and I began to read to escape from it. A major interest all my life has been natural history. Living in the middle of suburbia as I did, I used to have an absolute craving for everything that the whole conurbation of Southend wasn't. It was mainly satisfied through a novel by Richard Jefferies, called *Bevis*. I still think that's the major book in my life, although I can't read it any more. But I must have read it twenty or thirty times, from the age of ten or less right up until adolescence, when I should have been above such things. Something in that book represented perfection for me. It was set in the country. It was about adventure, doing your own thing. In the war, throughout my young teens, we lived in a village in Devon where I was profoundly happy. I could roam, I could 'live' *Bevis* in a way. I had a gun and a rod, and I could poach, and all that was marvellous. But then my father insisted we went back to Essex.

I recently took part in a BBC programme about another book that also had that effect on me: Alain-Fournier's one novel, *Le Grand Meaulnes*, or (*The Wanderer*, in English). I first read that at about the age of seventeen, and re-read it many times. I'd hardly finish it before I'd want to start again. That kind of obsessive relationship to one or two books is, I think, vitally important in a writer's life.

I went to a prep school, and then I won a scholarship to a public school, where I was a boarder. I became head boy of the public school and I did fairly well. God knows how this happens, but I was pushed into languages. (I often wish now I had gone into science.) I was reading the set book French and German classics (Goethe, Racine, and so on) by the age of fifteen, and they, in a way, also represented an escape. I can remember some of the set books we had then: some very hackneyed, sentimental 'classics' like Daudet's *Lettres de mon Moulin*. But they also had something of this same effect because their worlds were so remote from that of a public school in wartime: all the austerity we had then, and the brutality – the fagging and beating and all that sort of thing.

I've still got, upstairs, as a memento of the kind that punishes you, what we used to call, 'The Beating Book'. It records the number of boys I beat. I had to cane boys almost every day: as head boy I was responsible for the discipline of the entire school (600 boys). The private person escaped into the books.

By pure luck I studied French under an old man, now dead, to whom I'm profoundly grateful. (Every public school has one really good master like him, usually despised and disliked and laughed at by the other masters.) On the day it was announced I was to be head boy, this French master came and saw me (I happened to be ill in bed with something) and he made a very determined attack on the whole idea. He said, 'You're not who you think you are. You don't know who you are, and I thoroughly disapprove of your being head boy.' He tried to persuade me to say no; and I wouldn't do it. And he said, 'I've brought a present for you. Read this.' It was that anthology of Welsh and Irish verse, *Lyra Celtica*. I think it was the first time in my life I'd read Yeats, and ancient Welsh poetry. I knew of, course, what he was saying: 'This is the kind of person you are – you're in this book.' He knew that becoming a head boy in a system of which, he often told us, he generally disapproved, was wrong. He was absolutely right: but it took me many years to realise that fully.

I began to revolt against all this at the age of nineteen, after I left school and went into the Royal Marines, towards the end of the war.

Gradually I realised I'd been very heavily brain-washed. In a way, this is how I believe writers are made. It's much more fertile that you should be brought up in circumstances that are hostile to what you will become. The Royal Marines were very useful for me because I did very badly in them. I did become an officer, but I wasn't considered 'officer material': I passed out bottom of the course. The captain in charge called me in when the officer list was announced and said, 'I can tell you now, I'd give anything to be able to fail you, but your headmaster has spoken to the Commandant General of the Royal Marines.' So I got through on pure graft, really.

I hated the Royal Marines. The Corps is a very bullshitty, rule-obsessed, tradition-obsessed body of men. But at the end I was training people who were going to be commandos, at the pre-commando training school on Dartmoor. And there, I softened slightly. We lived most of our life on Dartmoor and you were, to a rather unusual degree, in charge of what you did yourself. I enjoyed that life because it was a very healthy one, and even more because one got to know Dartmoor and its natural life very well; and also many of the officers with me were slightly odd fish. It was supposed to be the worst job in the Marines. You were meant to hope you went aboard a ship, beat the retreat, and all that rubbish. At the end of my conscription I could go to university (I had a place at Oxford) or I could stay on in the Marines. I was slightly torn, I have to admit, but then one day Isaac Foot (Michael Foot's father – the Lord Mayor of Plymouth) came to the camp, and I was appointed his ADC to look after him. I put it to him and he said, 'Anyone who would give up a chance of going to Oxford for this is mad.' That was very important for me, because here was a person who was famous in Devon life and who I naïvely thought would say the very opposite. The next day I put in for early demobilisation.

I went to Oxford, for which I'm very grateful. There, at least, and at last, I was in an environment where the arts were 'normal'.

After Oxford I went to teach for a year in a French university, and I was invited in that year to go back to England (to Winchester, which is, academically, one of the best public schools) to teach French there. But I knew by then that I didn't want to be a university or public school teacher; I'd begun to feel I wanted to be a writer. On another occasion I had the chance of teaching English in the Royal Navy dockyards, and at the same time I was offered a job at

a Greek school. I took the job in Greece – though it was obviously
the wrong career choice. To become a writer you always take the
job which will offer you most time, or the job which looks as though
it will be most interesting, or the job that will take you abroad; and
that's seldom the best job in a careers master's sense. So I worked
in Greece for a couple of years. I came back to England and worked
in an adult education college. These were all steps down, so to speak.
Finally, when I was about twenty-eight, I took a job in a secretarial
college in North London. There, I was teaching English to foreign
girls; academically nowhere at all. But this was in fact a very
interesting job. I found that teaching Siamese, Icelandic, Peruvian
girls, girls from all over the world, about Shakespeare's plays, and
Jane Austen, can be an exciting, revealing experience. Many of them
came from claustrophobic and father-dominated societies, and
helping them open their minds was often a rewarding process. Like
watching a flower bloom.

I began writing in my last year at Oxford, in '49. I can remember
the very first thing I regarded as original: a translation of a well-
known French poem. And from that I began to write a few, small
(and very bad) poems of my own. Going abroad is very important
for young writers. When I went to France and taught in a French
university I started keeping a regular diary (another thing, in my
view, very important for any writer to do: it's our equivalent of bar
exercises for a dancer – very good training, and it also teaches you
to be observant, even slightly more honest about yourself). I began
to have definite instincts towards fiction. And then, when I went to
Greece, I wrote a book about Greece. It was a travel book, but I
had written one section as fiction. I sent it to Paul Scott, who was
an agent (he wasn't known as a novelist then). He said, 'I don't like
the travel book, but stick with the fiction – that's where your talent
lies.' That was a shrewd and helpful piece of advice. From then on
I really did concentrate on writing fiction. I also still wrote a lot of
poetry. I regard poetry, for a novelist, as another productive
exercise. At least it gives you some sense of rhythm in prose.

I decided to write about Greece, and I began *The Magus*, but that
gave me endless problems. One's first novel is always teaching
oneself how to write as much as anything else; and it was an absurdly
difficult idea for a first novel. I adored Greece, and I had a terrible
sense of loss when I came back. Writing about it was partly a way
of filling up that sense of loss. I had discovered one thing about

Greece – it's a very, very bad country to try to create in. It's
something to do with the climate, and the perfection of the
landscapes. You feel dwarfed almost before you begin, and then
inevitably you start hitting the bottle, or living the summer life there,
where it's too hot to think or do anything. But back in England it
was easier. I was then teaching at the adult education college, and
certain events in my private life gave me a basic scheme for the
novel, which I transferred back to Greece.

I regard a published book as a dead book. They are, if you like,
like crimes in your past. I'm not really an existentialist any more,
but I'm still enough of one to believe that you must accept these
things. *The Magus* was a crime in the sense that I had nowhere near
the equipment to deal with a massive subject like that. I never have
plans when I write and the trouble was that, during its writing, I let
myself be endlessly sidetracked. I also made a gross mistake at the
beginning in introducing a supernatural element. It took me many
years to see that was out of place, and I led myself into many
mistakes in the countless writings of it. It was written very much
under the influence of Alain-Fournier's novel *Le Grand Meaulnes*.
In the end I felt I had to cut out references to it.

I feel for *The Magus* the affection one does for one's first work.
I regard it as quite a good novel of adolescence. I wrote somewhere
that only adolescents could really appreciate it. I now get quite a lot
of indignant letters: 'Sir, I am sixty years old . . .' But I think that's
basically what it was, just as *Le Grand Meaulnes* itself is a novel of
adolescence. I suppose it pleases me in a metaphysical way in as
much as it deals with the man-God relationship. Most people hate
the hero of it – Nicholas, just as they hate the girl in *The Collector*.
It's surprising how many people have gained an intense dislike of
her. I get letters saying, 'When are you going to write *The Son of
the Collector*? Will you get another middle-class prig on the spot?' I
don't agree. She was meant to have some of the qualities of a prig,
but I did hope it was clear she might have become a better human
being. *The Magus* is being written by Nicholas long afterwards, and
so all the accusations which people spring on him are really written
by him. But obviously I failed there. I didn't get it across enough,
in the way I wrote the book, that this is a man looking back on his
sins and crimes.

It took me ten years to write *The Magus*. I wrote, in one month,
a very short novel, which became *The Collector*. I published that

first; but for me it's the second novel. I wrote it a little bit coldly. I realised I was getting nowhere with *The Magus*, and I had for my own sake to produce something fairly short and concrete, and which somebody would publish. So in that sense it was a deliberate exercise in the macabre, the perverted even. I quite like it. I would change one or two things now – but it's too late. I was first of all excited by the idea, because it's almost universal among male adolescents, although not often in a perverted form: not imprisoning somebody in a cellar – much more being shut up in a jammed ·lift with the person you can't approach in real life. This notion of some miraculous event happening that joins you or associates you very closely with the person that in real life you can't get near. That idea has always interested me. I was also interested to see if I couldn't marry the two characters in a strange way: their faults and their good qualities don't mesh at all, and that is why the tragedy takes place. This interested me as a basic pattern. I had great difficulty making up my mind to kill the girl. I think in the first draft she escaped, because the tyranny of the happy ending was on me. Also I had a very good editor, Tom Maschler at Cape, and he rearranged the text brilliantly in terms of suspense. Tom is not always kindly regarded in the publishing world, but he's a cracking good editor. He's an old friend now. I'm lucky also in that I have an agent whose judgement I respect, and I listen to both their criticisms, even if I don't always follow them. Tom is marvellous when you're going on a bit too much. His nose there is almost infallible, so I don't often disagree.

After *The Magus* I wrote *The Aristos*. That was mainly because I didn't like the feeling that I was becoming set as a novelist only. That book, I do slightly regret now. I find it rather naïve. It was in the wrong form; that was because I am deeply influenced by French literature. I don't regret it for myself because I think it's useful for a writer to get all his general ideas, however dreadful, down somewhere. Then you can keep them out of the novel. The novel doesn't take unmediated intellectual or philosophical ideas at all well. I hate novels that are clogged up with ideas, with long conversations that are endless arguments. I've never been very fond of Huxley's novels. I haven't read them for many years but I can remember not liking them. I'm very fond of Thomas Love Peacock's novels, but he also goes on too long in that way. I love narrative, and too many ideas choke the narrative. But of course, a writer must express his basic nature, both in a Freudian sense and in a more practical living sense – you must, willy-nilly, suggest that you're Tory or not, and things like that. But 'socialist' novels are better as socialist tracts. This is what I call mis-channelling: the water may be good but it's in the wrong channel. I would much prefer a good journalist like Jeremy Seabrook or James Cameron to put these ideas in journalism or in tracts than see them forced into a novel. The novel should be about characters and narrative. I hate to lay down laws – with the novel you cannot make any rules at all, because the test is always in the reading.

Next came *The French Lieutenant's Woman*. Novels often start with one image. I had this constant image, like a cinema still, of a woman in black with her back turned to me – that's all it was. I thought at first it was a widow standing in an airport lounge or something. But then because I could just see the end of the Cobb (the harbour at Lyme) from our garden, it gradually became a figure standing on the Cobb, and therefore an historical figure; and so gradually a Victorian woman in black, who was obviously in some way ostracised or exiled by the world she lived in. I now know who the woman in black was. Another book that has influenced my life, one of these mysterious books you like beyond any intellectual judgement, is an obscure and very short French novel called *Ourika*. It was written by a duchess who was a friend of Chateaubriand, the French Romantic novelist. Hers was the first good attempt by a white mind to get into an intelligent black one. Claire de Duras was as right-wing as you can imagine, but because of that streak in Romanticism that worried about human suffering, she created this black slave and lady's companion, whose life is tragic. It is a remarkable attempt to realise what it must have been like to be a black in the last twenty years of the eighteenth century. And now I see that my figure was really Ourika; but where my mind cheated was in not making the woman black – I simply dressed her in black. I didn't quite realise this until after the book was published, but I'm quite sure now that behind Sarah in *The French Lieutenant's Woman* is this fictional black woman, Ourika. (I translated *Ourika* later, and it was published in America.)

I don't like, and I never read, historical novels – I think they're boring, but for some reason I did rather enjoy writing this novel. And, having sworn I'd never write another, I'm doing another at the moment. We all know that if you say at some point in your career,

'I'm never going to write a detective thriller,' or whatever, sure as fate, within a year you'll find a secret longing to do it. I think *The French Lieutenant's Woman* is quite good technically. I doubt if it's as original as some people have been kind enough to say, but it pleases me as a work.

The next novel, *Daniel Martin*, pleases me much more as a novel that I wanted to write. I was very much harsher because I wouldn't listen to any criticism on it. My agent, and Tom Maschler, and Elizabeth (my wife) all wanted cuts, heavy cuts, and I said, 'No. This is my book, and it will stand as I wrote it.' I suffered for it, it was very badly reviewed. It's a sort of *Bildungsroman* – a story of how somebody develops in life. It covers a long span; and I just wanted it to be like that. I know there are too many digressions and asides, it 'goes on' too much. I deliberately decided I wouldn't go in for normal narrative cleverness. At the end I did quicken the pace a bit. The idea was really that all these events in one's past are equidistant in one's life. Of course, we tend to think chronologically, but in fact, emotionally, one's childhood is as close as what happened yesterday.

I wrote all the stories for *The Ebony Tower* in one year. I wrote them for relief in the middle of writing *Daniel Martin*, at a time when it seemed improbable that *Daniel Martin* would ever finish. I'm not a good short-story writer – I don't have the special knack that good short-story writers have. The idea was that they'd be variations on things I'd written about already.

Mantissa was a far from perfect book. It had the reaction I usually get now: half to three-quarters bad, a quarter good. It was written a little bit for other writers. It's about, on the surface, the problem of the muse: where one's inspiration comes from; and why, in the actual act of writing, things come that one could never imagine oneself thinking of. I've treated the muse as another human being – a woman because the other character, the writer, is male. The book 'behind' is Flann O'Brien's *At-Swim-Two-Birds*. That's another important book for writers, a novel where characters don't obey any normal rules – they step out of role. My characters put on all sorts of masks – a very dangerous thing, because, unless you say, 'He puts on a mask,' people think that everything said comes from you. There are only two characters, but they switch from one role to another, so at some points it's anti-feminist and so on; which one or two very naïve critics have taken as my own view. It's a very short novel, and is based on the French philosophical tale – the 'conte philosophique',

Candide, things like that. It's really a sort of in-house book. I didn't want it published by my main publishers – it was at first going to be a small press production – but they have you by contract: I have to show them any fiction I intend publishing and they have first rights on it. I also have a strong feeling that being a 'best-seller' is a terrible trap. You're expected to do nothing but produce more and longer best-sellers. In the past, such writers were allowed to produce minor things off the cuff, as *Mantissa* very much was. It was a kind of joke I tossed off among more serious things. But you can't do that now and remain 'respectable'.

I did a collection of poems a long time ago. I was friendly with a poet called Dan Halpern who was running this, then, very small press in America: it's now quite successful. It started as a magazine – *Antaeus*. Then he began building up a tiny publishing list, and asked me if I'd go in. That was vanity publishing; I know I'm not a good poet.

Neither am I a good screen-writer. I did the script for *The Magus*, and I must take some responsibility for the awfulness of the end product: I also helped in the final version of the script for *The Collector*, with William Wyler in Hollywood. I enjoyed the experience of Hollywood, and working with Wyler (whom I came to like); but it was not a good film. I respect the cinema as an art, but generally detest the ordinary film world – all its false glamour, its wastefulness, its egocentricity, its lies and compromises. Above all I detest all those worthy people who think being filmed must be the highest honour they can receive from life. As if one's books were not complete till then. For me, almost all films of books are really a kind of paperback edition, no more. I am grateful when my own have been well done, as with Karel Reisz and *The French Lieutenant's Woman*; but even then my heart stays with the book.

I don't place reviewers very high on my list of who matters in the writing business. Readers matter above all. I'm very lucky because hardly a day of my life passes without my getting some letters from readers. Total strangers feel impelled to write – often not so much about my books as about themselves, and some of the letters are very interesting. Even the 'anti' letters are often quite helpful because they define. They answer the question that every writer must be clear about: Who do I write for? I suppose I now get about three or four hundred letters a year. Over the years I have had a considerable response. That very good novelist B. S. Johnson wrote somewhere that he received only nine letters in fourteen years of writing (or fourteen letters in nine years, I can't remember); whichever it was, that was terrible. He seemingly had no contacts with readers except through friends – and they're notoriously unreliable. I wouldn't listen to a friend's opinion about a book for ten seconds. Either they gush, or they can't hide their resentment – they're the least impartial judges, in my view. Bad reviews you learn to live with. Of course they hurt you for a day or two. However sensitive and thin-skinned you are in reality, you must train yourself to shrug it off. That's lesson one. I do bear grudges against people who I think have been mean and untruthful; but you cannot blame anyone for sincerely not liking a book.

I don't have any ambition. I hope I'll write some more books, I wouldn't say novels. In a way I'm that bad thing, a satisfied writer. I have been very lucky in the way my books have been received and studied, as also in the way they've sold. I do quite a lot of 'foreword' work. I enjoy that. I'm doing two introductions now: for a collection of Hardy photos that have recently been discovered; and to a retrospective of a photographer, Fay Godwin, whose work I'm very fond of. The trouble is you are asked to do far more than you can cope with, so you're eternally writing, 'I regret . . .'

I suppose I live a very isolated life, in ordinary literary terms. I enjoy literary life and literary gossip very little, and literary publicity even less. I only know one other writer at all well, and feel very remote from the world of contemporary letters. This is by choice mainly; and a little also because of my success in America. One is not lightly forgiven that. If one talks about it, one is boasting; if one doesn't talk about it, one is being smug. One can't win.

There are aspects of writing I don't find enjoyable, such as the endless typing out. (I don't believe in the word processor.) There's a chore-like aspect to it, one has to develop a kind of peasant patience. But I believe in the endless re-typing – it does improve the book. It seems a waste of time very often, but in the end it's valuable. I do a lot of drafts. I even quite enjoy what they call 'writer's block', when you don't see your way round a problem. Again, because I have no money worries, I can take time with it. I think this is the way one ought to write. I tend to write texts, then leave them for two or three years. In a perfect world everyone would be able to do that.

The novelist's wife is one of the great ignored figures of the literary

world. She's got a permanent rival, one worse than any living 'other woman': it's a terrible situation to be in. I know a lot about Hardy's two awful marriages, and only the other day I saw *Tom and Viv* in London, about T. S. Eliot's equally grim experiences with his first wife. Eliot was to blame; as Hardy was to blame, and I'm sure almost all of us are to blame. I try not to put my work first, but it often has to come first because writing is a very slow process. It takes a hell of a lot of time to write a book. Also I spend a great deal of my life in books. I'm always happy to spend the whole day reading, and that, I know, is a bad thing for the person who has to live with you. And then there's the mail you get – fan letters, and academic letters. Everyone's interested only in you; the you that is a writer. This person, or public persona, 'John Fowles', has for several years now seemed to me very distant from what I really am – a distinctly foreign fellow, whom both my wife and myself agree we don't very much like, a cuckoo in the nest. But it's harder for her. I don't have any children of my own. I don't think I was ever a fit person to have a child; the children of writers are the second category of major sufferers.

The most important thing for me now is conservation. This is one quarrel I have with socialism: it's far too anthropocentric. What concerns me most is the way we're killing off nature. There's been a holocaust in the last thirty years in this country, but because it's so diffused nobody's really aware of it yet. The same thing is happening, of course, all over the world. I did collect butterflies as a schoolboy – but there were many more of them about then; the present dreadful situation hadn't arisen – there are six British butterfly species at the moment on the probable extinction list. In the 1930s you could walk into a field that hadn't been 'improved' (i.e.buggered) and there would be a mist of butterflies over everything. That's gone for ever now.

I also had an uncle who was an entomologist and I used to like to go out with him. I was interested, in my teens, in shooting and fishing, but that was always much more a way of getting out and watching nature. But then I had a change as big as I had after being head boy. I was about twenty-one, I was still in the Marines. I was very keen on wildfowling, a nice solitary form of shooting. I went out one day and shot a curlew. The curlew was wounded, and screaming as they do. I picked it up to crack it down across the gun, and somehow its beak or its head entered the trigger guard and fired the second barrel. I saw a hole in the mud only six inches from my foot. I had very nearly shot my own foot off. Since then I've never killed anything; and now I won't use insecticides or pesticides. In a way (many natural historians have said this) hunting birds and animals is a good way of developing one's love for them. Peter Scott's a famous case. He used to shoot like mad when he was young. Then suddenly that day comes when you know you're destroying beauty and you have no right at all to do it. You just can't do it any more.

I'm an atheist; rather a militant one. I'm a unilateralist in nuclear matters. Most of my views are Labour Party views (though the present Labour Party distresses me very much with its feuding over the last few years). Perhaps this defines it: I wish there was a Marxist party in parliament, on the other hand I'd be seriously worried if I thought it was going to gain supreme power. This is to do with my feelings about Marxism – absolutely marvellous on some things and absolutely wrong on others. I don't like the British class system, but I'm a conditioned victim of it. And of course (if you're being cynical) it is an enormously useful thing for a writer. Writing English novels without the class system would be a much harder job in many ways, whether you're against it or for it.

Usually I write when I feel like it. When I was going out to work I used to grasp at every free hour, but I count that more of an obsession than anything else. I wrote the first draft of *The Collector* in one holiday, in fact; in three or four weeks. Nowadays I fill my life with other work, so I've always got that to fall back on. I occasionally do very long hours: sixteen hours a day, even. Normally it's about five or six hours a day. Usually, in first drafts, I like long periods at it, but in revision I think it pays to do it in breaks and snatches. You come fresher to it like that.

I'm the 'sort of' archivist-and-historian of Lyme Regis, so I spend quite a lot of time on local history, doing petty jobs like indexing, typing out old manuscripts, and the rest. Our local museum is a voluntary set-up – run by amateurs like me. I do get some personal return from history. I'm just doing a pamphlet at the moment on thirteenth century life here. I enjoy the reading I've had to do to try and imagine what it was like then. Being an archivist is also enjoyable because new bits of information are always coming in: old papers, deeds, photographs, things like that. I enjoy it very much although it's totally useless in most ways from a literary point of view. But you can't live uniquely in books.

I'm not a scientific natural historian – I don't write down observations or anything like that. I have, I suppose, a rather 'poetic' relationship: I just like being in nature and knowing what I know about it, and also rather liking what I don't know. My garden here, mess though it is, is very important to me. We're in a mild climate so things flower all round the year, and we've got some quite rare plants. I feel intensely close to the plants, birds, animals and insects who share this place with me; much closer than to most human beings, who would own me or be owned. I don't much like the notion of ownership. My friends and family think this is all a private domain for me; a little private world. I think they don't understand.

I'm in favour of Arts Council grants. I'm not for a state co-operative publishing house. I don't mind co-operatives like Writers and Readers, but I have seen it proposed that we should all be under one master in terms of publishing; and I'm against that, very definitely. The problem is how you award grants; who you award them to, and who does the awarding. I would guess, as human beings are involved, it will always be corrupt and wrong in places, but I would personally accept that. If out of ten grants seven are wrongly given there are still three people who deserve them. The problem is the question of ability. The writers who most need help are the writers at the beginning, without the published proof of ability. I don't know the answer, I don't see that there is an answer. But it's worth taking the risk, even though most of the grants will go to the wrong hands. I suggested once that the money richer writers pay to tax (sixty per cent of what I earn goes in tax) should go to help writers in need. I wanted PLR to do that (bestseller writers should not benefit) but when I suggested it in public it met considerable resistance, which rather surprised me.

I'm against writers who feel forced to live abroad in tax exile. That simply says you're so greedy you want all your money. It also shows a lack of confidence in yourself, that you can go on earning money. And the worst thing, of course, is that you're exiled from your mother tongue. I think that's death. Every writer fears that one day he or she won't be able to write. I don't have a neurosis about that. But again, this is the peasant side of me: I think I know about seasons, and bad years, and lying fallow, and all that rural side of life. Sometimes you must get bad crops, and it's patience really. Stendhal said that genius is nine parts obstinacy. That's very true. I

always say this to young writers: 'Patience, patience, patience.' I get
so many letters from writers aged twenty, twenty-one: 'I've just
written my third novel and again it's been rejected.' And I feel this
is so idiotic: the novel is the hardest and longest of all the artistic
trades to learn. I don't believe, under the age of thirty, that anyone
has much chance. You need at least another five years after you've
left university to begin to think about it. In a way it's an old man's
trade.

* * *

Richard Jefferies' *Bevis*, as I said before, was a very important book
for me. And also Alain-Fournier's *Le Grand Meaulnes*. Voltaire's
Candide is a very great novel. For me it has a perfection of form,
and a tone that stays in one's mind like certain flavours or tastes.
I'm very fond of Daniel Defoe, particularly *Robinson Crusoe*. I like
Defoe's enormous narrative drive. And his plainness, his simple, on-
driving way of writing novels. And his faking too. I love the way he
can simulate reality in *The Journal of the Great Fire*, and books like
that. I greatly enjoy that deceitful part of novel writing where you
have to trick the reader into thinking you were actually there, or into
thinking that they're reading real history.

I very much like a novel by Golding called *The Inheritors*, about
primitive man; It's a masterly bit of intuitive imagination, a feeling
back to a reality of which we know very little. *Housemother Normal*,
by B. S. Johnson, is a small masterpiece. He was, I think, much
underrated. For me the best fairly recent American novel is Bellow's
Herzog; it has a wisdom, a sense of history, a European quality I
find lacking in most American fiction. They are very good at doing
the present, what it feels like to be alive now; but impoverished, I
believe, elsewhere, in the past. Nabokov's *Ada* I admire very much.
That's another book for writers; a novelists' novel. I haven't read
Malraux's *The Human Condition* for years, but I did think that was
a very fine novel; although I don't know if I like *him* very much. I've
always found all of Peacock's novels enjoyable. Flaubert, too.

There are countless French writers I could choose. Flaubert is
probably the greatest in a technical sense: sentence after sentence
dropping perfectly. I do find that pleasing, partly because I can't do

it myself. Again, I think it's doubtful whether he was a good human being, but then I suspect most novelists are rather unpleasant people. Hardy, for instance. I like Hardy very much as a novelist. And as a poet, too. The major poet in my life has definitely been T. S. Eliot, although I've never liked at all what I know of him as a person, or of his philosophy. But he did have some unique magic with language, an ability to write lines one cannot forget, and there are very few who can do that; Yeats is another, I suppose.

* * *

I can't believe that literature actually changes society. But what it can do (I have learnt this in part from readers' letters) is change how people think and feel; and perhaps it's changing how they feel that is really the social power in the novel. You can help to liberalise people through the novel; and liberate them a little. I remember some of us at my school were complaining about the set books in French. That old French master I spoke of gave us Céline's novel to read, *Voyage to the End of the Night*. (He'd probably have been sacked if he'd been found out.) That's another very great novel by a rather unpleasant man: 'pornographic', full of foul language, and so on. I can still remember the shock of struggling (a lot of the French was over our heads then) through it, the shock that someone had actually written all these things. The same, when you're young, with more normal classics. That does open your mind. Suddenly you realise there is something beyond examinations in a book – you see what the 'grown-ups' are talking about.

I had it with Jane Austen, I remember, when I was at Oxford. One day I suddenly saw what she was truly about. And I can remember having that same experience with various poets, like Dylan Thomas. You discover what other people see in them. I think this is a vital experience, what education is (or should be) truly about: being led out of your much too personal and self-imprisoned adolescent view of life. That's an important value and function of literature.

Another value, I would say, is sheer pleasure, both conscious and unconscious. Being, willy-nilly, 'lost' in a book; but also being able to analyse how the words are chosen and arranged, and working out what effect they are having on you. I don't know if most readers bother to work it out; but I think even the simplest, most innocent reader does, sometimes, ask, '*Why* is this happening to me?' I keep asking the academics to do more work on what goes on when you're reading. It's the great dark area in literature. Evelyn Waugh is a relevant case. One half of me hates almost everything he stands for, but another half admires his writing. I have this dilemma: do I hate this writer because of his evil or crabbed views of life, or do I admire him because he is clever with words, funny even when he's being foully rude and inhuman? Philip Larkin is another case. I know at once that he is a very considerable poet, with a marvellous felicity of phrase; but so much of what he stands for I find repulsive: his hatred of children, his hatred of everything foreign, all of that. I find his views often really unpleasant, but he expresses them in a style nearer to perfection than any other English poet or writer today. It's an old problem in writing; the Devil somehow hires the best voices. Meanwhile, we wait.

Lyme Regis, February 1984

NIGEL GRAY'S COMMENT.

John Fowles is a shy man, not at ease with people he doesn't know well. Paradoxically, his copious knowledge of and exuberant enthusiasm for literature, history (ancient and local) and natural history make him a magnetic and stimulating companion. Although in his fiction he never writes in a propagandist manner about his political and social beliefs, no sensitive reader can fail to be impressed by his humanity and respect for life. To talk to him is to be left in no doubt about his honesty and sincerity. Perhaps self-consciousness of his straightforward manner, combined with his lack of ease in public, contribute to the tendency to use the masks so typical of his novels.

Before meeting John Fowles to interview him I had only known him through an occasional correspondence. I guess his willingness to put himself in the position of interviewee – a position he doesn't relish – was to do with his genuine concern to help struggling writers. In the event I took to him immediately and felt at home in his rambling and interesting (though not ostentatious) house. I was honoured too with a tour of the delightful garden which slopes south towards the sea, and which, more importantly, is tilted thereby towards the sun, where daffodils were already in bloom in February. I was very impressed, in my child-like way, with the piles of garden rubbish John keeps for the badgers to burrow in at night, with ancient species of vegetable he helps save from extinction by growing each year, with a very rare tree he nurtures there – the only one of its kind in the world outside China.

That summer, in France, I made the acquaintance of Hugues, a charming man, who has since become a close friend. In return for the tenancy of a little cottage he looks after the garden of his rich neighbour. Hugues speaks no English, and my understanding of French is severely limited. (For a long time I thought I'd been told I spoke French like a Spanish cow – although lately I've discovered that what I was probably being accused of was speaking French like a Spanish Basque.) I understood Hugues to say that a tree in the garden was one of the oldest in the world. I hurriedly sent off leaves to John telling him of this amazing discovery, thinking perhaps he would want to journey to France to see it with his own eyes. John sent me a postcard to inform me that while it was indeed true that this species of tree, the Ginkgo biloba, was one of the oldest known, it was in fact extremely common, and could be found lining the streets of New York and other great cities.

In 1985 John published his second historical novel: *A Maggot*. It contains the mélange of compelling story-telling, mystery, erudite detail, informed chat, and erotica, that Fowles fans have come to look forward to; it was widely acclaimed. He is, without doubt, one of the major novelists of our day. *The French Lieutenant's Woman* won him both the Silver Pen award and the W. H. Smith Literary Award.

At the time of writing, John is, sadly, in hospital.

John Fowles was born in a suburb of Southend-on-Sea, Essex, on March 31st 1926.

John Fowles' Book Choice:

Bevis Richard Jefferies
Le Grand Meaulnes
   Alain-Fournier
Robinson Crusoe Daniel Defoe
The Inheritors William Golding
Housemother Normal
   B. S. Johnson
Herzog Saul Bellow

Ada or Ardor Vladimir Nabokov
The Human Condition
   André Malraux
Nightmare Abbey
   Thomas Love Peacock
The Sentimental Education
   Gustave Flaubert
The Well-Beloved Thomas Hardy
The Waste Land T. S. Eliot

Books by John Fowles:

The Magus
The Collector
The Aristos
The French Lieutenant's Woman

Daniel Martin
The Ebony Tower
Mantissa Poems
A Maggot

Non-fiction:

Islands
   (Photos by Fay Goodwin)
The Enigma of Stonehenge
   (Photos by Harry Binkoft)

The Tree
   (Photos by Frank Horiat)

Chapter Seven
BARRY HINES

My dad was a miner. My mum was a housewife. I had a very happy, conventional working-class childhood. It's a curious area, South Yorkshire; it's a strange juxtaposition of the industrial and the rural. Hoyland Common was just a collection of two-up-and-two-downs, with a little council estate on the side, surrounded by woods and fields; there was a pit at the bottom of our street where my dad worked: yet it was very close to Barnsley and Sheffield and Rotherham. In some ways we had the best of both worlds, but looking back on it I suppose it was a rural childhood. Most of my time when I wasn't in school was spent in the woods and fields, and I think that's where I got this love of natural history which I've been able to use in my work.

The fathers of all my friends either worked down the pit or in the steel works in Sheffield or Rotherham. All the mums of my friends were housewives; none of the women seemed to go out to work. It was very much a man's world. It was all very physical. Work was always dirty and dangerous. My grandfather was killed down the pit when I was seven. It was a rough sort of background. The heroes were fighters and sportsmen; and when we were older we were judged by how many girls we were knocking off, or how much beer we could drink.

When you look back on your life there are milestones. I suppose, for me, the first milestone was when I passed the Eleven Plus (it was called the Scholarship then). I took this examination in February and did a little essay and some sums, and then off I went in September to this grammar school five miles away with a few others who passed. But most of my friends had failed and gone to the secondary modern school just five minutes walk away. I was suddenly taken away from this very safe, close community where nearly everyone was working-class. There was only one street of middle-class houses. They seemed posh then, but looking back on it they were just 1930s semis. The men would have been in lower management at local steel works, but

there was a definite class difference between them and us. When I
went to the grammar school there were more of 'them' all of a
sudden. I never really fitted in at grammar school. I never really felt
like an academic boy. I was a very aggressive boy at school. It was
my way of hitting back, of objecting to whatever they were doing to
me. The teachers and most of the middle-class children seemed to
be 'on the same side'; they seemed to know all the rules. I loathed
most of the subjects, and what made it worse was that when I came
home at half-past four or so, my mates were out playing. They'd
done for the day. I was supposed to spend the evening doing
homework. I spent four or five years skiving, and planning how I
could get homework done without doing it officially at home. It was
always done in the school lavatories or on the bus coming home, or
on the bus going to school next morning. There was just one barber
at Hoyland Common, and when you went to him it was a two or
three hour job, so rather than waste time I used to do my homework
in the barber's.

It was very much a split world. The only thing that made it
tolerable was Games and PE lessons. I just wanted to leave as
quickly as possible. When my mates left secondary modern school
at fifteen I wanted to leave with them, but my mother insisted that
I went back to school for another year. My dad wasn't really
concerned about academic success. He left school at fourteen and
went to work down the pit, and he lived all his life in Hoyland
Common, whereas the day after my mother was fourteen she was
put on a train to Manchester. She was in service there to a doctor.
Then she came back to Sheffield and she was in service here. She
had seen the middle-class at first hand; she knew what they were
like, how ambitious they were, and saw the way that their children
were treated. Like a lot of working-class people, she wanted her
children to become middle-class, to 'do well for themselves', as they
always say. So it was my mother who said, 'You're going back to
school for another year, Barry, to get some 'O' levels.' I managed
to pass six 'O' levels, then I went to work at the pit for a while as
an apprentice mining surveyor. It was in the office. I was on the
staff. It seemed apt for a mediocre grammar school boy.

All the time I was at school I wanted to become a professional
footballer. I was a good player. I was a good athlete as a boy. One
or two clubs were interested in me. I was playing for Wolves Juniors
– they had a northern nursery team near Barnsley. The trouble was,

they played Saturday mornings, and I had to work Saturday mornings. It was one or the other – so I gave my job up. Well, my mother wasn't too pleased about this. I started thinking about it as well. I wasn't a star, and I wanted to be a star. I wanted to be like Denis Law or Bobby Charlton. A lad of my age called Alec Jeffrey played for Doncaster Rovers in the second division (he had a couple of bad injuries; I think he was finished by the time he was twenty). I can remember watching him and thinking, 'I'm not as good as that.' I can remember seeing Denis Law play for Huddersfield Town when he was sixteen. He wasn't just playing for the first team, he was *starring*, and I thought, 'I want to be as good as that.' – and I wasn't. So I thought, 'Well, if I don't make the grade, what'd be the next best thing to be?' So I thought, 'Why not become a PE teacher?' It seemed like a pretty cushy sort of job. It didn't seem like work because I'd always regarded work as being dirty and dangerous. At school I'd seen the PE teacher in his shorts up the field in summer, or doing a bit of basketball, or joining in the football games, and I thought, 'God, he gets *paid* for that.' So I went back to school, managed to scrape a couple of 'A' levels, and then after a year working at various labouring jobs I finished up going to Loughborough as a PE student. That was the second milestone.

Up to this point I'd never taken literature seriously. It was just another lesson to me. I was no better at English than I was at anything else, and also, I think, I resisted it. I resisted the books that we had to read because it was just another manifestation of 'them' against 'us'. The books were always about the ruling-class. The big problems in the books were: the servants; what coach they were going to use and how many horses were going to pull it; keeping the silver clean. It didn't concern me. I didn't care about it. I wasn't ready for books by Jane Austin and George Eliot. I read them now in my own time, read them for pleasure, but I wasn't able to make the imaginative leap. You can't leap straight from the *Beano* and the *Dandy* and the *Rover* and the *Wizard* to *Pride and Prejudice*. Well I couldn't, anyway. I wanted to know what it was like for a teddy-boy in Barnsley or Nottingham or Newcastle. I wanted the subject matter to be about 'us', about 'our people' instead of 'their people'. My heart used to sink at the sight of those heavy tomes coming out of the cupboard. They all looked like bibles. Every book weighed as much as a house brick, and when you opened them there'd be 5000 words on a page. If I'd been able to read books by David Storey and

Stan Barstow and Alan Sillitoe when I was fifteen or sixteen I think I'd have been less resistant to literature.

I went to Loughborough hardly having read anything, almost a determined philistine. My whole life had been taken up by sport. That's all I cared about. I was a sports fanatic. So Loughborough was the right place. It was like going to Sparta. All we did there most of the time was play games. It was terrific. But funnily enough it was there of all places that I started reading and started doing a bit of writing. I think one of the reasons was a feeling of inadequacy. For the first time, I became friends with people who came from a different class. When I was at school they were mostly middle-class boys and girls, and I got on all right with them, but I went back home to my own mates. But at Loughborough I became friendly with people from middle-class homes who shared my interest in sport, and that created a bond between us. They were more academic than I was. They were good at sport, but a lot of them hadn't had that professional ambition that I had. They wanted to be PE teachers, whereas I wanted to be a footballer. I'd played for England Grammar Schools; I'd played for Barnsley in the 'A' team and in the reserves. Some boys went through school and their ambition was to be a PE teacher the way some want to be a Geography teacher. They'd followed a more academic path, and some of them had done English at 'A' level. Most of the students weren't as narrow as I was, and I felt this very quickly.

I started going into the library and reading books at random. I can remember liking Dylan Thomas: I think it was the richness of the language. Now, it's too rich for me. It's a bit like Christmas pudding – a little of it goes a long way. Then I went on to Hemingway, and I appreciated that, in the end, more. It seems like a contradiction, but what attracted me was the sparsity, the simplicity, the clarity of the language. I can remember reading James Joyce's short-stories, *Dubliners*, and being tremendously impressed by them. I liked Scott Fitzgerald as well, and I got on to Orwell's essays very quickly. It was a matter of tasting everybody, and enjoying tastes of them. It was like a whole new world opening up for me.

While I was doing all this reading, we did an English course and we had to write up exercises. It was like being back at school – we had to write about: 'A Windy Day'; 'What I did in the Christmas Holidays'. Because I was becoming interested in language I enjoyed writing these little pieces, and one of the lecturers, a man called

Ernest Frost who was a novelist, spotted something, and started encouraging me. He told me to have a go at writing one or two short-stories. I had no idea what to write about. He said, 'Write about little incidents that happened to you as you grew up – little things that you remember.' I suppose I was influenced by the writers I enjoyed, but that didn't matter. I think that if you continue, you do find your own voice. I was enjoying doing this writing, and I can remember reading that Orwell essay, 'Why I Write'. He says prose should be like a window pane. That was a very important essay.

I got one or two pieces in the college magazine, and on the strength of that I decided I wanted to be a writer. It was at a rather juvenile and romantic level, like some people want to be rock stars when they can't even play a guitar, or want to be ballet dancers when they're about fifteen stone. You want some miracle to occur, some fairy to come down and touch you with her wand so that a sparkle comes out of you, and then you're going to be it. It was all very much at that level because, what did I know about writing? – Nothing. I suppose I thought it would wear off, but it stayed with me.

I started my apprenticeship at Loughborough – reading, and writing these little pieces. Then I went to London for a couple of years as a Physical Education teacher. I carried on reading, and I started to go to the theatre. For most working-class people things like that come much later than for most middle-class people. There's no tradition of the theatre – apart from Christmas panto. I can remember going to the Aldwych and seeing Brecht, and to the Old Vic and seeing Shakespeare (we'd had to read the plays round the class at school – a certain killer of Shakespeare, that). I started going to serious films for the first time, like Bergman films. It was another kind of apprenticeship. I was being introduced to the arts.

Then I went back to Hoyland Common. I was teaching PE in a new secondary modern school on a council estate in Barnsley. But all the time this idea that I wanted to be a writer had stayed with me, and I thought, 'Well, a time must come when I've got to try and prove it and put some words down on paper.' By this time I had realised that this business about hanging around waiting for inspiration didn't seem like a good idea. I was very functional about it. I applied sporting principles. I knew that anybody who had got the basic talent at cricket or football or athletics or tennis got better by training and practising: so I went into training. I was always very professional about it; from the word go, I took it seriously. I used to come home from school, have my tea, and then I had a sort of clocking on time at three minutes to six or whenever it is that the shipping forecast comes on. That was when I went upstairs and did my two hours stint. First of all it was a couple of evenings a week, and then I used to write Sundays as well (I was still playing football on Saturdays). I think that was very valuable: doing it regularly, and learning how to sit still. Sometimes I did sit there for two hours and come down with the sense of desperation at not having done anything; but I would still go up there the next time, hoping something would happen.

The first thing I wrote was a radio play. Well, that's what it became. To me it was just a play. It was based on an old man at Hoyland Common. He lived rough in a shed on the allotments. He earned a very precarious living, getting people's coal in. In the mining villages the coal that came from the top of the pit wasn't bagged up. If you ordered a ton of coal, it came in the back of a lorry and was tipped loose outside your house. So then you got it in yourself, either down to the coal shed or into the cellar or wherever. This man used to come round and say, 'Do you want your coal getting in?' And some people would say, 'Yeah.' Old people would do. He charged a few bob. There was coal being delivered every day somewhere in the village, so he'd have a few bob a day. I suppose he ate at the fish and chip shop, and then he'd go to the pub in the evening and have a half of bitter. People used to give him clothes. Any cast-offs, people would say, 'These'll do for Joe.' He was a well-liked man, really. The kids made fun of him, but adults never did, because he was a fixture in the village. I wrote this play about him (I don't know where the idea came from): somebody came to the village and, instead of him getting the coal in when he wanted to, they tried to put it on a regular footing, to make a business out of it. It all became highly organised, and he couldn't cope. It was a curious play. It was an epic, when I think back on it. When anybody starts off and they send me their work, and I see it's in pencil and it's all crossed out, I groan. I think, 'Oh, deary me. Here we go. I can't bear it.' But mine was almost like that when I sent it in. It was written in broad South Yorkshire dialect, which is like a foreign language. It was like Chinese. I saw in one of the Sunday papers that they'd appointed this new producer, Alfred Bradley, at the BBC in Leeds, who was looking for new writers. It was a very happy coincidence for me and for several other northern writers who were just starting out at the time. So I sent this play off. Alfred read it and sent it back, and he said, 'Have another look at it – I think there's a play in there somewhere.' So I went through it and got myself an hour radio play out of it.

That gave me tremendous confidence – having the first thing accepted. On the strength of that I gave up my job and for several years I just taught part-time. I don't know how I had the nerve when I think about it. I was just married, just got a mortgage – but I wanted to be a writer. I think there's something about writers – they have that single-mindedness, a dedication, a ruthlessness, which I think is not altogether admirable. It's good for the writing, but I don't know if it's good for the people close to you. You live your life in blinkers. The work's everything. I probably didn't consult my wife about it. She was always very helpful; I can't remember; but if she'd said no, I'd still have done it – I was going to be a writer at all costs. The only thing that would have stopped me would have been lack of talent.

After the radio play, I wrote a novel called *The Blinder*. During this time Alfred Bradley ran a programme called *Northern Drift*, which was smashing. There isn't anything like it now. It was for short pieces: poems, sketches, little stories, the sort of thing that there isn't a conventional market for. It used to go out live from Leeds once a month on Sunday mornings. I got a few pieces accepted on this programme, and I used to go over to rehearsals on Saturday afternoons. I told Alfred about this book I was writing, and he said, 'When it's finished, let me have a look at it.' He read it and said, 'I'll let Stan Barstow see it.' Stan's a big friend of Alfred. So Stan read it. I'd not met Stan then. He phoned me up and said, 'I'll send it to Michael Joseph for you if you like.' So Stan sent it off, and they took it. That was wonderful. There's never anything like the acceptance of the first novel. It must be like winning a Cup Final medal. A telegram came to the school I was teaching at (from either Stan or Alfred – I can't remember now): 'Michael Joseph would like to get in touch with you. They've accepted *The Blinder*.' It was about a quarter to four. School had just finished and I was going to umpire a cricket match. I was beside myself. I didn't want to go out. I'm sure it was the shortest cricket match on record because all I wanted to do was go home and tell my wife: I was going to have my first book published! Everybody was out lbw. No matter where the ball hit them, in front of the wicket or not, it was 'Out!' Everything was, 'Out!' – both sides: at least their umpire couldn't accuse me of favouritism. I think the score was about 4–2 at the end. It was all over in about twenty minutes.

The Blinder was partly about football. It was the subject I knew best. After the book had been published I went off it. For years I rejected it and was a bit ashamed of it. I've tried to analyse why, and I think the reason was, it felt as if it didn't wholly belong to me. It felt almost like a composite 'northern' novel. Those northern working-class novelists I mentioned earlier came at the time I began reading and writing, and it seemed to me, looking back on it after several years, that it was partly their novel as well, as if we all belonged to the same team, and it didn't have my individual stamp on it at all. So I rejected it and thought, 'No, I don't like that book.' But I think, now, I underestimated it. I think it's better than I thought. What it has got is a lot of vitality. It's a very vigorous book. It's plain. It gets on with it. I don't think there's a lot in it – but it tells a good tale. I think it has got more of me in it than I originally thought. I wish later books had got as much vitality as that one had. I did enjoy writing it more than anything I've written since. It was sheer pleasure, I think, because I was so naïve; I'd no standards; whereas now, having written seven, it feels more like hard work. I haven't got that energy that I had, that sheer vitality that you have in your youth. I've got other things now that I hadn't then, but there's some things that you can't recapture. In the same way, an eighteen year old footballer's got something that a thirty year old footballer hasn't got, but the thirty year old has now got something that compensates for the vigour and dash that the lad has. But even so, you shake your head and say, 'I wish I'd still got a bit of that.' You've got to compensate in more crafty ways.

After that I wrote a novel called *A Kestrel for a Knave*, which was an important book for me. I wanted to write a little book about education. I was starting to become more involved in politics. As a boy I was always instinctively anti-authoritarian, like a lot of working-class boys and girls are. You're against authority. You don't know why. But somehow you know that authority is against you as a class. Coming from a mining background I've always been aware of the miners' struggle. You're brought up with that. My dad wasn't a political person at all; he voted Labour but he never talked about political theory. But he was always against authority; always felt that 'they' were trying to get as much out of him as possible, and that he wasn't paid enough. He knew about capitalism instinctively without being able to talk about 'surplus value'.

I was always aware of the class struggle. It was part of me when I grew up. I knew about safety and danger in the pits because my grandad was killed down the pits. Also, we were surrounded by woods and fields: a lot of those woods and fields were private; a lot of the land was private land owned by Earl Fitzwilliam. So we used to go into 'private' woods and the gamekeeper would chase us out. It seemed absurd. We didn't seem to be doing anything wrong. So there was the gamekeepers, and there was the authority that my dad always seemed to be fighting at the pit – the deputies and the overmen and the manager, and there was the history of the miners' struggle. Teachers were obviously part of another class. The police didn't seem to be sympathetic to our class. They were on a par with the gamekeepers. They always seemed to be patrolling, protecting the interests of somebody who wasn't us. At school I hated prefects. If a prefect were to tell me to move on, just touching me, he was in danger of being smacked in the mouth. I thought, 'Here's another police force doing the dirty work for the teachers.' Alan Sillitoe wrote well about these destructive working-class people who're against authority but who're not *for* anything. They're not able to channel their energies into anything constructive or to see any kind of alternative.

I went into teaching for all the wrong reasons: I just wanted to perpetuate my adolescence and carry on playing football and running round a track and doing a bit of gymnastics and so on. But I got interested in education and I got involved in the NUT, and I started reading about politics and the theory of it all. And I wrote this little book, *A Kestrel for a Knave* which for me was all about the Eleven Plus, about the unfairness and inequality of it all, and about the way your background and the school you go to determines your class level in society and what's going to happen to you afterwards. It was obvious to me as a boy that more care and money was being spent on us at the grammar school than on my mates and my brother at the secondary modern school. Although the schools were built at the same time, the grammar school was bigger. It was grander. It had a portico and steps up at the front. It was pretending to be an Athenian temple. The secondary modern school could have been a biscuit factory. We had fields. They had a pitch. We had a gym. They didn't have a gym. We had tennis courts. They didn't have tennis courts. We had a uniform. They didn't have a uniform. It was just so obvious. Even though I didn't take much advantage of it, I got my education at the expense of that eighty percent or so who hadn't passed the Eleven Plus.

My spiritual home was the secondary modern, I suppose. When I became a teacher I taught in secondary moderns and comprehensives, and I wrote *A Kestrel for a Knave* because it seemed crazy that all this talent was going to waste, that all these boys and girls had been branded as failures, and that so many people, over generations, had been scarred and injured for life because of what happened to them at school, because at ten they were told they weren't any good and sent to schools which didn't develop their potential, so that they grew up feeling second class citizens and spent their lives on their knees. It's like James Connolly said, it's no wonder the great seem great, because the working-class have lived their lives on their knees. I was beginning to realise some of this when I was in my mid-twenties, and I wanted to show it in this little book about the boy with the kestrel hawk. Although the boy has a job to read and write, when he gets some motivation and he steals this book full of complicated, esoteric falconry language, he masters it and takes this kestrel and trains it to fly to the lure. He's a very skilful, very talented boy, but he'll probably get no 'O' levels. There's no 'O' levels or CSEs in falconry, unfortunately. But there may as well be. It seems to me as relevant as Religious Studies or Latin or Greek. For me it's a political novel. *The Blinder's* not: I think there's some instinctive political attitudes come out of it – the boy has this hatred of authority, he makes fun of his teachers and he hates the employer (that was me, and it was my dad), but with *A Kestrel for a Knave*, the politics had been analysed before I wrote it.

After that there was a disastrous book called *First Signs*, which was a mess. It was far too didactic. Looking back on it now, I suppose it had some of my best writing, but definitely a lot of my worst. But I learned a lot from it. It was a book about a young man who leaves university and bums around the Mediterranean for a while; enters teaching for, I suppose, the same reasons I did; gets involved with the NUT; and comes back up north, and so on. But it's me pulling the strings – Tom Renshaw doesn't develop as a character in his own right. But from that book, what I did learn is, that if you're going to write political fiction, the politics have to be integrated into the narrative rather than occasionally surfacing and wallowing like some great whale. In *First Signs*, the whale spouts for a few pages, then it sinks below the level of the page and I get on with the story for a bit, and then up it comes again. Here comes the next lecture! Here comes the political commercial! I hope I learned from that. But there are some nice little bits in it about the family, about how Tom comes home and sees his mum and dad after several years away.

Then I wrote a television play called *Speech day*. It was like *A Kestrel for a Knave* without a hawk, in some ways. I think the trouble with *A Kestrel for a Knave* was that there were too many loopholes for people who would like the failings of society to be put down to human failings. They could always say, 'Yes, but if he'd come from a better home; if his dad hadn't left; if his mother had cared for him more; if he'd gone to a better school; if his teachers hadn't been so unsympathetic: then he'd have been a better boy; he'd have been more interested in school; he'd have got five 'O' levels then and he could have got a job as an apprentice mining surveyor.' In *Speech Day* its a boy who wasn't in the bottom stream; who *is* going to get one or two 'O' levels and CSEs; who came from a good home background; who wore a blazer; who went to a modern comprehensive school; the teachers weren't monsters; yet when he leaves school he's still going to be on the dole. I was trying to close all the loopholes. Why is that boy, who's done all the things we've told him he should do, still on the dole? I'm just trying to make people think: 'Well, why? Perhaps there are political forces that put people on the dole at certain times; perhaps it's not just individual failings.'

When Tony Garnett was working as a producer for the BBC, he read *The Blinder* and asked me if I was interested in writing a script about football. I said, probably, but I couldn't do it at that time because I was in the middle of a novel about this boy and the hawk. A year later he phoned up my agent and said, 'Is that book finished?' She said, 'Yes, it's in proof.' Tony read it and came up to see me about it. He said, 'What about a film directed by Ken Loach – are you interested?' I was delighted. If I'd had a choice of people to have made the film, they were the ones. They'd done *Cathy Come Home*, and two of three of Jim Allen's early films. Tony said, 'Look, I'm not interested in falconry – I want to make a film about education.'

So I knew we were on the same wavelength. Then Ken came up, and we tried to raise some money for it, and eventually *Kes* was made. It was a very productive time for me, both artistically and politically.

After that came *The Gamekeeper*. It's just a quiet little book. I suppose it's more of a documentary than a novel. What I mean by that is that there's not much of a plot to it. I just record a gamekeeper's life, more or less. I start in February when the pheasants are born, and finish it in November when the syndicate of aristocrats and businessmen come to shoot them down. I think it's a strong book. It's my favourite really. What I like about it is that sometimes you can hit on a theme where you don't have to spell it out. I think it's always stronger if you can show it in action. I think that's a good rule about writing: 'Show me – don't tell me.' I always try to keep that in my head. In *The Gamekeeper*, I can show it. The gamekeeper doesn't have to come out with any political manifestos; I just show him at work. You just look at things, like where the gamekeeper lives and where the duke lives. You show them on shoots, and you show the relationship between employer and employee. You show what the gamekeeper's going to have for his dinner and what the duke's going to have for his dinner. And nobody can say, 'Oh, but you're exaggerating there.' I can say, 'Look, that's how it is. I've seen it.' The book's just written in a very quiet, matter of fact way, just pointing it out, and I think that's one of the reasons it works. It's about the countryside, and I'm a great lover of the countryside. It's nice to have written a country book. Some time in the future I'm sure I'll go back to live in the country. I'd like to have a go at another country book.

After *The Gamekeeper* novel was written I wrote two films, *The Price of Coal*, for the BBC. After they'd been produced my publisher said, 'Would you write a novel from those two films?' I said 'All right.' I can't remember being wildly enthusiastic about it, simply because so much of the energy had been expended in the films. When you're writing a film there always seems to be several drafts, and I'd seen rough cuts and fine cuts, and seen it on the television, and I suppose, really I'd done it. But I could see that if I didn't write a novel soon there was a chance I might not write a novel again. Three or four years had gone by since *The Gamekeeper*, and really I can't say I enjoy writing novels, but I get more satisfaction from writing novels than I do from writing scripts.

There's something about the density and complexity of a novel that I find extremely challenging. I thought I could use it as a way of getting back into training. I had the scripts to work from, but it was hard work simply because I couldn't bring anything new to it. I'd no longer got my original pictures. The pictures I'd got were from locations. I could see the actors' faces. I could hear the actors' voices. But anyway, I did it, and I think it's not too bad. I think it works. But I wouldn't want to do it that way again. You don't get that same kind of detail that you do if you write the novel first. I find that when I'm writing a novel I write it much slower than a script simply because you've got to put more in. A lot of detail in a film can be put in by the designer and the cameraman and the director. You might write: INTERIOR. OFFICE. DAY. Desk, chair, plant on the window-sill. Whereas in a novel you might go a little bit into what kind of plant it is. And once you've started putting what kind of plant it is, you might think, 'Is it in flower or not?' and mention a little bit about the flower, and if you're not careful a couple of petals will have fallen on the window- sill, and a shadow might have fallen and it might have made a pattern against this and that. So I wrote *The Price of Coal*, and it did get me back into it. So it was worth writing for that. Also I think it was worth writing because it's a printed record. One of the frustrating things about writing for television is that you can make a film, and a lot of good work's gone into it by the writer, the producer, the director, the cameraman, the whole team, and it goes out once. If you're lucky you might get a repeat out of it. But then it's dead. It seems a dreadful waste of work. I think about what's lying in the vaults at the BBC and ITV, and all that work that people put in – a year's, two year's work sometimes. They ought to be shown regularly like plays are shown regularly in the theatre, or films in the cinema. At least *The Price of Coal* is in printed form, and it's a faithful adaption.

Then I did the screenplay for *The Gamekeeper*. By this time, Ken Loach had moved to ATV and Tony Garnett had gone freelance and gone to America. So Ken directed *The Gamekeeper* for ATV.

After that it was *Looks and Smiles*. That took a lot of getting off the ground. It started as a script. A French company put some script money into it, and a German company put up half the budget, but we couldn't raise any money here. I'd got a draft of the script and a year had gone by. It was time when unemployment was becoming an important issue and I thought, 'I'm not wasting this.' So I did a novel from the draft. It was all right doing that, because it was still all mine. They were still characters I'd invented. The locations were mine. Three-quarters of the way through the novel, Central TV put the other half of the money up so I finished up with a novel and a film. But if we'd raised the money for the film straight away I'm sure I wouldn't have written the novel from it.

After that I wrote a novel called *Unfinished Business*, which I'd had in my head for years and years. It's a recurring theme of mine: unfulfilled potential. Most people don't have the chance to keep their options open because they leave school at sixteen and go into dead-end jobs, or they go on the dole which is even worse. If you go on to higher education you've got a better chance of finding something that is satisfying.

I got the idea for this book when I was Writer-in-Residence at Sheffield University. I did some work there with the day-release miners; men who worked on the coal face and did labouring jobs down the pit. They were all ages, from their twenties right up into their fifties. Some of them had seen this poster in the pit baths and thought, 'I'll have a go at that.' Four days at the pit were better than five – it seemed like a good idea to have a day off at the university and see what it was all about. Many of them had been constricted all those years in the pit village knowing little more than their work and their family and the pub, but that seed had lain dormant within them. They were studying subjects like Union History, and Industrial Relations. They had to read books and do essays, and some of them found they quite enjoyed the challenge of it, and over the three years they were there, they grew. Some of them went on to Ruskin, and colleges of higher education, because once you've done that, it's difficult to go back on the coal face and resume your former way of life. I thought, 'There's a story in there somewhere.' For years I thought of it in terms of a man doing a course, and the problems it creates within the family. And then, somewhere along the way, I thought, 'It's much more complex and interesting if it's a woman.' I know there are some men who do fifty/fifty in the house, who're really involved with their children, who bath them and read to them and everything; but there are also a lot of men who don't get involved – the father tends to be peripheral. I thought, 'If the husband leaves, it's a big wrench, but what if the wife goes on this course and then leaves home? What about the children?' So I wrote it from the woman's point of view. She goes to university, and

WHISTLE

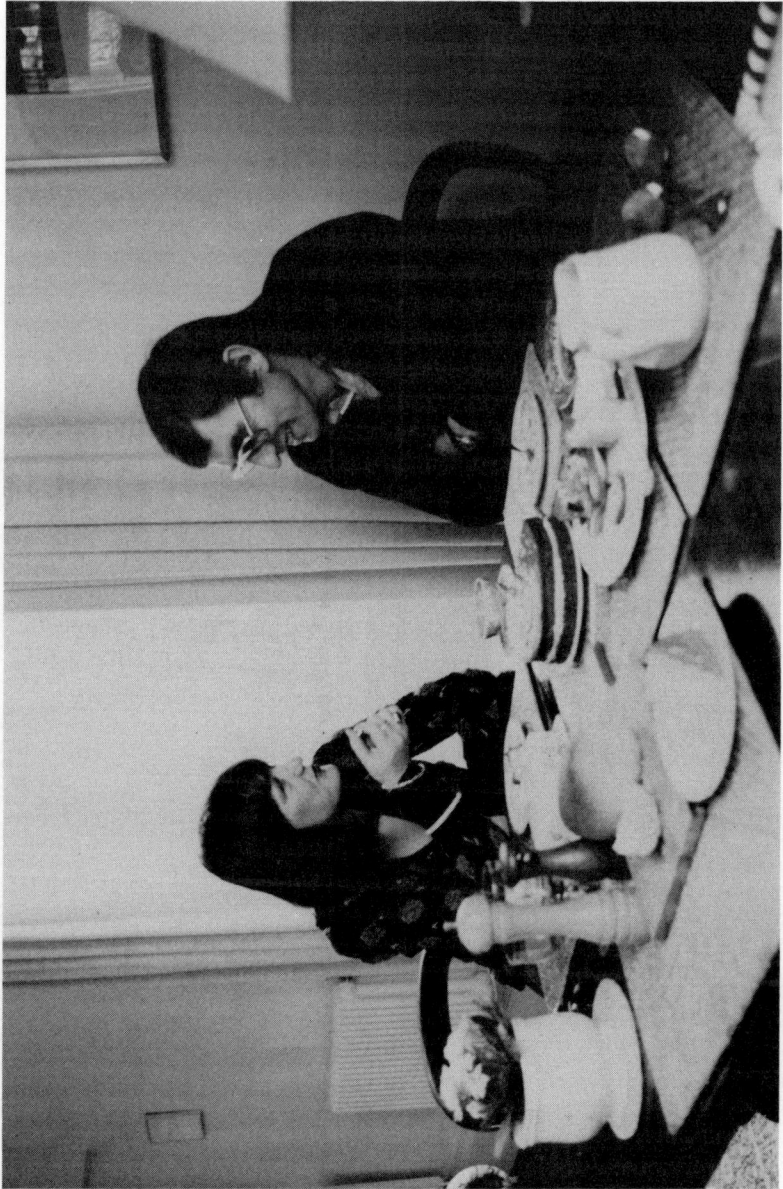

blossoms intellectually, and grows away from what she'd known.

I've been writing a script for the BBC this last year, which I've just finished, about nuclear war. It's from the point of view of two families; one working-class, the other middle-class. It's a drama-documentary. The producer, Michael Jackson, came up to see if I was interested in writing it. I wasn't sure at first, then I thought, 'Yes, I'll have a go at this. There'll be areas here, particularly the scientific parts, that I know very little about. I'll have a go and see what I can make of it.' I found it extremely demanding and exhausting, but I do believe in challenging myself.

To use a cliché of the football managers, I take each game as it comes. I've got one or two ideas in my head. I'm never full of ideas, never brimming over with them. I've just had one or two but no more. Luckily, occasionally, somebody's come to me with an idea. For example, this film about nuclear war. That was a year's work, and I've still got those two ideas I've been holding back in reserve. I might now have to draw on one of those, so I've only got one left, but then in the meantime somebody might come to me with an idea, and I might get another idea of my own. So it's all very precarious and nerve-wracking. I do find novel-writing particularly exhausting. Orwell said, 'Writing is a horrible, exhausting struggle, like a long bout of some painful illness.' People think that's an exaggeration, but I don't think it is.

I'm not sure why I do it. I think there's some sense of wanting to do something personal, wanting to achieve something in prose writing and in script writing that I would want to achieve if I had been a sculptor or a footballer: being good at the art of it, being good at my craft. If you make tables you want to sell tables – you don't want them all piling up in your cellar. You want to make a living out of it, but also you want to exhibit your craft. But it's more than that. I would like to entertain, and I would like to enlighten as well. There is a political motivation in my work. I'm trying to entertain the reader and at the same time show what's wrong, and sometimes try to present a tentative alternative, to show that there may be a different way of living, a different way of organising society for the benefit of us all rather than just for the benefit of a few. It's a difficult thing to explain because if you're not careful it all sounds dogmatic and pedantic. At one time I would have said that I want to be an entertaining propagandist, but propaganda always seems so crude. You can see it in street theatre. You put a top hat on and suddenly it's the evil capitalist. I'm not knocking that, I think there's a place for it, but I want to be a subtle propagandist, to integrate it into the structure in a much more complicated way. That's what I'm after: the shark under the surface threatening, rather than the whale spouting off on the surface. I think that's the aim: strike and withdrawal, before the reader or viewer realises what's happening. Otherwise it can be counter-productive. You can put people off by being too didactic. I've done that in the past, and I'll probably do it in the future. It's very difficult, if you are concerned, to control that anger, to control that concern. It can come over too strong without the writer realising it.

I work office hours. I try to start for nine o'clock, but usually it's about half-past, and then I work through until some time after five with just an hour for lunch, a coffee break in the morning and a tea break in the afternoon. I like to work away from the house. For many years I did work at home but I found there wasn't enough contrast between the daytime and the evening. Also I got a bit fed up with my own company. If things were going wrong I would go and make a cup of coffee on my own, or have lunch on my own, and it was always in my head – I could never get away from it. I'd finish at teatime and then I'd go up and have a bath or change my clothes or something, trying to make some kind of difference between the working day and the evening. At the moment I'm Writer-in-Residence at Sheffield Polytechnic, but even before this fellowship started I was working there. I quite like having an office where I can always have a cup of coffee with somebody, or I can have a chat with somebody at lunchtime about something else but my own work. And then I enjoy going home in the evening. I can leave my work there. I get on better when I'm away from home because there's no other distractions. If you go out to work there's nothing much else you can do – apart from fiddling about and sharpening your pencils and looking out of the window. But at home there's all kinds of things you can do: you can take the dog for a walk, cut the grass, pretend this needs doing and that needs doing, and if you're not careful you spend the day fiddling about.

I'm a very slow and clumsy and laborious writer. It takes me a long time. I work in long-hand and I do a lot of drafts. When I put the biro down at five, and clock off, I've usually got something down on paper, but a lot of the day I just seem to be messing around. I seem to have to work myself up into a panic before I can write anything, and there's no steady pattern of writing during the day. Sometimes I just find it's too hard, and that builds up inside me and then it's like a release of tension when I put it down. I find now that I work best late afternoon. For a long time I used to have this romantic idea of working in the morning and having the rest of the day off, taking the dog walks on the moors, or reading, or doing some gardening. If I did that, I don't think I would be able to do enough. A sprinter spends hours warming up, and then it's all over in a few seconds – it's a bit like that with me. It takes me all day to warm up, and then about three o'clock I start, and I concentrate for about two hours, or part of that two hours. There's just a few hundred words a day, that's all. People might say, 'But that's not much,' but it's surprising how it builds up if you work regularly five days a week. It's the consistency that matters as far as I'm concerned. If you're writing a novel you can get discouraged by the sheer task ahead. When I go home in the evening, I'm content if I know where I'm going to start next day. It's a bit like building a wall in a way – you just lay a course of bricks, and after that you lay another course, and then you lay another course, and then eventually you stand back and the wall's been built. At the outset, if you thought, 'God, the size of that wall I've got to build!' it would be just too enormous to contemplate. But I do find it hard work, particularly writing novels. After a while it does get wearying, just carting it around in your head all the time. It's a very wearing process.

I think I need aggravation. Quite often, when things appear to be going too smoothly, I go out of my way to make things awkward. There's a destructive element in me which I need in order to be creative. With the break-up of my marriage, things weren't obviously going wrong, but what I could see was a predictability about it which I think I shied away from. I think, in the end, I sought trouble, I created bother, really. With me there's this need to pursue emotional experience even when I know it's dangerous. I find it very difficult to justify, knowing all the hurt I've left behind me, but I've had to do it. It's all to do with the writing. I'm very tentative about expressing it because it sounds so cruel and destructive. But I think, without being melodramatic about it, being a writer *is* a pretty painful way to live. I think a lot of writers would say that. If you want life on an even keel I would never recommend being a writer. I find it's all ups and downs. I think it's what writers get a high on, get their kicks from. When it's good it's really good, but when it's bad it's awful. They prefer the lows and the highs rather than the security of a steady job and a pension and knowing where they're going to be in five years time. Sometimes you yearn for that, but if a fairy came and said, 'All right, then, I'll give it to you,' you'd shoot the fairy stone dead. Really you don't want it. Writers want everything. But they can't have it, and they can't come to terms with it, quite often. They bang their heels on the floor like kids do – throw a tantrum. I feel sometimes like a perpetual adolescent. Other times I feel like an old man. It's a curious mixture, but yet I want to carry on feeling like an adolescent in some ways. I want it all. I want to grasp the experience that there is in order, I suppose, to be able to make better books and better scripts. Saul Bellow's title, *Seize the Day*, is as good a motto as any for a writer. Seize the day, or seize the experience, but seize whatever comes along, and try to make the best of it without causing too much pain. Orwell, in one of his essays, says that most people have given up personal ambition by the time they're thirty: they've become family men or women, and all their energy goes into the family. He says that most people are not acutely selfish, but writers don't come into that category. He says that scientists, artists, politicians, successful businessmen, are selfish, and they're in it for their own ends and they're going to pursue their own careers in spite of anybody or anything: nothing's going to get in their way. He puts writers in this category, and I think he's right. Some people seem to live by little step ladders or little stepping stones. They look back and say, 'I was there when I was twenty-five, and now I'm thirty I'm here, and when I'm thirty-five I'm going to be there.' And it's all somehow predictable, and they're following a very narrow, constrained, unimaginative path. Part of me wants that, but another part of me wants to run a thousand miles from it. So really, if I'm put on the spot, I don't want that at all. I want to do what I want to do at all costs. I think that's the top and bottom of it, and I'm going to.

When I need to know something, I read up about it, or I go and talk to people. With the nuclear film I'm working on at the moment, the producer works in the science features department at the BBC so he's very knowledgeable. He was in touch with scientific advisors both here and in America, and he kept sending me piles of scientific information. There was massive research on this film. I had to assimilate a lot of scientific knowledge in order to write the script. More than I needed probably, but it gave me confidence. Hemingway

said something like: 'If you know it, you don't need to put it in: but
if you don't know it, somehow the lack of confidence shows and the
reader is aware of it.' For *The Gamekeeper*, I had a wide knowledge
of natural history, but I didn't know anything about the details of a
gamekeeper's life. I took out a subscription for *Shooting Times* for a
couple of years, and read other country magazines, but I had to know
what a gamekeeper did every day. Luckily I knew somebody who
was a gamekeeper and I went around with him for one day a week
for a year, and he took me on shoots. I just helped him to do things
and saw things the way he would see them. I helped him to set traps,
and went with him when he was doing work with his pheasants, when
he was releasing them and catching them and handling them. If I
want to write about a factory, I phone a factory up, tell them what
I want to do, and go and walk round. When I write about it, very
little of that experience will show, but it doesn't matter as long as it's
in my head. I can then choose what I want. If I haven't been, I
haven't got that choice of sounds and sights and smells. For example,
in *Unfinished Business*, Lucy's husband's a welder. There is one
scene showing him at work, but even if I'd left this out, I would still
have needed to go to a factory to know what it's like to be a welder.
What I wouldn't have got right was the noise. When I went in this
factory the thing that struck me was the noise. It meant that people
had to keep shouting at each other. I was able to write about that.
When Phil comes home the noise is still in his ears, and it rings in
his ears for hours. That was the only detail I used, but you always
pick up little bits when you go out. It's invaluable. sometimes you
think, 'I know enough about it. It's too much bother to phone up
and then go on a bus for ten miles. It's cold today.' But I always resist
that. I always go out and talk to people as much as I can. People are
quite helpful. I think they're fascinated in a way. I've just started a
little thirty-minute play about this lad who plays truant and spends
all his money in an amusement arcade, so I went to an arcade in town
the other night. I've been in umpteen amusement arcades with my
own children at the seaside, but this time I was on the look-out. I
don't know what I was on the look-out for, but I was looking at it
with different eyes. I went in and saw the manager walking around,
and I told him what I was doing, and he told me one or two things
that were quite helpful. The play is set in the headmaster's study.
There's no scene in an amusement arcade. But out of that visit I got
something that was really valuable. So for me it's essential that I go

out and research as closely as possible. I have to be able to see it and feel it and hear it and smell it before I can write about it. My writing is full of detail. It's all what people see, what they do, what they say, and where they are. There's nothing internal about my books. It's all on the surface. So if I don't get that part of it right, it fails.

I find an agent handy just for handling the finances. I haven't got the patience for it, or the energy. And with contracts, especially film contracts, there's so many clauses that if you don't know what you're on about I think you could be cheated. Just by chance you might write this little book or this little film and it might take off, and if you're not careful you could have made a fortune and you find you've signed it away to someone else. I find an agent helpful, and it leaves me to get on with the work. I have an accountant to handle my tax for the same reason. I don't want to think about it because I worry about it. It's a great effort to read a tax form. I get irritated by it. My instinct after five minutes is to rip it into pieces and kick the table or go berserk. All my energy goes into writing, and once I've done that I don't want to be faced by any forms. I don't like writing letters for the same reason. I write dreadful letters. I'm irritated when I'm writing the letter because I don't want to write any more when I get home in the evening. I suppose my publishers have always treated me honourably, but publishers are in business to make profits, so they pay you as little as they can get away with. I can't earn a living just writing novels. My novels don't sell enough. I write modest novels that sell moderately. They don't sell in any great numbers. But if you break down the costs, the writer comes out bottom of the list, which is absurd. I suppose the ideal is writers' co-operatives. I earn my living from television and films plus the novels; and occasionally a fellowship – that's always helpful.

I think state support is very important. It's very difficult to earn a living as a writer. There are good books that are published that don't have a wide readership. I think we ought to accept that, and that you can't judge everything by market values. Massive grants are given to certain theatre, opera and ballet companies because, presumably, it's felt that what matters first are artistic values, not commercial values. I can't see why the same couldn't happen with books. Perhaps there could be a state publishing house. But however it's done there ought to be a lot more money available for writers (what literature gets is always a drop in the pond anyway) and it ought to be used much better than it is. I think it's disgraceful that there are poverty-stricken writers: published writers of proven quality. And the Arts Council should be taking risks. Everybody should have the chance to fail. If people are serious, and they have the time and opportunity to write, they'll learn from that. Just having written a novel gives you confidence. That's money well spent, because you don't know what seeds you're sowing. From that investment you will get good writers. Grants could also go to small publishers so that they can find writers and commission work. There should be a whole network stemming from the Arts Council.

* * *

Scott Fitzgerald was an early influence, particularly *The Great Gatsby*. I think it's a perfect little book in its way. There is an air of longing, of seeking something intangible, that I find very appealing. I remember being impressed by *The Naked and the Dead* when I first read it; the sheer force of it, it think. In a way I resented Mailer's experience. He went to war. He had something dramatic to write about. What did I have in my poky little life? (A lot as it turned out.)

I thought *Catch 22* a stupendous work; page after page of brilliant idiosyncratic intensity. I like Jean Rhys's novels, to go to the other extreme. Wistful little books, filled with longing and unfulfilled promises. Evelyn Waugh and Anthony Powell are both fine prose writers. There is an elegance and simplicity about Waugh's work that I find brilliant. I don't like to admit it really, because politically I'm against everything the man stood for.

I've read a lot of Kurt Vonnegut. *Slaughterhouse 5* is a terrific book. Vonnegut makes you laugh, makes you see things from a different point of view, and you think, 'How does he do that?' He writes in a very economical, accessible way. He makes complex ideas seem simple. Not simplistic; simple, so that you can understand them. John Berger does that too. I enjoy Orwell's essays and journalistic pieces. They are full of good sense. He, too, makes complex ideas accessible. He's good on the business of writing and use of language. He has had an influence on my own prose style.

Hunter J. Thompson's *Fear and Loathing in Las Vegas* is a book I've read several times. I keep lending copies out and never getting them back. The book is hysterical, with form and content perfectly matched.

* * *

I think literature extends the imagination. You can learn things from literature, about countries that you don't know about, about jobs that other people do. It can move you. When I read a book I always feel I'm in partnership with the author, and not only does it tell me things I don't know about, but a good book can tell you things about yourself. A good writer will sometimes put things into words that for the reader has just been a feeling that you've never been able to analyse or pin down, and you think, 'God, I've felt that – I've often felt that.' It can make you feel less lonely. I think that's the difference between watching television and reading a book. Watching something, however good it is, is passive. You just take what they give you. When you're a reader you contribute as well. If it says she sat on a chair, it's a different chair and a different she who sits on it, so we all bring something to the characters, to the rooms, to the countryside or whatever, whereas when she sits on the chair on the telly it's the same she and the same chair for everybody. I think literature feeds you.

Sheffield, December 1983

NIGEL GRAY'S COMMENT.

You cannot talk to Barry Hines without being aware of his sansculottism, his commitment, and above all his passion: also, conversely, a defensiveness that is never completely relaxed. You get the impression that he never gives himself fully, that he always holds something back. He has that sharp intelligence and aggression typical of many working-class people, overlaying a surprising sensitivity and meticulousness.

I would imagine that his novel, *A Kestrel for a Knave*, (filmed and paperbacked as *Kes*, has done more, since its publication in 1968, to interest ordinary young people in good literature than any other single book. *The Gamekeeper* is a novelist's version of that wonderful image which captures so clearly the essence of the late sixties: a blossom planted in the barrel of a gun.

I included a section on *Kes* in *The Silent Majority* – a study of the working-class in post-war British literature, which (apart from two or three slim vols of unimpressive poems) was my first book. Barry wrote to thank me, saying how rare it was to find a critic or reviewer who understood what his book was about. That book was published fifteen years ago, and was the beginning of a valued friendship.

One memorable evening I chaired a meeting at which Barry and Archie Hill were reading and talking. Archie was reactionary in the way of so many working-class people: against the bosses, but as fervently against the unions – as articulate, aggressive, proud and passionate as Barry – the author of a marvellous autobiography, *A Cage of Shadows*. They were like a pair of fighting cocks, verbally at each other's throats, and often on their feet, eyes blazing, fingers jabbing, fists flourishing, and me between, keeping them apart. I don't know who would have come out on top had they set to, physically, but Barry unequivocally won the war of words.

I interviewed Barry during the winter of the miners' strike of '83/ '84 – the beginning of Thatcher's campaign to destroy the power of the unions in Britain, part of her scheme to reintroduce the evils and injustices of Victorianism. We drove out of Sheffield to a nearby pit and asked the men there if we could cross the picket line to take photographs. Barry told them his name, and was immediately recognised as the author of *The Price of Coal*, although this was already some years after it had been shown on television. He was welcomed with great warmth. (When Barry introduced me as, 'my friend, Nigel,' I got a more derisory reception.)

In 1984 the BBC broadcast Barry's television film *Threads*. It was a powerful and imaginative depiction of Britain in the aftermath of a nuclear disaster, and it proved to be a valuable contribution to the re-vitalisation of CND.

Since then, things have not gone well. He separated from the woman he was living with, and is now on his own. He has completed a good deal of work, but as yet has not seen any fruits from those labours. A BBC television film about the miners' strike, to be directed by Ken Loach, was oddly aborted for reasons unknown. He is more optimistic about other television projects: a film about a rock band; a domestic drama about a redundant Scottish miner who moves to England and gets a job in a nuclear power station; and a series about a Welsh slate quarrymen. Hopefully all should be shown on television in the next year or two. He hasn't started on another novel.

He feels that England has now become 'a vicious, shabby place with the smell of fascism in the air'. And who could argue with that.

Barry Hines was born in Hoyland Common, near Barnsley, on June 30th 1939.

Barry Hines' Book-Choice:

The Great Gatsby
  Scott Fitzgerald
The Naked and the Dead
  Norman Mailer
Catch 22 Joseph Heller
The Sword of Honour Trilogy
  Evelyn Waugh
The Ragged Trousered
  Philanthropists Robert Tressell
A Dance to the Music of Time
  Anthony Powell
Slaughterhouse 5
  Kurt Vonnegut

The Collected Essays, Journalism
  and Letters George Orwell
Fear and Loathing in Las Vegas
  Hunter J. Thompson
After Leaving Mr. Mackenzie
  Jean Rhys
Good Morning, Midnight
  Jean Rhys
The Joke Milan Kundera
A Seventh Man John Berger
A Fortunate Man John Berger

Books by Barry Hines:

The Blinder
A Kestrel for a Knave
First Signs
The Gamekeeper

The Price of Coal
Looks and Smiles
Unfinished Business

Television plays and films:

Kes
Billy's Last Stand
Speech Day
Two Men from Derby
The Price of Coal

The Gamekeeper
A Question of Leadership
Looks and Smiles
Threads

Chapter Eight
DONALL Mac AMHLAIGH

I was born in a village just outside Galway City. My father was a professional soldier – a Limerick City man. He'd been through the entire First World War, and afterwards was in the old IRA, in the East Clare Brigade, in the War of Independence. After that he gravitated to the Free State Army, though he was always very happy to say that he never saw a shot fired in anger in the Civil war. We had a certain amount of moving about the country, because my father was from time to time transferred: (Galway; the Curragh camp in Kildare; Limerick City; Cork; back to Galway; and then to Kilkenny) which accounts probably for my rather mongrel accent.

During the 1930s, when people were really hard up, we didn't see the worst of the times because my father had a regular job. But then, during the war years (the Emergency we called it in Ireland) things were pretty bad all right. I had to abandon my education at a relatively early age and go to work for ten shillings a week in the woollen mills.

My parents never had much formal education but both of them were avid readers. My mother had a reasonable grasp of what had literary merit and what hadn't. My father was less discriminating. He read novels by Denis Wheatley, and Rafael Sabatini (a very popular novelist of those years – *Captain Blood* and that sort of thing), as well as decent literature at the same time. They were both fairly familiar with the classics, with Dickens and people like that. Even working-class people without any formal education read a lot more in those years than they do now. Certain literary allusions wouldn't be lost on them as they would on many well-educated people today. Musically they were quite literate too. My father used to be fond of the opera, light opera in particular, and music hall as well. We weren't entirely culturally impoverished. I would say that the only cultural intake for most urban working-class people in Ireland in those years was the cinema, but rural Ireland almost entirely escaped the Hollywood cultural domination. People hadn't the means or the money to travel into the cities to see the cinema. There was a great cleavage – the towns and cities were dominated by British and American cultural ideas, but poor rural people had their own culture up to a point. I wouldn't go so far as to say it was as rich as the culture of the Irish-speaking areas – *they* had the richest oral tradition in Europe – but they did have a coherent, passed-down heritage. We shared in that up to a point. My father could sing old Irish country ballads, at the same time he was familiar with the music hall tradition of England: Marie Lloyd, Dan Leno and all those.

My family weren't Irish-speaking, but as a child in Galway I heard a lot of it spoken by adults, and so, when I began to learn it later on, it came to me pretty easily. All the children in the village spoke English. The parents consciously spoke English to them. They didn't want them to be, as they saw it, burdened with Irish. But from a very early age I acquired a taste for it – from as young as five or six. In later years, I spent three years in an Irish-speaking battalion – it was my finishing school, if you like. If anybody asked me to present a rational argument for the preservation of the Irish language, I don't know whether I could do it. If you asked a man why he liked a certain piece of music I don't think he could give you an intellectual reply. Many people make a conscious political decision that they must learn Irish because it is an integral part of our republicanism, of our separatism; but it wasn't a political decision with me. I liked the sound of the language, I liked the people who spoke it. I'm greatly saddened by the decline of it in those areas where it was spoken.

We never really lived with my father for any length of time. He was away so much that eventually, when he came out of the army, his arrival home was regarded with something like dismay by myself and my mother. It was the intrusion of a stranger. I suppose we resented him because we didn't know how to relate to him. Quite honestly, I never did relate to my father except over a few drinks. That was the only time the ice was broken; the only time we had some sort of common ground. That was very common in rural Ireland. The father and son might work in the hay field all day and exchange a few remarks, but there was always an uneasy feeling. Perhaps it was to do with a sort of sexual repression – because the man you were working with was your progenitor or something. I was about sixteen when it dawned on me how I came to be. I was smitten with shame, horror, revulsion and sadness. 'My God! How could people's parents be guilty of such an act!' It seems ridiculous now. To be fair to the Church, it doesn't officially teach that – but it's like a concomitant.

I wanted to write from a very early age. Even at school, if I was half good at anything at all it was essays. I was always conscious of scenery, of heather, mountain, bog, lakes, of wanting to put it on paper; but I never had the linguistic resources to do so. I haven't today. I'm very bad at descriptions of scenery. Like a very bad painter who wants to put something on canvas, I wanted to encompass these scenes, to get them down, to make them live, to hold on to them as much as possible. Some days you see Galway Bay absolutely lucid, unmoving, with that peculiar breathing stillness in the air, and the Clare mountains opposite standing out with perfect clarity, and the Aran Islands appearing to be above rather than on the water. Even as a kid, I wanted to be able to describe things like that. If I'd had any talent as a painter, that should have been my métier. I never did manage to achieve that facility with words.

Another unfulfilled ambition was to write good short stories. Somebody's definition of a short-story was 'a story that's not long'. I don't mean just that, but a story that has 'poetry and punch' as Sean O'Faolain says; something that would live, and remain in your memory. There's this terrible gap between what you want to do and what you're capable of. I claim that I'm a born writer in as much as I can't leave the blooming thing alone. If I don't do it for four or five days, I itch to be back at it. At the same time, this doesn't confer any talent on me. I'm all too painfully conscious of the few things I can do reasonably well and all those things which I can't do at all. It's a very chastening, very saddening, humbling thing really, when there's something you would dearly love to do well and you know you can't do it anything like as well as you would wish.

When I left school I became a waste-wool sorter, which is the lowest rung on the ladder in the woollen mills. It was my job to go through all the sweepings, picking out the foreign bodies; then the waste was shipped off to England for the making of some inferior cloth. There was a great affinity between the people working in the textile industry in Ireland and those here in England. They spoke about places like Oldham and Rotherham and Bradford in much the same way as artists, I suppose, speak about places in Paris where you go to see pictures. All the incredibly antiquated Victorian machinery in these mills had originally come from England. The machines were kept running round the clock during the war (despite the fact that the necessary bits and pieces were hard to come by) by a brilliant German engineer – a fascist by the name of O'Callaghan. His father was Irish, his mother was German, and he was German through and through.

I had a facility then which I've lost since: I could spin verses off with no trouble at all. It came naturally to me. I could write old-fashioned verses and ballads at the drop of a hat. In fact, people would say to me, 'Write a poem about such and such a thing,' (they'd call it a poem). I used to bombard the local paper with these rubbishy efforts, and they printed them, although of course they never paid me. I also wrote a long, rambling novel. The only good that came out of it was that that period of my life formed the basis of another novel which I wrote later in Irish, so it wasn't completely lost. Oddly enough, I was writing verse mostly in Irish, and prose in English. I don't honestly know why. This novel of about four hundred-odd pages, written in close-packed writing on both sides of the page, I sent off to the Stockwell Press in Cornwall – they advertised for manuscripts and if they were half publishable at all they would ask the author for a fee. They wanted £80 in 1945. It would have been over a year's wages so that was out of the question, which is just as well because it was sheer rubbish. I got a lot of encouragement from my mother, probably (if for no other reason), because it kept me at home at nights and out of mischief. Whatever critical faculty she possessed didn't extend to my writings.

The next two years I spent writing a rambling western novel. I don't know why I committed the cardinal sin of writing something I had no knowledge of. I gave it to a professor of English in St. Ciaran's College in Kilkenny, and when I got it back I was mortified to see that he'd gone through it with red ink correcting all the grammatical errors and had made no comment whatever on the content. The manuscript disappeared later on, which is just as well because it would make me cringe with embarrassment now.

I left the woollen mills and went into the army. I wrote very little in the army: occasional short pieces, and songs in Irish – ballads in the traditional mode.

I came to England when I came out of the army because there was no work. If there had been work I would have stayed. I didn't want to come to England at all. When I came here first I thought, 'My

God – how will I stick it?' The place seemed so insipid and boring and uninteresting. My initial impression was of how illiterate, on the one hand, English working-class people were, while on the other hand they seemed to have a level of sophistication that we lacked. I would say that even middle-class Irish people had a certain naïvety about them, a certain sense of wonder which was lacking in English people. They were bursting with self-confidence – we went to the other extreme: the chip on the shoulder. I didn't seem to have a lot in common with them. I couldn't relax with them or enjoy their company very much. The kind of thing that most of the English lads were going to do – play skittles, or throw darts, or talk endlessly about football – didn't interest me in the least. It seemed to me that we were on a different wavelength completely. I stayed among Irish friends almost exclusively. There wasn't any question of being lonely. This town was flooded in those days with young Irish men and women. They had their own club and they thronged the pubs and the dance-halls. You could live a completely expatriate life among your own people.

I came to Northampton because there was a job waiting for me as a nursing orderly. The National Health Service advertised widely in Ireland. It was live-in and four-pounds-seven-shillings a week. It was a godsend. It meant that I just had to find my fare and get here and then everything was taken care of. I soon began labouring, because in those days, in the Irish communities, there was a stigma attached to a man being a nursing orderly. The attitude was that if he was any man at all he'd be out working on the buildings or working in a factory earning big money, or he'd be on the farms or some place. I should have had enough maturity at the age of twenty-four to withstand that, but in any case I wanted to get out and earn more money and be with the lads. For the next ten years I was working long hours. I had a habit of going home every Christmas and staying there till the end of February which took care of any money I might have saved over the year.

After coming to England I turned against the whole idea of writing. There was a very crass, materialistic atmosphere in those days. You admired men who could work long hours and earn big money, and it seemed to me that writing and all that related to it was a complete waste of time; it was the stamp of a ne'er do well, a man who had no worthwhile qualities, and idler or a dreamer. I didn't write anything for about ten years – except my diaries which

I did keep up, but I didn't see them for a moment as being a literary endeavour. They were fairly cryptic, a lot of them, although they were the basis of *An Irish Navvy*.

I started writing again in 1958 when I was thirty-two. The urge resurfaced. I mangled good ideas in several short stories which I wish I hadn't written then; but the notion came to me so strongly I wrote them and had them published. I was writing in Irish. It wasn't a conscious choice. I just wanted to write in Irish. Then, because I'd written a number of articles and stories, I was asked by a publisher in Ireland if I would do a book. That was *An Irish Navvy*. I wish I could have the opportunity again, or that I'd had somebody to guide me. I wrote it in three months while I was working on the construction of the M1 – and I didn't have any discipline. I had plenty of energy. I could work, battering away at the old typewriter at night, but I didn't rewrite a single line. I only did one draft. I wouldn't for a moment presume to do that today. I'd write four, five, six drafts, but then I just wrote one rough draft and sent it off. I didn't stop and think, and remove things, or bring out the full richness of them. Very often, when I tired of a thing I just arbitrarily moved on to something else. I just picked my way through the entries in my diary. It was a marvellous opportunity thrown away really. Hardly anybody had written anything in that area. Even with my limited resources and talents I could have made it a memorable book. I failed to do that because I didn't have the gumption. That's something I lacked through a lot of my life. Quite honestly, when I wrote it I didn't believe for a moment it would be published. And I certainly didn't believe it would be translated into English. It's still in print in Irish, and English. The respected poet of the 1930s, Valentin Iremonger (who is now the Irish Ambassador in India), translated the book and brought it along to me to vet. I just skimmed through it. If I'd had any savvy I'd have gone through it and deleted things, suggested alterations and things like that, but I didn't. I think, even at that stage, I didn't conceive for a moment that it would ever be published in London. I find it a very chastening experience to look through the book today.

I'm not entirely happy with the translation. The ending is an example of my use of a certain dialect, the nuances of which the translator wasn't aware of. I describe an exodus of people from Dun Laoire just after Easter on the mail boat. The last line of the book says, 'We're a great people, surely', which on the face of it sounds a sort of chauvinistic remark, as though for some odd reason we should be exalted above everybody else, but it's a quite different meaning from what I wrote. I would have translated it: 'We're a rum lot, surely', 'We're a queer old crowd', something like that. In the book I told a little story about how an Italian maid got annoyed with myself and an Englishman in the hospital. We were sitting having a cup of coffee and she wanted to polish the floor around us, so, in exasperation she said, 'All Irish dirty, all English lazy'; and this Englishman replied, 'All Italians dirty *and* lazy'. Now the translator used the word, 'riposted'. I wouldn't consider that a wise choice of word. 'Riposted' is a stilted, literary word. It doesn't accord with the Irish original. There were a number of things like that. It's ungracious of me to pick them out maybe, especially when I consider the poor job I made of the book. I think he served me pretty well on the whole. It never occurred to me to do the translation. Nobody suggested to me that I should. At that stage anyway, I don't think I would have been very good at it. I don't think I had enough feel for the writing of English at that time, even for a simple, straightforward job like a translation. I would have been inclined to make it too wordy. I would probably have been parodying or copying somebody else. I wouldn't have had the gumption to be myself. For some reason or other I could be myself writing in Irish in a way that I couldn't, up to fairly recently, writing in English.

I didn't begin *An Irish Navvy* until after I was married, although I'd written a number of articles and stories before. Going back to writing was due to a culmination of things: the wish to write was growing stronger; and there was the fact of not having to share a room with four other men. I must have been a sore trial to my wife at that time. We were newly-weds, and yet I spent maybe two or three hours every night, six or seven nights a week, plugging away at the typewriter. I wasn't much company for her, no doubt. She would prefer I'd chatted to her or something like that. There was no television; we didn't have a radio even. I suppose for a newly-married man it wasn't the proper thing to spend night after night writing. But once the idea of the book had been suggested to me I wanted to do it.

When I finished that I went straight into another book: *A Soldier's Life*. The publisher knew I'd been in the army and the suggestion came from him. It was more a directive than a suggestion – he told me to get cracking right away, and I did. Although the material wasn't so rich, in many ways *A Soldier's Life* was better than *An Irish Navvy*. It was better written, although at the same time not a patch on what it could have been. It was a wonderful opportunity. I was the only Irishman who had ever written a book about the Irish Army, so I had a clear field. I might have done a better job if I'd had a bit of gumption and I'd paused and thought about it. I had notes to refer to, to refresh my memory, but I didn't have any clue what writing was about. I didn't know what I was doing really. I was just battering down so many hundred words a night without for a moment saying, 'Where am I going?' It wasn't meant to be a novel, although sometimes it's described as that, but I could have brought in the characteristics of a novel in such a way as to build up a picture, rather than a diary effort moving from thing to thing without any predestined course. It had more form than *An Irish Navvy*: you join the army; you do your training; you go through a process of acclimatisation; you see your date of release approaching and regard it with mixed feelings; and you leave. Willy nilly, it has a certain artistic form or shape. When *An Irish Navvy* ended, it didn't really end because that life was going to go on and on, but when your army days are over, they were over.

They have a saying in Ireland: 'Ní bhfuair duine ar bith an da shaol,' ('Nobody's got the two lives'), but if I could get the two lives I would love to go back and write those books again; I'd be confident then that, even if they weren't great literature, I could leave two very worthwhile efforts behind me. The material was there at my hand to be shaped. Even the best novels can be surpassed by another novel which is rather like them – you're in a very big pool when you write novels – but I was writing something that was uniquely my own. A lot of it was broadcast before it was published. The late Frank McManus, the author of several memorable novels of Irish country life, said it was among the best radio scripts he'd ever produced. The material, for some reason or other, was ideally suited to radio. It was probably because of my simple style. I didn't attempt for a moment anything high-flown or literary. I never used a single word I wasn't familiar with, that wasn't in everyday use among Irish-speakers. The book is less rich than it might have been, than later books. There wasn't any attempt at real literary expression.

I wrote both books in 1959. The next book wasn't published until 1965. It was two and a half years writing – two and a half years of utter slavery, of real hard work. By then, I knew where I was going wrong. I knew I wasn't putting the work into it that I should have done. By then, I had read a tremendous amount in Irish, and I knew what the resources of the language were, what could be said and what couldn't be said. I'd realised it wasn't enough to write just one draft of something and stick it in the post. I'd realised you'd got to work hard at it, and improve it, read the thing aloud, strive for style and effect. The novel was called *Diarmid O Donaill* – it was an autobiographical novel based on a year in a teenager's life: leaving school; growing up; experiencing what so many people have written so much better about: Irish Catholic upbringing, with all its richness and its hang-ups. It was my own story to a large extent. I would say it was probably a dismal failure, a pretty poor book all round. I don't think anybody ever pretended it had a lot of merit, but at least it was the watershed for me. It was the book in which I cut my teeth on writing – I learned what it was all about, so that anything I wrote subsequently (while it may not have had the appeal of the first two books) was certainly better written. I think Diarmid O Donaill could be rewritten yet (maybe in English), but I was disappointed that, for all the effort I put into it – rewriting sentences and pages again and again – it didn't achieve the same impact as the earlier books. Probably people weren't looking for that sort of thing from me. They were content with my folksy reminiscences, and they probably didn't want me trying to do something which other people could do much better. It did win a small prize in '65 in the Oireachtas, which is like the Irish Eisteddfod – a literary and cultural thing held once a year. That was like a consolation prize.

After that, I began to write short-stories for Irish monthly reviews. Some of the stories appeared in a collection called *Sweeney, and Other Stories*. There again, that wasn't too favourably received. Some of the critics were fairly harsh. The stories were told with little art; much more could have been made of them. It's the kind of book I'd rather not have written, quite frankly. I translated some of the stories into English, too. In Irish you sell around the two thousand, two and a half thousand mark. There's a fairly well assured readership. I think there's probably more commitment on the part of Irish-speaking people to buy books. Some people think in terms of thousands and thousands of readers and say it's not worthwhile doing it unless you get ten thousand people read you, but I'd prefer to be read by a thousand even, if they were discerning, and if what I wrote was good enough.

I began toying, in a desultory fashion, with a novel. Then I put that to one side to write a short comic novel called *Schnitzer ó Sé*. It seems to me that there are certain comic aspects of everyday life, like the airs and graces folks give themselves; and the way some people manage to be dignified and ridiculous at the same time (I often thought that about my own father – he had a certain spurious dignity; you get it in drunkards – that ridiculous dignity of drunken people). It seemed to me that these were facets of life that might be worth exploring. And I thought it was time to break out of the confines of the personal experience. (It's a thing I would like to do more and more as time goes on.) The idea came to me at work one day. I think I'd been reading about an Austrian writer called Schnitzler. I suppose it's a form of chauvinism really: because it's a German name it struck me as being quite comical. I thought that, coupled with an Irish name the effect would be more comical still. I was shovelling ballast on the railway down at Wolverton. I began stealing off, and taking notes on the idea of a very naïve, semi-literate type of character from rural Ireland (a sort of person I've met very often, and which to a large extent would have components of myself) who for some odd reason begins to write poetry and makes an impact on the literary world. I started on it bit by bit. I wasn't quite sure where I was going, but eventually I got it in some sort of shape. It was quite handsomely published in Ireland in late '73.

I then went back to the novel, which, conditionally, is called *Exiles*. It is a very ambitious project really – it was to be the first of a trilogy in fact. It hasn't been published yet – they're having some difficulty because of its size. It is a very long novel – it would be about a five hundred page book. I was on and off that for years. I don't like to think how long in fact. I will say one thing about it (if I may allow myself any self-congratulation at all): it has a degree of competence that a lot of the other stuff hadn't. I think for the most part it is pretty well written – as good as I could make it at the time in any case. And it is definitely the result of a lot of hard work. Many of the pages have been written ten times over. If hard writing makes easy reading then that should be the case. That was a real, conscious effort to produce something of worth. Apart from the style of the book, the goal was to try to articulate Irish working-class experience in Britain over the last thirty years or so. The people at home have written so many stories and novels about the perception of life in

Ireland, and the Irish Americans have done the same, but scarcely a thing has come from us, the Irish in Britain. You might wonder why, when little islands like the Aran Islands produced Liam O'Flaherty and Brendan O'hEithir, and the Blasket Islands produced two or three good autobiographers who have written classics. *Twenty Years A-Growing* and *The Island Man* were translated into many languages. And yet, all those thousands and thousands of Irish who came here, and went through the experience of adjusting to a new country and the trauma of settling into a new way of life with different values and all that, have written scarcely a thing about it. I thought maybe I could, in a sense, make good the omission. That's why I worked so hard on the book.

There's four strands to the book. There's an archetypal, great big hulking, macho Connemara man who's earning fantastic money in digging tunnels and trenches. He's a married man with children in Ireland who's quite content to send home so much money every week, but doesn't want to be burdened with the responsibilities of wife and kids. In a sense he's almost retarded you might say, in that he's a grown man who expresses himself through his ability to outwork other men, and to fight in pubs and dance halls at night. It's a mark of immaturity no doubt, but yet a type that was so common it deserved expression. His wife takes her own stand. She decides she's going to join her husband with her two children. She sends him a telegram so he can't back out of it. He meets her at Euston station at half six in the morning, and his first greeting is, 'What in the name of Jesus is wrong with you!' He thought that with four pounds a week, living in the West of Ireland, she should be quite happy; but she wanted the fulfilment of married life with her children and her husband. Another woman, past the first blush of youth, has come to England because there's no possibility at all that the man she's engaged to will marry her. His aging mother refuses to have any other woman on her floor. (This was a very common thing in rural Ireland. In the 50s we had the highest bachelor rate in the world, I think.) The first part of an autobiographical section deals with the pauperised Ireland of the 1950s when we stood around street corners; when you weren't even sure of fourpence for the pictures; when you could long for a pint of beer and not have the money for it; when you became a cadger even if it wasn't in your nature, because there were a lot of chaps coming back from England with money. You'd 'plámás', as we say in Ireland: you'd flatter them

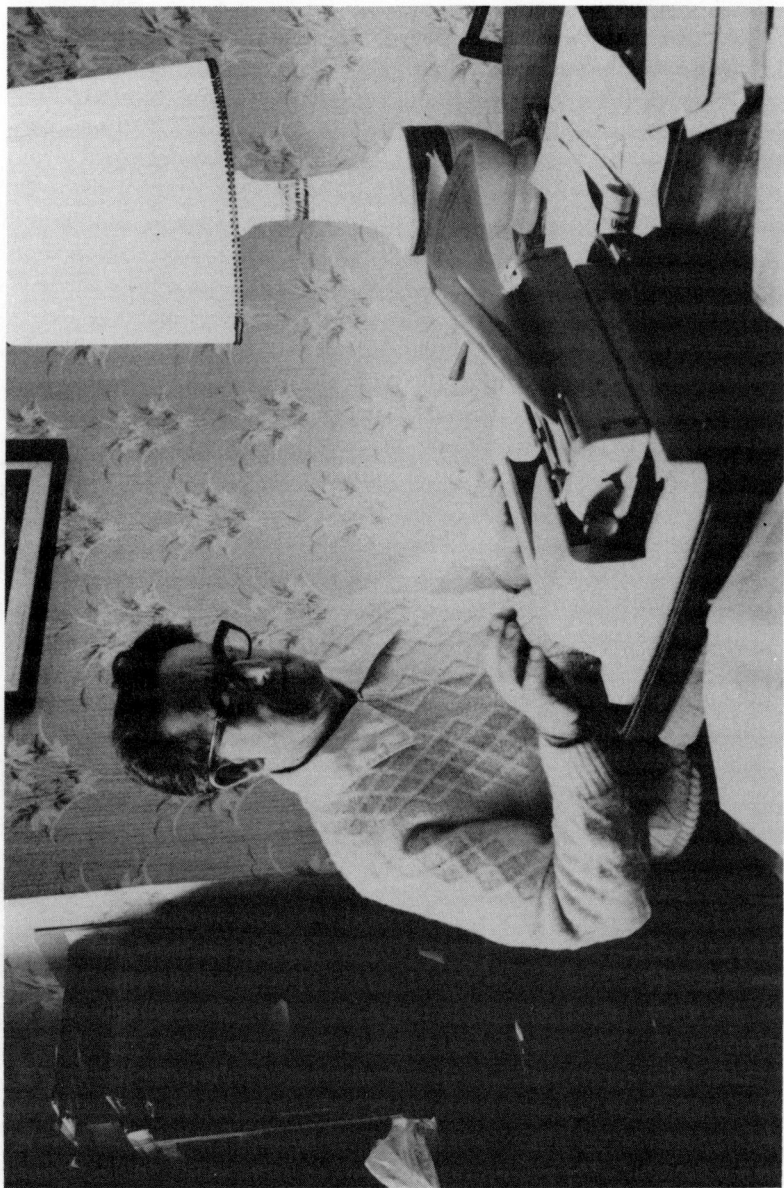

shamelessly for the few odd pints you'd get off them. It's given me
a lasting insight into the young unemployed. I can understand why
they would thieve – because of the feeling of not having what other
people have; of being outside the pale in a sense. A girl-friend was
out of the question. A girl's father would say, 'Let him get a job
first, before he thinks of keeping company with you.' We got to
know a different type of girl – unfortunates, I would call them:
orphans, or girls who had a difficult upbringing, or who'd been sent
to work for the nuns. Very often the poor creatures were wronged.
I remember one night, while I was still in the army, meeting a girl,
and I said, 'Shall I see you home?' She said, 'I'm starved.' I said,
'I'm hungry too.' So we put our money together and we bought a
small loaf. And we ate the loaf sitting on an old shelf of rock over
the back of the house where she was a servant. It seemed a kind of
oddly sacramental thing to do. I suppose I should have written a
story about it really.

By 1967 I'd started doing quite a lot of journalism. I was asked if
I'd write for *The Irish Times*. I write regularly for *Ireland's Own*,
The Irish Press, and *The Irish Democrat*. It's taken time from my
creative writing. If I could have done without, perhaps it would have
been better. I'm not writing a lot now. I'm fifty-eight. I haven't got
the energy. I had so much energy when I was younger that it was a
pleasant change, after a hard day's work, to be sitting at a typewriter.
I used to think what a pleasant relaxation it was. That's changed
completely. I can still do a pretty good day's work, but I couldn't
turn round and tackle a short story at night. It seems slavery now.
I can do a bit for *Ireland's Own* – a simple little article on current
affairs or something like that.

Since *Exiles*, I've only translated *Schnitzer ó Sé* into English. I
don't think I'd ever have translated it except that the pressure came
from the outside. I was quite half-hearted at the beginning. And then
an Arts Association grant came along which meant I could devote
four months full-time to it. I did that pretty conscientiously. I worked
hard on it and I did a lot of drafts. I'm still aware that lots of it could
even yet be rewritten, but maybe you could go on like that for ever.
Except for the odd short-story, it's the first thing that I've translated
into English. I'm glad I did it, but you can only do so much and I
think I'll continue to write in Irish rather than attempt to write a lot
in English. I don't know why, but I get more satisfaction out of
writing a page of good prose in Irish. I've got a conscious

commitment to the language. I think some of us now will have to do something or it's going to disappear. The very fact that the future of the language is not assured has made me more determined to write in Irish, to do my little part, to keep it going if possible. On the other hand, I think if somebody said to me, 'We're going to publish *Exiles* in English if you make a reasonable fist of it,' I would be tempted to do it.

In the summer I got back to work with a large building contractor. At fifty-seven years of age I was lucky to get taken on, work being as scarce as it is. The older generation of building workers here have a saying: 'Keep your hat on, they're sacking the old 'uns!' but oddly enough the increasing casualisation of the industry with less and less guaranteed conditions means that very often older men get taken on by subcontractors or labour suppliers on a short-term basis. Employment agencies who recruit labour and supply it on a casual, day-to-day basis, and take their cut for this service, are proliferating now, and there is a generation of building worker on the scene that knows nothing about the concessions and rights which we took very much for granted when I began in the industry more than thirty years ago. Things like lodging allowances, wet-time, proper overtime rates and proper safety regulations. Casualties have risen sharply in the building industry over the past few years and there is a serious shortage of safety inspectors to visit the sites.

I write for the same reason some people drink heavily or go to the football match every week. It's something I want to do, and I don't know if I can give any rational explanation why. If I don't do it for a number of days, I feel I should be doing it. A blank sheet of paper sets me off. It doesn't have to be anything worthwhile even – a little article or cameo. A day in London, and I'm itching to record my experiences. I'm probably more of a journalist than a creative writer.

From time to time I get ideas of writing different types of novels and stories. Everyday, several times a day, I get ideas that are not at all clearly defined about things I'd like to write. Sometimes I think I'd like to write a novel in which things can be seen from three or four perspectives, maybe centred around one man who's receiving letters from three or four people. In my case, lots and lots of people write to me because of my column in *Ireland's Own*. Some of these people know each other, or know of each other. I'm very often a clearing house for their ideas and things they've got to say about each other. There's a novel by Nathaniel West called *Miss*

Lonelyhearts. It's about this man who takes up the temporary job of doing the Miss Lonelyhearts column in a women's magazine. At first he's sceptical and bored; he feels the whole thing is ludicrous. But the realities of life impinge so strongly that he nearly commits suicide in the end. It seems to me sometimes that there's both a comic and a tragic side to things: so many people with unfulfilled ambitions who're, up to a point, filled with envy of each other; so many people striving for a little recognition in the world, constantly crying out for more attention and more acclaim. But I couldn't really use that material. I suppose the measure of your commitment as a writer would be whether you would be prepared to hurt people's feelings.

I may well finish the trilogy. Or maybe just a sequel to the first novel. That would be a novel of social comment, if you like, to do for the Irish in Britain in the mid twentieth century, in a sense (if I may make a presumptuous comparison) what Dickens did for the poor of London, or something like that. Not entirely from the literary point of view, but also from the social history point of view: to record attitudes and feelings and ideas; to get people's perceptions of, if you like, post-Christian England, and the reassessment they had to undertake. (To a large extent they'd been burdened with the historical knowledge of the wrongs that Britain had done to Ireland over the centuries. That biased them, or put them on their mettle a little. Then they had to come to terms with the niceness, the sort of inherent goodness, that you find in most ordinary people of all nationalities.) In a sense I'm privileged (because of my lack of education and because of not being in an upper social bracket): I have access to these people's thoughts and minds. Historians have written books about the Irish in Britain without ever really knowing the Irish immigrant labouring class. They can quote you the number of people who came to Skipton Hiring Fair, but they can't tell you what those workers felt and what they thought. To finish the trilogy though, I would need to be at it full time so that I could allow myself maybe five or six hours a day.

Then there's lots of other things I'd like to do. I'd like to write good short-stories. I'd like to write plays, but I think I lack the technique. I probably don't know enough about stage craft. I've written a number of one-act plays, none of which were any good. I had one play on television. That was something that almost wrote itself. It was well received. I haven't any clear-cut notions of where I want to go. Sometimes I think I'd like to do something experimental. In fact I think of too many things really because I know I haven't got the time to do them now. I couldn't ever imagine that I'd reach the stage when I wouldn't want to write at all.

I wouldn't set out consciously, as a lot of socialists would, to write something that was an indictment of any social ills that I saw – or I haven't done so far. I think if I had the ability, I'd like to write something bitingly satirical about the affluence and sheer bloody waste of the Common Market countries, while little mites die, crying out for their bread, all over the world. If I had the resources, linguistic or otherwise, I'd like to do it, all right. But meantime a lot of my writing is seen from the point of view of the person at the bottom of the ladder: the labourer; the servant girl; people like that. The very fact that I write about them, I think implies concern for them. I couldn't write about the very affluent scene, with people drooling over menus and talking about the number of courses they've had in the meal. I'd describe myself as a socialist in as much as I think socialism is better by far than capitalism. (Although you might very well be better off in a rich, capitalist country than in a poor, mismanaged socialist country.) I may be too lazy to attend meetings and read all I should about Marx and everything else, but I'm a socialist in that I believe socialism is a better and more humane way of approaching the problems of life than what we have in Britain today.

I suppose if this country was unjustly attacked tomorrow, I would lend myself to the war effort, if you call it that. But most of us, even though we've lived in Britain, and seen our children grow up here, could never give our hearts to this country in the same way we could to Australia or New Zealand or some place like that, because of the history, and the thing in Northern Ireland. You just can't shrug them off and say that we make too much about them – the loss of the Irish language; the Irish culture; the planned, systematic anglicisation of the Irish; the ill-treatment of the Irish over centuries; all these things. On the other hand you couldn't blame the ordinary working-class English person for them. I certainly haven't got any anti-English feelings, and if I had, I hope I haven't got a shred of them now. The 'British' thing, the idea of British domination and all that, I do dislike. You still see examples of the chauvinism (we saw examples during the Falklands). We have that feeling, on the one hand, of a certain amount of gratitude, if gratitude isn't misplaced, that we got work here when we couldn't have got it at home, and that on the whole we've lived reasonably well here and not been subjected to anything worse perhaps than the Irish joke. On the other hand, there's the fact of finding ourselves in a country we might perhaps rather not be in. This ambivalence finds its way into my writing. It's certainly in *Exiles*.

* * *

I'm an indiscriminate reader. There are so many books which I should have read, and might never get around to reading. I like Sinclair Lewis, the American novelist. I thought *Babbit* was a great portrayal of a mercenary businessman, although for all his crassness, the human being shone through. *Mainstreet*, I thought was a good portrayal of American life, too, although nothing very much happens in it. I always thought it was a very worthwhile exposé of what affluent America had done to people.

I like the short-stories of Frank O'Connor – a master of the form. Stories like the unforgettable *My Oedipus Complex*, which tells of a small boy's resentment and jealousy when his soldier father returns to civvy life. *Guests of the Nation*, too, is a memorable story, about the conflicting claims of dogma and humanity. It is believed to have supplied the idea for Brendan Behan's play, *The Hostage*.

A lot of things in Irish have influenced me. Mairtin O Cadhain's *Cré na Cille* is a novel (if you want to call it that) told entirely through dialogue. It's set in a cemetery, and as each person arrives for burial, those who are waiting underneath are avid for news of life above. The wrangling and talking continue as much as in the upper world, and a composite picture emerges of Irish village life, showing all the nastiness and inanity of people. It was savagely attacked by some critics when the book appeared in 1949. O Cadhain owes a great debt to the Russians because it was only after reading Russian writers that he realised what he himself should be doing: writing about his own people (who resembled the Russian peasants very closely).

Another novel which I found memorable is *Tarry Flynn*, by the poet Patrick Kavanagh. It's the story of a rather indolent, poetically-inclined young countryman, much given to daydreams and fantasy. It's one of the most authentic pictures of Irish rural life in the 1930s;

DONALL Mac AMHLAIGH

187

the descriptions of the Monaghan countryside are unequalled, and the people are portrayed without any of that patronising sentimentality which all too often marks the work of those who write from the outside; there's none of your silly Anglo-Irish whimsy. As in the writings of O Cadhain, these are the people of rural Ireland as they really are: the hunger for land, the rural cunning, the reality of life, the inhibiting nature of a rigidly-structured society, the ambivalence of people towards the dominant institution – the Church. It's only a slight novel in a sense, but a very endearing one.

I enjoyed *Goodbye, Mr. Chips*, by James Hilton, which is an odd choice. I read that with quite an affection for a type of man who was miles removed from my state of life, and whose politics and attitudes I wouldn't much approve of. It has an implicit class stance, but it surmounts it somehow or other and the people come through. That must be some measure of the author's gifts.

I liked Sean O'Casey's autobiography. The books are extremely enjoyable to read, and they are invaluable for the picture they give of the ferment of political and literary activity in Ireland, in Dublin in particular, in the years leading to Irish independence, and the sad disillusionment that followed. What O'Casey thought of the great literary figures of the day is all here and makes delightfully vindictive comment. O'Casey, like Brendan Behan who came after him, seems to have been something of an inverted snob, by which I mean that while professing not to be impressed by the high and mighty, he was very sensitive indeed to how they regarded him, and nurtured imagined or real grievances with all the solicitude of a mother nursing a new baby. I suppose if he had been less human he might also have been less great as a playwright.

Another book which had a certain influence on me is Mervyn Wall's *The Unfortunate Fursey*. It's a comic novel which mightn't make sense to someone who wasn't brought up in Catholic Ireland in the 1940s. We in Ireland had this, probably quite erroneous, notion of a mythical Golden Age when there were no wars or anything like that in Ireland; when everybody was devoted to learning. It was true up to a point. Before the Danish invasion the people had become very peaceful and there were a lot of monastic establishments, but I think the Golden Age wasn't as golden as we make out. But, growing up in the 1940s, with the horrible censorship which they had in Ireland at that time, with a narrow, inward-looking Catholic Church wielding such an inordinate amount of power,

WT—N

people like Wall rebelled. *The Unfortunate Fursey* is about a monk who, because he has a bad stammer, can't get out the incantation which would drive the Devil away. The Devil alights beside him on his bed and poor old Fursey is so petrified, he can't shunt the quare fellow off by saying the magic words; and because old Fursey isn't able to get rid of him the Host of Darkness gets a foothold in the monastery with disastrous results.

I think Anthony West's *The Ferret Fancier*, is a very good novel. Benedict Kiely's *Dogs Enjoy the Morning* is a brilliant tour-de-force: the language is scintillating, richly textured, a joy to read; and the novel is constructed with the utmost craftsmanship. His most recent novel, *Proxopera*, deals with the Northern Ireland situation, and in a manner which did not endear him to a lot of Republicans. A County Tyrone man, he is greatly saddened by the Northern conflict.

Women in Ireland today seem to have almost taken over the field of the short-story, and among those I like best is Maura Tracy, a County Kilkenny girl whose collection, *Sixpence in her Shoe*, portrays the small, rural, domestic scene with that keenness of insight and faithfulness to detail which women seem more capable of, very often, than men. Francis McManus, a Kilkenny man, wrote good novels which dwell on the small scene, the microcosm; there is a wonderful evocative quality in his writing. *Watergate*, is a classic really. *Flow on Lovely River*, is another.

I like comic literature. Jaroslav Hasek's *The Good Soldier Schweik*, that great anti-war novel, I could read over and over again – the story of a very reluctant conscript whose only weapon against the machinations and lunacies of the military mind is his seeming idiocy.

I could read George Orwell over and over again too, not just for the meat of what he has to say – his essays are as interesting now as they were forty years ago – but also for the readability of his prose.

* * *

I suppose good literature sharpens our perceptions of life, and helps people to see things in a way that they hadn't quite seen them before. A purely escapist novel, however brilliantly put together, seems to me a waste of effort. I wouldn't wish to write anything like that, myself. I would rather try to do something which someone, on reading it, would pause and say, 'But that's it, that's how it is, that's how one feels... ' There's an old saying in Irish, 'Chuir tu do shuil thar do chuid' – literally, 'You put your eye beyond your share' – meaning that people aspire to things which are beyond them. That is demonstrably true of a great many writers or would-be-writers, people like myself, who know very well what it is they would like to do, but whose limitations put that achievement beyond them. So you just keep slogging away at that which can be at once a joy and a despair.

Northampton, October 1983

NIGEL GRAY'S COMMENT.

Donall Mac Amhlaigh (pronounced MacCawley) is a modest, unassuming man. For a labourer, he is not a big man, but he is strongly built, and a studio photographer once complained that his hands were like bunches of bananas. He has emerged as a natural leader and spokesperson for the Irish in Britain, and he has always courageously spoken up on Irish issues, despite occasional hostility from the host community and periodic vilification in the local gutter press. The constraints of family, and his chosen commitment to the typewriter, go against a natural (and very Irish) tolerant friendliness and good-natured garrulousness. His conversation is always a pleasure: intelligent, informed, compassionate, and enriched with a wealth of anecdote. But beneath it all one detects a man who is rather sad, unfulfilled; someone who perhaps no longer, ever, feels completely at home anywhere.

I first came to Northampton as Writer-in-Residence in 1977, and met Danny soon after. And as well that I did, or the ten years I've spent in this town would have been far emptier and lonelier than

they have been. Tom Paulin once said to me in a letter: 'Give my
regards to Dick Davis if you see him. I've just read Mac Amhlaigh's
classic book – Northampton must be packed with writers.' Dick had
only stopped off for nine months and was long gone. And then there
were two. If only Tom Paulin had been right. Danny claims that the
Northampton disease of apathy even infected the Irish people who
settled here. In truth, the Irish Club is little more than a drinking
barn.

Most of the drinking Dan and I have done together has in fact been
tea – in his kitchen or in mine. On a number of occasions we have
shared a literary platform – something the romantic in me sets great
store by. Dan was born in County Galway in the south. I was born
in County Antrim in the north. By coming together politically,
socially, culturally, I feel that, in some small, insignificant way, we
are uniting our poor, bleeding, little country. But then, the longest
journey begins with a single step, as the sage said. I am leaving
Northampton two days from now. I shall go with little regret, other
than my sadness at putting distance between myself and this good
friend.

Since 1983 *Schnitzer O'Shea* has been published in hardback and
paperback editions, and *Deoraithe* (*Exiles*), has been published in
Irish. Despite some good reviews neither book achieved the impact
Danny would have liked. His main creative output has been a
number of short-stories. He has about fourteen now which have not
yet been published in book form. He may bring out another (his
third) collection in Irish soon, although he feels some reluctance to
part with them just yet. And he would like, some time, to publish
the best of them in English. *An Irish Navvy* has recently been
broadcast on radio again, in twenty episodes.

Donall Mac Amhlaigh won the Henessy Literary Award in 1974;
an *Irish Post* Community Award for Literature in 1979; and the
Oireachtas Award for Fiction in 1981.

He was born in Co. Galway, on December 10th 1924.

Donall Mac Amhlaigh's Book-Choice:

Babbit Sinclair Lewis
Mainstreet Sinclair Lewis
The Collected Short Stories
   Frank O'Connor
Cré na Cille Mairtin O Cadhain
Tarry Flynn Patrick Kavanagh
Goodbye, Mr Chips
   James Hilton
The Autobiography of
   Sean O'Casey
The Unfortunate Fursey
   Mervyn Wall

The Ferret Fancier
   Anthony West
Dogs Enjoy the Morning
   Benedict Kiely
Sixpence in her Shoe
   Maura Tracy
Watergate Francis McManus
Flow on Lovely River
   Francis McManus
The Collected Essays, Journalism
   and Letters George Orwell
The Good Soldier Schweik
   Jaroslav Hasek

Books by Donall Mac Amhlaigh:

Dialann Deorai
Saol Saighdiura
Diarmaid ó Donaill
Sweeny, agus scealta eile
Schnitzer ó Sé

Beoir Bhaile
Deoraithe
An Irish Navvy
Schnitzer O'Shea

Chapter Nine

ROGER McGOUGH

I was born into a Catholic family of Irish descent. My mother's name was McGarry. She had eleven brothers and sisters. On my father's side there were eight brothers and one girl. We lived in a working-class area in north Liverpool which was called Litherland, near the docks at Seaforth. I had one sister. I went to the local primary school and then to St Mary's College, which was a well-respected and highly disciplined Irish Christian Brothers grammar school. It was fiercely Catholic and quite repressive in many ways, but at the time you felt you were lucky to be there. I was never interested in literature at school. I used to enjoy English Language, parsing and all this sort of business, but literature didn't mean a great deal to me, and in fact I failed 'O' Level English Literature because I hadn't read the books. When I went into the sixth form I did French, Geography and History merely because those were the subjects I did best at. I had no interest in any of them. In the eyes of a working-class family like mine the best thing you could be was a priest, and after that a doctor would be very good, and then a lawyer. Probably a teacher would be all right. So that was the level you were supposed to aim at. I was quite interested in painting and drawing, I enjoyed that, but a choice had to be made early on at school: it was either Latin or Art. The ones who weren't considered to be so clever were the ones who went to Art. If you were good at art you were supposed not to be academic. I'd have loved to have done Art really, and gone to Art School.

It was in the sixth form and the first year at Hull University that I started getting interested in theatre. In late adolescence I became very excited by ideas and philosophy and writing, and the *idea* of the writer, the *idea* of the artist. At university I did French and I read Baudelaire, Rimbaud, Nerval, and some other French poets, and the thing struck me was not only the poetry (because I wasn't terribly good at French anyway and I read them in translation) but the fact that it was a way of life. I suddenly realised what art was, what painting was, what writing was – it was people devoting themselves to something with an almost religious intensity. I suppose I was to a certain extent, an outsider, I always felt very much an observer, and when I read the poets, and about their commitment, I certainly felt something in concert with them. I realised what I was – I was a poet. So I started writing poetry. I suppose that's a funny way round really.

My first poems were written at Hull. They were very much the sort of thing that adolescents write: 'Am I outside of Life? – Am I its nucleus?'; some love poems. I'd been very little exposed to poetry. The only poetry I'd had was Palgrave's *Golden Treasury*. I'd also done verse-speaking. My mother had sent me off to elocution lessons to learn to speak 'properly', and there used to be verse-speaking competitions: like learning *Jabberwocky* and standing up in front of people and reciting it aloud. At Hull, Philip Larkin was the sub-warden of the hall I was in. I'd never heard of him before I got there, but he was a *writer*. He was a very shy, private man – I didn't talk to him at the time. But he was a man who had had a book published. He was a poet, and I thought that was great. I decided that would be my ambition: to write, and have a book published. I started writing poems feverishly, just for myself really, and showing them to people round about. There was a university poetry magazine, but that seemed to be full of Latin words and very literary-scary sort of poetry. It was very much a class thing: there was no way I could write for that. All the poems I published were in the university newspaper.

I still had this thing that my parents had passed on to me: it was no good just being a writer; if you were going to be a writer you'd got to be very good. If you were going to be an artist you had to be very good; to be an actor you had to be very good. It wasn't in the scheme of things not to be good at what you did. (Presumably, to make money; I suppose that's what it amounted to.) My dad worked on the docks; all his brothers worked on the docks; and all the brothers on my mother's side; none of them had had a good education. They had all had to leave school at thirteen or fourteen, so they wanted achievement for the next generation. My mother enjoyed reading and imagined she had a flair for writing, and she encouraged me. When I went to the library, my father used to ask me to get a book for him. He was afraid of libraries; he was embarrassed about going in; he didn't know how they worked; so he'd ask me to get a book – about the sea if possible. Sometimes I'd bring him back one he'd had before and he'd say, 'It doesn't matter. I'll read it again.' I was in that generation that was growing up just after the war – that achieving generation that included the Beatles, Hockney, Barry Hines, John McGrath and all those people who became successful in fields in which their fathers hadn't dared trespass.

I was scared of the poetry establishment, I suppose. Instead of just sending poems off to magazines, it took me a while to think I was good enough. I used to think, 'They'll find me out.' I think the first poem I had published was in a magazine called *Tomorrow*. It was edited by a gentleman who has since become a critic and not my closest friend. One of his quotes in the seventies was: 'The trouble with poetry today is not the poets – they can't help being bad; it's the editors and publishers,' not realising in fact that he'd been the one to first publish some of us. I think I must have read in a student newspaper that this magazine was looking for poems. There was a fellow you had to send off to in Oxford, and I thought, 'I don't know anyone down there, so that'll be all right. If I get published that'll be nice. If they know who I am they won't publish me.' They're the sort of fears you have. Publication gave me a real lift, although at the same time it didn't matter in a way. It was nice to get published, but I'd decided that I was a poet; that was my vocation. Whatever I did as a profession didn't matter because I was a poet; that was the pact I'd made with myself. I was into reading and getting to know what was going on in the theatre. I would like to have done drama at university or something creative, but I just did Geography and French; so when I went back to Liverpool, I got a job as a teacher. I lived in central Liverpool, Liverpool 8, which was the area where lots of students and villains and painters and prostitutes and professors lived. It's a very small area, but unique in a way; so I met everyone who was around, which included Adrian Henri and Brian Patten and lots of others. Although I was still an outsider, suddenly I felt I belonged to a group.

I went straight from university to a teaching job in Kirkby where I led a double life – conventional during working hours and then assuming a different persona outside of it. I used to keep a canvas bag with me with my jeans inside and my dark glasses, and after school I'd go into the toilets and emerge as this blind butterfly. After work, in coffee cellars and pubs, a group of us used to write plays together, and it was very exciting – although none of them were ever really finished. It was the time of Mike Horowitz and Pete Brown and Adrian Mitchell doing readings, and the American poets, Ginsberg and Ferlinghetti – the Beat generation. Because it was classless or American, it was all right. Most of the poetry I read at the time which influenced me was French or German. Poets like Guillaume, Appolinaire and Christian Morgenstern – they were surrealists really; with few equivalents in English. I started doing readings around Liverpool, and I was very much involved in other things. I sent a collection of poems off to Faber, and then Penguin. They came back, but with quite encouraging letters. I'd sent some poems off to Larkin, for whom I'd developed a great respect, and he'd also been very encouraging and said, 'I don't see why you shouldn't get published.' I sent some poems off to *Encounter*, and *London Magazine*, and they'd come back, and I realised there was very little market for the sort of poems that I was writing. Then I got some work published in *Ambit*, which was edited by Martin Bax. That was really the first magazine I was involved in. I remember doing readings in Manchester with Tony Connor and Jack Marriott, and I really felt then like a poet because it was organised by a literary magazine, and there were my poems in the magazine, and I was reading them. I felt somehow then, I was definitely on the road. I remember going into bookshops and reading magazines and books of poems, and feeling that it was very important that these things were in print. We were doing readings around Liverpool, and there were big audiences each week, and it was fun to do, and it did keep the writing going (although I think it would have kept going anyway), but getting a magazine with my name in it was thrilling.

I did a reading at the Everyman theatre which was then called Hope Hall, and John Willett came. John Willett, the writer and Brechtian expert, was then the assistant editor of the *TLS*. He came to me after the reading and said, 'Do you have an agent?' The agent he recommended, took me on, and I got a book together. Michael Joseph published this book which was, *Summer with Monika, and Frinck*, a series of poems and a novella. *Frinck*, was about a singer who leaves Liverpool (it's similar to *Summer with Monika* in a way, because it's about a love affair), doesn't make it, and comes back. The book wasn't very successful, but it was published in America with an awful front cover saying, 'The most exciting writer/performer since John Lennon... runaway winner of the Liverpool Poetry Festival, star of *That Was The Week That Was*, etc. and other horrific fibs. Sphere did the paperback over here without much success. It was all messy. By that time the book, *The Liverpool Scene*, had happened. Rapp and Caroll published it in '67. It has poems by me, Adrian, Brian, Pete Brown, Spike Hawkins, Mike Evans, Henry Graham, with photographs. Trendily packaged, it was dedicated to the Beatles, with a quote from Ginsberg on the back saying: 'Liverpool is at the present moment, the centre of the consciousness of the human universe.' It got *Daily Mirror* cover, and a lot of publicity, which really got up the nose of a lot of people, but it certainly sold the book. Then the Penguin *Mersey Sound* came out. They chose the three of us: Adrian Henri, Brian Patten, and myself. Having the Penguin book out was really important – we were part of a 'Modern Poets' series which involved a lot of 'proper' poets; so that was very good. We felt part of a tradition rather than a 'pop ephemera'.

I taught for two years at St. Kevin's in Kirkby, and I did a year and a half at a place called Mabel Fletcher College. I taught English and Games and Catering French. They were mainly student nurses. It was great actually. Then three of us (John Gorman, Mike McGear and me) went for an audition and got offered a Saturday night, live television series called *Gazette*. We thought, 'Great – chuck the job and we'll go and do it!' So then *The Scaffold* was launched. I didn't do any more teaching for about two years, and then, in a quiet time with *The Scaffold*, I went back to doing one day a week for a year, and that's the only other work I've done.

The Scaffold was originally a poetry-orientated theatre group – perhaps the first alternative cabaret revue. All the sketches were quite poetic in a way, but also satirical. Gorman was a very good comic. You need a good comic presence and good writing, and that's what we had. We always got very good reviews at the Edingburgh Festival – the best reviews I've ever had in a way. I wrote most of the material, and so I used to write myself most of the funny lines, but it emerged over the years that John was the funny man and I was the straight man, but these things took time to come. Mike was Paul McCartney's brother (still is, in fact) and Brian Epstein was our manager and we started making records, one of which was *Thank You Very Much* which was a hit, and *Lily the Pink* was number one, then *Liverpool Lou*; suddenly we were into a different area. It created a sort of trap really. It made money and all that, but I could have done without the hits. I'd rather have stayed with the theatre.

As it was, we got side-tracked, and had to wear white suits all the time and have a band.

Eventually we had more material than we needed. We had enough stuff, so why bother rehearsing new material? We were just repeating ourselves, so, as a writer, I felt we had reached the end. Then we did a show with the Bonzo Dog Doodah band. That was fun, and we thought it would be good to work together, so we teamed up. That was refreshing. We brought in Andy Roberts. We called ourselves *Grimms* – that stood for Gorman, Roberts, Innes, McGough, McGear, Stanshall. They were the original people. It was like *The Scaffold* extended. We went on tour with a mixture of sketches, and poetry with music, and rock and roll. Then Zoot Money joined us, and Brian. By this time there were about twelve in the group. So there was no *Scaffold* any more. The manager was getting gigs for *Grimms*.

Incidentally we'd got our own office in Liverpool – a place called 'Scaffoscope' – with a secretary working there, and we put all the money we made from the records to try to build an arts centre in Liverpool. We lost it all and got ourselves into all sorts of mess.

Eventually *Grimms* wound down. There were too many people in it. All chiefs and no indians. Since then I've lived off reading fees, and royalties, and television (I seem to do a lot of children's educational television, sometimes presenting, sometimes writing), a lot of radio work. Recently I've been writing lyrics for *The Wind in the Willows*. An American company are doing it as a musical. That was a a nice little job. It was one of those projects that come out of the blue. An American called Bill Perry had done a television series about modern English poetry called, *Anyone for Tennyson*. He found my work and liked it, and ended up doing a whole half-hour programme of my work, with Jim Dale performing it, and so he got to know me. This was a few years ago. When this project came up, he was the musician involved, and he put me forward as the lyricist.

I do quite a lot of tours overseas. Most years I go somewhere: Greece, Australia, America, France, Holland. I used to think, 'Other people get translated, but not me.' I used to feel left out. But I suppose one thing about poetry is that it doesn't translate very well. When I do a reading to a non-English-speaking audience, some poems work great, for example the tennis poem '40-Love'. Last year I was at the Sarajevo Festival in Yugoslavia. Sometimes the readings would be in a great hall or auditorium, sometimes they'd take you

to a factory making stockings, and all the people would sit in the
canteen. I'd read the poem swivelling my head from side to side and
there'd be no response. Then the girl would stand up and translate
it, and they'd all fall about. I tend to choose the poems that I think
will throw a stone into the lake; usually something that's got a story
to it. There was a Russian poet there last year. He was actually the
secretary of the Russian Writer's Union. He looked like Rod Steiger
– he was very powerful looking, and he'd stand up there and chain-
smoke and read and he put on this great performance. The people
loved him. I asked my translator, 'What are the poems about?' She
just shrugged and said, 'The usual.'

When I look back at the early stuff – the bad poems are bad
poems, but the better ones I still like – it's just as though they were
written by another man. On the recent 'Mersey Sound' reunion tour,
I read some of the poems from my early book which is something I
rarely do, and it seemed like reading poems by a very much younger
man; I didn't have those feelings any more. But they worked, I
think, for what they were at the time. I had one book, *Watchwords*,
which I've asked not to be reprinted any more. In that, there were
so many poems written for a particular time. Most of the poems were
written for a weekly television programme called *The Eleventh
Hour*. 'This week we want a poem about backing Britain.' 'This
week, a poem about the permissive society.' They might be
interesting sociologically, and bits of them work as poetry, but not
enough to stand up. *Summer with Monika* was very early, and that
was heartfelt, and it had enthusiasm and verve, and a great energy
went into it. There were some good poems in it, and some less good.
I wrote so much at that time, and some of it wasn't any good. Later
on, I re-ordered it and changed it. I got caught up in running words
together and developing a style, and the early poems suffer from
that. I got better at it as I went along – it got a bit tighter in a way.
I suppose early on, the excitement of writing, that feeling; 'Hey! I'm
writing a poem!' showed a bit in the poems. When things didn't work
later, they probably didn't work for other reasons. Nowadays I do
lots of drafts. I do more and more revisions as time goes on. I write
more revisions than poems now, whereas in the beginning, I used to
write more poems than revisions.

Writing has been slow this year since I had *Waving at Trains* out.
I wrote some of the best poems after it had been accepted because
of the pressure of having to come up with something a bit stronger.

The fact that the book was going to come out focussed me on to it.
I haven't done a lot that is any good since then. I've done the lyrics
for *The Wind in the Willows*, and I've also been doing a lot of poetry
readings, which I'm stopping doing now. Brian and I felt that there
were too many readings and not enough work, so hopefully I'm
going to get some writing done now.

To some extent things are changing all the time so I've never had
a real routine. Until last summer I still had a place in Liverpool, and
there's been so much toing and froing I was almost peripatetic. I had
a house up in Liverpool with my desk and my books there, and yet
I was writing mainly in London, on the kitchen table. Since July I've
actually moved into a new house in London and I've got my desk
and stuff here, so now I do tend to go up to my room to write at my
desk every day. The day starts with going in and doing my letters
and phone calls and getting that out of the way, and then I try and
work through. I don't go out for lunch. I don't drink during the day
or anything. I may go for a run or I may go up to the gym, but my
working hours tend to be during the day. Of course it's dependent
on the kids as well. I used to find that I quite liked working between
five and seven, but when I have the boys here I can never do that.
They're only here at weekends now, so that's different. There's been
no pattern really over the years. It's always been a matter of adapting
to whatever situation I'm in. I used to work a lot late at night. Now
I tend not to because Hilary's got to get up early in the morning to
go to work.

The only effect of success on my personal life is that I get more
mail of the 'Here's some poems – tell me how to get them published,
by return of post,' sort of thing. I get a lot of those; over a couple
of dozen a week. I answer them and try to be encouraging or
whatever. It's very difficult. I had one yesterday. He didn't send the
poems – just a long letter. He's a working-class writer who can't get
published but who thinks his work is important. It was quite a big-
headed letter in a way, but it had to be because he was saying he
thinks he's good; and he can't understand it, and how do you get
on? I had to write back saying, 'I can't help you. I'm a writer, not
a poetry editor.' I know what they want me to say – what I wanted
when I sent some poems off to Larkin: they want me to say, 'Hey!
You're a genius!' That's what everyone wants really. All you can say
is, 'Keep sending stuff off and hoping, and if you believe in yourself
– eventually... ' I'm conscious that people are going to listen to what

I say, and get annoyed, or be flattered or whatever. People expect
something more from me. That sometimes puts me in a difficult
position. If you buy somebody a drink they think you're throwing
your money around; if you don't buy them a drink they think you're
being tight-fisted. With *The Scaffold*, of course, it was worse – you
were public property for a while. That was not nice. People expected
you to behave in a certain sort of way. At least now it's a quiet sort
of thing. If people do recognise me they don't usually say anything,
or if they do, it's usually something nice.

It's upsetting when you get bad reviews. I'm always disappointed.
I rationalise now and say, 'Why is this a bad review?' I know that
I'm going to get bad reviews from certain people. There's a kids'
book I did called *Sky in the Pie*. There's some good things in it, and
some less good. Charles Causley did a smashing review of it; even
though he was complimentary he also said that one or two of the
poems were a bit sentimental and that he wouldn't have included
those. And he's right. But an enemy reviewer would have quoted
from those poems and said they were typical of the book. I've come
to realise that it's a matter of being philosophical about criticism.
But what happens now is that certain critics don't review you at all.
A silence. Part of you gets upset and annoyed, but another part says,
'When you stop selling books and people stop coming to readings –
that's the time to worry.'

It really chuffed me psychologically when I first got an agent.
Having somebody there actually working on my behalf made me feel
like a 'proper writer'. I'm dyslexic really, when it comes to money
and contracts. I can't read contracts. I find them boring and I don't
want to read them, so I do find it very important to have an agent
looking after things. I know a lot of writers feel bad about paying
the ten per cent, especially if the work comes to you direct.
Sometimes someone like Penguin comes straight to me. They say,
'How about doing this book? We'll give you so much advance.' And
you give it to your agent, and they get ten per cent. On the other
hand it comes to the time, like with *The Wind in the Willows*, where
you're dealing with an American company for a start, and all sorts
of things could go wrong – that's when they earn their money. It's
worth having someone there who you can talk to about the work
and who can distance you from people. As well as a literary agent,
I have an agent who looks after my performance work. I don't like
saying 'no' to anybody. People ring me and say, 'Can you come and

do this?' I say, 'Go through Steve.' And Steve will arrange it. It provides a sort of buffer.

There should be money available for the arts. I think Covent Garden, the opera and ballet, get too much money, crazy amounts of money, purely for a middle-class diversion. That money could be put into people. You:ve got to have your writers and your painters, and they've got to be supported. In this country we see art as luxury, the writer as an idler – unless he's a commercial success, then everybody loves him (except the purist critics, of course). Last year I was in Cornwall, and I went to see W. S. Graham who lives in a tiny little house with an outside toilet. He's an amazingly talented man, but he's got no money. The thing he's doing is not marketable. There are standards, but the Arts Council could subsidise a poetry list and support more magazines. That's where the life-blood of it is. Then your writers won't feel lost, won't feel they're sinking into some sort of oblivion.

I have a tendency to see both sides to every question. I used to see that just as a weakness. I was never able to come out on one side and say, 'Yes, that's what I should believe.' But it can sometimes be a strength; otherwise you get blinded. There are certain basics, of course. Wealth is unfairly spread around, and people, once given it, hold on to it. The poor would do the same if they were rich. People hold on to things until they're made to share; and that's what's got to be done. Things like the Falklands War I find horrific; things like wars, aggression. We're living in a world where the need to be seen to be aggressive seems to be important. That macho thing I've always mistrusted having seen so much pain and hate caused by it: from a highly political international level, to a basic one-to-one level – the physical or mental violence you get in your personal relationships.

I still feel as though I'm a Catholic. That upbringing affects the way you react. I'd like to think that I'm optimistic and caring and that that comes through in my work. And I think that what would make some pieces of writing work better than others might be this *feeling* in it. What you're really writing about is yourself in relation to other people, and so much poetry I see around is removed from that. You couldn't very well tell what the person thought, other than that the writer doesn't like people, or mistrusts people, perhaps even despises them. I don't think *I* do. In my work there's a concern which leads to sympathy, or something like that.

I occasionally go to mass and confession. But since I've moved to

London I haven't found a parish. It was a social thing. I still say my prayers, and meditate in short bursts (- if that is possible). It's just something that's driven into you when you're young. In times of trouble we used to say 'Hail Marys'. In times of celebration we said 'Hail Marys'. That's part of my life I suppose. I'm not talking religion here – it's almost a naïve thing. You're trained to be aware of yourself if you're having evil thoughts. If I catch myself being uncharitable or envious or something, I try to stop myself. That's fair enough. I am envious and uncharitable obviously, like the best of us, but I try to stop. My childhood was spent in those days when you couldn't eat meat on a Friday. On Friday night we used to go up the pub, and then get some meat pies, and walk the streets till twelve o'clock before eating them. We felt good about that then. They were the rules, so that's how we did it. It was sometimes as easy to keep the rules as to break them. They were the fabric of our lives really. It was always superstitious Irish religion, but it was a structure that kept people going and made them very happy. You couldn't knock it. But it was never very thought-out. My parents were a bit embarrassed by some of the writing I was doing when I was younger because it was sexual. I don't know if I could have published *Holiday on Death Row* had my parents been alive. The Church, I can't wholly agree with. It's only a clearing bank or a travel agency or something like that really. So many of the priests I knew, were not very bright, and were biased often. Well-meaning, but unsympathetic and uncaring sometimes, they were really just God's bouncers.

I was never subjected to violence as a child, but I was expected to be mannish or boyish. My father was very masculine. He was a very strong man. I think he always wanted me to be a footballer. He wanted me to be strong, and I wasn't. I was not very good at the things you were supposed to be good at, even like trying to help my father mend things, or help decorate. He always used to get impatient with me because I used to mess everything up and go away. And sensitivity wasn't regarded as a virtue. I remember I cried once when I was 'too old to cry'. I'd had a crewcut and he kept on to me, and I broke into tears at the tea table. I suppose in an artistic family they might have realised they'd got a sensitive child and encouraged him, whereas I don't think that was recognised. It was looked on more as an illness: 'Feed him plenty of cod liver oil!' I think I was quite well-balanced, but if anything was wrong with me it was always something 'nervous'. I used to get nervous twitches and things like that. Any illness I had was psychosomatic. I don't know why. As the only son, a lot was expected of me. I was expected to be good at things. It was to do with my generation. We were supposed to be the big achievers. There were lots of cousins who came after me. I was the eldest – the first one to go to grammar school (no one in our family had ever been to a grammar school), the first one to go to university. There was no one for me to follow. Of course, that meant no one to be compared with, but on the other hand no one to advise me what to do, or how to do it, or how to behave.

I hope I've reacted against it with my boys, but I sometimes find myself quoting what my father said to me. I think everyone does that. The boys have always played football, because they want to do what their mates do. I play football with them and encourage them. The elder one's starting to want to read more now, and that's good because I can encourage him in that. But I'm fairly relaxed with them, I think. They're not pushed into too much.

I don't have any ambitions for myself really. I'd just like to continue to write poems. Cape keep saying they want to do a *Selected Poems* at some time, but I'm in no hurry for it. Sometimes I have an idea for a novel or an idea for a film, but there's nothing I'm really burning to do. There's nothing that makes me feel frustrated because I'm not doing it. I've never felt that. Things seem to come along. There's a lot of variety, which is something I enjoy. I'd just like to be producing solid poems really. I seem to get waylaid by a lot of flotsam and jetlag: all these readings, and gadding about. I did a play or a revue for The Lyric, Hammersmith, every year for a few years. Then I was offered the part of the narrator in *Blood Brothers*, the Willy Russell musical, but that would have been too much – although it would have been very interesting to do. I do one thing and then I get fed up with it. I do too much theatre, and then I want to go away and do something on my own. But when I've been on my own for a bit I'm hopeless. I get worried and want to get out and meet people and do a bit more theatre.

In the theatre, although I've been successful in terms of managing to fill the place, there's never been any offshoots: no West End transfers, no Spielberg films, no T-shirts. Usually it's been slammed by the critics, and critics are more important in the theatre. So even though I enjoy theatre and working with other people, I've never

had any success out of it. I've had my fingers burned a bit. Some of
the things I've done, I'd like to do again properly. There are shows
I've felt haven't had the life out of them that they should have done.
Lifeswappers, something I wrote as a television and theatre play,
was never done properly on stage. *Monika* has never gone the
mileage as a theatre play. I hate having things around that haven't
been done properly. It's simpler with my poems. The responsibility
is totally mine. But with theatre, success so much depends on the
director, the cast, and on so many other elements. If the elements
don't come together it can flop. So that's one ambition: to re-do the
things that haven't been done properly.

I'm very conscious of the fact of not living in Liverpool where I
was so much a part of things. I used to see writers come to London
and write plays about Liverpool, and it was all wrong – so dated. I'm
hoping I won't be like that because I'm so conscious of it. I've no
wish to be a spokesman in exile. Things change. I miss the jokes and
the gabble and the camaraderie, but sooner or later I had to leave
Liverpool. I think that most of what I write is fairly imaginative, it's
not often reportage, so it probably doesn't matter where I live. I
don't have a car (in fact, few poets seem to be able to drive), I still
travel by tube and trains and buses, so I'm still going round listening
and watching to some extent. I grew up with a very strong gang in
Liverpool, but when I go back I realise everything's changed.
They're all married for the second time, and they've got kids, and
some of them have stopped coming out. The ones I see now tend to
run pubs and clubs, and even they're changed in the sense that
they're settled. I've made new friends down here now.I think the
move was inevitable.

When you go to Liverpool and you go in a pub, someone's always
got a joke. There's always wit. It's the same thing in Ireland. English
people say that the Irish are dumb, but that isn't true. Irish people
are often so witty that the English don't understand what they're
saying. It's the same with story-telling. Irish people are great story-
tellers, and sometimes there's almost a surrealist element: things
aren't what they seem, and so they're often misunderstood by your
average, educated English person. But Liverpool's a hotpot of Celtic
people: the Irish and the Welsh, and the way they use language is
always variable.

I didn't set out to be witty or entertaining. I was just writing the
poems. It's probably something to do with my background,

something to do with Liverpool. And also something to do with being working-class; with being sensitive among people who regard sensitivity as a weakness, where you can't be seen to be too serious about anything (except politics). 'The polystyrene fist in the velvet glove' – that's me. Afraid of being seen as 'intellectual', you end up with a joke. 'I was only joking really.' I think particularly my early work was like that. It was one of my faults, I think, that early on almost every poem had a punch line. Eventually I learned to get rid of that. I don't know what the ratio between funny poems and serious poems is. Some are just serious and some are just jokes, but the best poems are somewhere between the two. The humour certainly makes them popular. People come to a reading because they know they'll enjoy it and have a laugh. But if there were only the funny poems, they wouldn't come back. What brings them back, I think, is the serious element which is what really holds my work together. That's what I like to think. But there's some sort of snobbishness – 'If it's funny and it's popular it can't be very good.' Even well-meaning teachers say to me, 'I use your work a lot to amuse the kids, and then I introduce them to real poetry.' 'Thank you very much!' And they think they're being nice to you! What are 'real poems'? There have been good writers who could be funny *and* serious.

It always reminds me of when my grandmother was dying. We were all gathered round her death-bed. I had this black hat which was lying on the seat beside me. The priest came, and he said hello to us, and he gave her Absolution, and then went off. And then my aunty said, 'Oh, he's forgotten his hat,' and grabbed my hat and ran off with it. I shouted, 'No, It's not his – it's mine!' and everyone laughed. And it's like all this hysteria comes out of something very serious and rather sad. When something funny happens it intensifies the situation. I think some of my writing is like that. It's a sort of strangled chuckle in the dark.

The only creative writing teaching I've done is for a couple of days, or a couple of weeks; a few lessons of hyper-creativity and away leaving the teacher to get on with the nitty-gritty. It's not like teaching all the time. I think I would like to see Creative Writing as something separate from English Literature. It has always seemed to me that English Literature is like History or Geography. It's not like English as such. Creative Writing is an art form – it should be a separate subject like Art. Writing poetry, writing short-stories, play-acting, all that is to do with language. It should be taken apart from English Literature. People are always surprised that I didn't get English Literature 'O' Level. They say, 'But you're a poet.' It's nothing to do with being a poet. English Literature is to do with assimilating, comparing and dissecting. Nothing really to do with creation. Being a poet is to do with using language. The skills are different skills.

The poets who mean most to me are Morgenstern, Rimbaud, Baudelaire, and Nerval – and T. S. Eliot actually. I remember discovering *The Waste Land* and *Prufrock*. *Prufrock* staggered me – that 'patient etherised upon a table' image. It knocked me back. It was the first modern poetry I'd read. I liked reading Gerald Manley Hopkins, and listening to Dylan Thomas. I heard *Under Milk Wood*, which sparked me off to go and read the books. I found that very refreshing and marvellous. I remember, too, seeing Robert Frost on television reading the poem about stopping in the woods; and hearing Adrian Mitchell; and hearing Christopher Logue and being quite impressed by him. A lot of the first influences were aural in fact. I liked a lot of American poets, like Cummings and Patchen. And I enjoyed sharing readings with people like Pete Morgan and Tom Pickard.

I read a lot when I'm travelling. I like Anthony Burgess, Graham Greene, Kurt Vonnegut. I was in America last week. When I first arrived in New York I was waiting for my suitcases, and standing next to me – there he was; white hair and a white moustache. And I did something I never ever do. 'Excuse me, it's Mr. Vonnegut? – Aren't you Kurt Vonnegut?' He said, 'He's certainly somewhere, but he's not here.' And as I crept away, I remembered who it was: the novelist Jacob Lind! I'd met him at a Methuen party only months before.

* * *

Good literature can move you sometimes, in the way you can be moved by a painting, or by a piece of music, and the way it moves you is difficult to explain. With poetry you'd think it would be easier to explain because the medium that's moving you is words. But it's difficult to express in the same way that it's difficult to express the way music works. On one level, it's something that happens between words; it's some kind of sharing with other people. It's something that is part of some microcosm, some part of the universe. It's not to do with telling stories quickly, which is what you get on television or film. It's something very private, very still, very charged. It's made out of something you use every day, some part of the language which suddenly crystallises, solidifies, and shimmers, and jolts your whole being into some sort of sense of yourself in the universe. Sometimes in the writing you can do that to yourself and you get that feeling, that shimmer, without knowing quite what it is. It's something to do with the magic and pattern of life.

Or something.

London, December 1983

NIGEL GRAY'S COMMENT.

Roger McGough's work is deceptively extrovert. The apparent simplicity of his poems disguises their competence. The relaxed manner of his readings disguises the excellence of his performance. The most immediately striking features of his poetry, the word-play, the wit, disguise its underlying sensitivity and sadness. In private, Roger McGough is gentle, quiet, and guarded. The vigour, the humour, the accessibility of his poetry accounts for his tremendous popularity, of course, but there can be few living poets who can equal his ability (see his poem *Funny Sort of Bloke*, for example) to say so much, so simply.

I first saw Roger perform at an evening of Liverpool Poets at the Round House in London – I suppose it would have been in the very late '60s. I do know that what for me was memorable about the evening was his contribution. I can't remember when I first met him – it was too long ago: it must have been when I was a supporting poet at a reading where he was topping the bill. In any event, that is a role I have enjoyed on a number of occasions. I can't say that there are many people I enjoy playing second fiddle to – but as a poet, Roger is certainly one of the few.

Since '83 Roger has produced half a dozen books as well as continuing his work on radio and television. At the moment he is adapting a short story by Nabokov for a dance theatre called 'The Kosh', as well as working on a new collection of poems for children. And perhaps, most importantly of all (with the help of Hilary) he has recently produced Matthew Joseph, and is now enjoying late afternoon fatherhood.

Roger McGough was born in Liverpool on November 9th, 1937.

Roger McGough's Book-Choice:

Le Bâteau Ivre Arthur Rimbaud   *Breakfast of Champions*
Les Fleurs du Mal   Kurt Vonnegut
   Charles Baudelaire   *Absolute Beginners* Colin McInnes
The Love songs of   *The Unfortunates* B. S. Johnson
   Alfred J Prufrock T. S. Eliot   *Private Angelo* B. S. Johnson
The Outsider Colin Wilson   *Revenge of the Lawn*
                                        Richard Brautigan

Poems by: The Beats; Dylan Thomas; Charles Causley; Philip Larkin; Christian Morgenstern; Jorge Luis Borges; Edwin Morgan; Stevie Smith; Sylvia Plath; Adrian Mitchell; Bertolt Brecht; Jacques Prévert; John Berryman.

Books by Roger McGough:

Frinck, A Life in the Day of, and Summer with Monika
Watchwords
After the Merrymaking
Out of Sequence
Gig
Sporting Relations
In the Glassroom
Summer with Monika
Holiday on Death Row
Unlucky for Some
Waving at Trains
Crocodile Puddles
Melting into the Foreground

For children:

Mr Noselighter
The Great Smile Robbery
Sky in the Pie
The Stowaways
Nailing the Shadow
An Imaginary Menagerie
Helen Highwater

Chapter Ten

PETER VANSITTART

My father died before I was born. I have not the least idea what he did. I suspect nothing very much. He must have been very young – I think in his early twenties. My mother never mentioned him and soon married again. Although I'm fascinated by history, I have no sense of family. My mother (though she wouldn't have been pleased to hear it) played very little part in the growth of my imagination, such as it is. I didn't see much of her. Those were the days, certainly in the class which I inhabited, where, apart from coming down for half an hour after dinner you didn't see your parents much. She would go out to meet friends for coffee about eleven, then probably spend the afternoon playing tennis or golf, would be out to dinner two or three times a week, or out playing bridge, or dancing. She thus contributed little to my development. Parents were just people in the background who paid the bills, and on the whole I was rather pleased about this. When I first read Freud in the early Penguin editions in the 30's, I gaped at the idea that I should be in love with my mother and hate my step-father. I was mildly bored with both. I didn't really know my mother until I was over thirty, though she was, in many ways, an outstanding personality. She composed a bit of music, had great personal courage, fine taste in furniture, flowers, and, on the whole, in books. But we were never close. To the end of her life, which was only about eighteen months ago, I found it very difficult to talk to her about anything that mattered. As an intimate, she didn't exist; nor as an influence (except very unconsciously) other than that she sent me to certain schools and chose my governess.

I was first taught to read, a very important and dramatic thing for me, reasonably early. At about six and a half I realised that I was not spelling things out loud, but reading to myself in silence. I owe that to somebody who had a position in the household which is now totally forgotten: the nursery governess. She could only have been about eighteen or nineteen, but she taught me to read, and herself would read me stories, or tell me the plots of stories: for example she would tell me the plot of *Macbeth*, with vivid quotations. It all seemed very exciting. And she would show me musty volumes of Dickens with extraordinary pictures – or so it seemed to me: Steerforth lying dead on the sand and the hungry waves coming in to eat him up, and that sort of thing. I got a sense of books being mysterious, remarkable worlds, of enormous importance. I was very impressionable and certain incidents, certain sights which I saw on the streets, seemed sooner or later to find an analogy in books. A shadow on the nursery window would connect up to a picture of Fagin looking in through Oliver's window. It was a very literary and literal attitude towards life. I remember writing a newspaper in invisible ink, about the age of seven, and trying to sell it on the streets of Southsea – without success. It was written, I think, in lemon juice, and you held the paper in front of the fire to make the writing come out. I remember writing plays, and I would stand on the sofa acting them out. I don't remember a time since learning to read when I wasn't attempting to write.

My early years were spent in Southsea. It was a naval town, with Portsmouth next door. There were marvellous children's parties at Christmas. The children would be rowed out, and then climb up the sides of the great battleships: *The Renown, The Repulse, The Hood* (all of which were sunk by the Japanese some years later), and you were welcomed on board by the bluejackets dressed as pirates, and the naval officers' cabins were turned into 'shops'. You could just go into a 'shop' and take a parcel, and then go into the next and take another – all free of course. There would be over a thousand children. I hated children's parties but this would be quite different because you didn't have to sing a song, or do fearful games like Hide-and-seek, Charades, Sardines, or Blind-man's-buff; there were too many of us. One ate and drank to blow-out proportions, and then watched films of Laurel and Hardy, or Felix the Cat, or Chaplin. The parties were for children of officers and friends of officers. (It was always 'them' and 'us' as it is in any society.) The bluejackets knew their place – but they were marvellous with us children. Of course it didn't occur to me in those days to question the organisation of society.

There was an exception to this. You couldn't go out into the streets in the 1920s without seeing masses of beggars. They were blinded, or maimed in some form or another, and would be selling

matches, or bootlaces, or playing musical instruments, often with a
monkey or a dead-looking dog with them. They were of course, the
men who'd won the Great War. They would come along to your
house and put their foot in the door and not go until you'd bought
something. They might whistle derisively when they saw me in a
school blazer. I wasn't quite certain what the Great War was, but
there seemed to be something very discreditable about having won
it, because here were these people with their grand medals (which
for all I know may have been hired for the occasion), who'd clearly
been brutally treated, and yet seemed to be starving on the streets.
It was something I never forgot. Years later I did an anthology on
the First World War, and the basic motive behind it was this
appalling memory of when I dreaded going out for afternoon walks,
because of these sights. It seemed to me even then that there was
something monstrously unfair about life. I can remember very
vividly that when Field-marshal Haig died, in households like my
parents' there was gloom and despondency, but from the slum areas
there came what sounded suspiciously like cheering. Haig was
awarded £100,000 and a peerage, whereas the chaps who'd really
done the work got fobbed off with wretched little pensions, and
sometimes no pension at all.

At boarding school, particularly at night in the dormitories, the
mythology of the First World War was told and re-told. (There were
certain great myths. The sinking of the Titanic was another; there
was a famous silent film called *Atlantic* which was full of gruesome,
and indeed more or less truthful, accounts of what actually
happened.) In that night world, it was a matter of fervent belief with
us that the Kaiser in person, in the Market Square of Brussels, cut
off the right hands of Belgian schoolboys, so they'd never use a rifle
against Germany. It would never have occurred to us not to believe
it. I was not an imaginative child, but such things sunk into my
imagination, and later on became images I could use. I remember
my first headmaster telling me that, when war broke out, he had two
boys whose parents lived in India. In September 1914 he got a parcel
from India, and inside was a loaded pistol with which to shoot these
two boys when the Germans reached the channel ports. It's the sort
of thing one wouldn't have questioned. I don't question it now. I
imagined a nasty little scene where the headmaster would give out
the morning prayers and arrangements for the day and end up, 'By
the way, I almost forgot – I want to see Marshal major and Marshal

minor in the cellar; for a very few minutes.'

I've got a very bad memory of the past forty years, but exact
recollections of childhood between the ages of about five to
nineteen. I can recall at will almost every day. I know the names and
most of the addresses of my six hundred or so fellow pupils, together
with many of their birthdays. My first school was an old school
(which still exists) reaching the end of a régime. For the first two
years it was very Victorian; a good deal of bullying; very harsh hours
of work. The assistant masters' common room had a glass door so
the authorities could see that the young men weren't up to no good.
It was a tough, even primitive régime, in which one act of kindness
might last for the rest of one's life. At cricket supper in the summer
term, we had a marvellous blow-out with trifles and jellies, creams
and cakes. Most of the regular food was totally disgusting, but the
cricket supper stood out like an oasis in the Sahara and I never forgot
it. As this was my first school, I had nothing to compare it with, and
assumed that the whole child population suffered exactly the same.
And there were bits about it I liked. I had certain advantages: I was
big; I could look after myself; I was good at games – unusually good
at football; and I made myself good at cricket for which I had no
natural talent, but I was fascinated by it, and became, in due course,
a fast bowler – extremely fast and extremely bad; but it was a
marvellous feeling – hurling oneself free of the earth at nervous
batsmen. On the whole I fitted in, and still have two close friends
from those days. In 1930 the school changed, in the sense that the
neo-Victorians retired and much younger people took over. We lived
in a Queen Anne country house with enticing woods, ponds,
meadows, and there was an atmosphere of frivolity, and a fruitful
experimental amateurishness. I felt very much that the masters were
on my side. It now seems to me that I had the best and the worst of
private school life – the light and the dark – which taught me that
there is no single principle in the universe: the creative and the
destructive fight each other, and existence tends towards cycles. I
learnt that however despairing I am, and of course I despaired at
times, because of some sort of balance in the universe, things will
change sooner or later: no doubt later, often much later – but change
they will.

From when I was seven, my mother and her husband lived abroad
most of the time. He was 'in oil' – like a sardine. So I was parked
out, both in boarding schools and in other people's houses, all of

which was of enormous value to me. I used to get my full share of misplaced sympathy – a wretched child sent away at seven to a terrible boarding school! But I loved almost all of it! In many holidays I was with a country doctor and his wife in Devonshire, and this was the happiest time of my life. He and his wife were too busy to bother about my daily routine: they were wise, generous, and they trusted me. I had almost total freedom to go where I liked, to read what I liked. I would cycle perhaps twenty-five miles for a game of tennis or a cricket match, or exploring hills, villages, moors. There were books all over the house. I sometimes felt the doctor and his wife had taken very literally Bishop Heber's remark, that a gentleman always buys three copies of any book: one for his library, one to read himself, and one to give away to his friends. (If that was taken literally today of course, authors would have less to worry about.) I was always very indiscriminate about my reading, and still am. When I first began to use the public library, all the books had the same binding – the original covers and jackets were torn off and they were shoved into a black, rather forbidding cloth, so that the library itself seemed to be a temple to some dark, mysterious and slightly furtive deity. But as all the books looked exactly the same, I had a vague idea that they were all the same book, so I would read Franz Werfel, Mrs Henry Wood, P. G. Wodehouse, Hugh Walpole, H. G. Wells, Jakob Wasserman, as if they were all the same author, though often puzzled by the extreme changes of style, and the lack of continuity in the story. This wasn't actually such an absurd approach to literature. I would read *Pegg's Paper* or Carlyle's *Revolution* simply because they happened to be there.

All this – the country doctor and the Devonshire freedom, the Great War, the varied experiences of school, left me with a sense that life is capricious but also bizarre – it can deal out great pain, but it can also give unpredictable, often undeserved rewards. I was a rather shy and affectionate child, and on my very first day at school I arrived early, too early. There was nobody else in the corridors except a rather good-looking boy, so, from politeness, I went up and spoke to him – and at once got a couple of black eyes. He was the school bully, outraged that anybody younger than himself should dare address him. That gave me a shock from which I've never entirely recovered. I'm not being over-dramatic, but such a rebuff had never happened to me before. Even the beggars on the streets, once you actually spoke to them or gave them a coin, were at once appeased; but this total unfriendliness that might have cost me a tooth made me very wary. On the whole, I now dislike people when I first meet them: I'm mentally cowering, and people are guilty until they've proved themselves innocent. It wasn't a bad lesson to have learnt – but I could have learnt it in a less spectacular way.

Although I was quite capable of playing my part in the rugger scrum, and could stand up to fast bowling, in terms of mortal combat with bare fists I've always been timid. I don't think I had the instincts of a bully, though I suppose, like everybody else, I usually wanted to get my own way, not least when I was a prefect. The Public School is a much abused organisation, but in general I learned a great deal from it, including a responsible attitude to power. Intelligent teachers wished me well; didn't impose themselves on me over-much; gave me advice when I wanted it; answered my questions honestly; tactfully nudged me forward, for example, by giving me books to review for the school magazine.

I was reading a great deal but in a rather unadventurous sort of way. I tended to read books over and over again, and was extremely unsophisticated. I was at school with the future historian Denis Mack Smith and others, who would be saying, 'Have you seen Wyston lately?' meaning W. H. Auden, or, 'I saw John the other day,' and John was John Betjeman, or, 'Edith rang me up,' and Edith was Edith Sitwell. Whether true or not, all this passed me by, even though I eventually edited the literary magazine. I did not appreciate Joyce, or Eliot, of whom I'd never heard at school, or E. M. Forster whom I had heard of, indeed had to study for an exam, but who meant nothing to me till later. It was very much the conventional schoolboy writers. Buchan, I read over and over again. A book which made a lasting impression on me was *The Four Feathers* by A. E. W. Mason. H. G. Wells, I admired, particularly his short-stories and world history. I read a lot of biography, but again in a very indiscriminate way. I would read a book called *Twelve Monstrous Criminals*, beginning with Nero and ending with Crippen; or Famous Trials. I remember Duff Cooper's *Talleyrand* engrossing me. (Talleyrand's remark, which I read elsewhere, that mankind is given speech in order to conceal his thoughts, has always stuck in my head.) In those days I myself was extremely tongue-tied and inarticulate. I didn't like being left out of parties and occasions, but disliked still more being included. I would sit at masters' gatherings not understanding much that was being said, about Henry James,

Matisse, Gielgud, but being treated as if I did. Because I had a certain gift for words (words unaccompanied by thought) I had a reputation, which I hadn't earned, as being a potential writer. I could string words together, but if some busybody said, 'Yes, yes, yes, but what do you actually *mean*?' I was, as I would have expressed it at the time, stumped.

I found it very difficult as a small child to realise that words could have more than one meaning. An expression like, '"Hurrah!" cried Charlie.' seemed a contradiction in terms. It was many years before I could make sense of imagery and metaphor, and look at literature painting and sculpture in any way other than literal. My attitude towards painting was entirely anecdotal. I loved such paintings as *The Last Day in the Old Home*, or *When the Danes Came up the Channel a Thousand Years Ago*. They seemed to me major art. I was astonished by Hieronymus Bosch, and the peasant paintings of Brueghel: but allusion, imagery, obliqueness, I couldn't understand. This would prove a major handicap, and I've often wondered how it could ever be that I had ambitions to write novels. I never had any ambition to write poetry. I did, at my first school, actually write one line of poetry of which I was unnecessarily proud. The line was, 'Squelching through the gulch, Mombassa,' and I repeated it whenever possible to stupefy superiors. But phrases struck me, phrases from certain hymns, from certain sermons. I remember a voice crashing through some vast church in Hove: 'Was not such love worth more than all the gold watches of Johannesburg?' I, of course, preferred the gold watches, but the resonant words enthralled me. Unconsciously, I was absorbing a great deal – consciously perhaps, rather less. I would read a great deal of history and biography, and dozens of second-rate novelists: Lion Feuchtwanger, Wasserman, Werfel, Dumas, Victor Hugo. Much of the history I picked up was from misleading historical romances. I believed anything in print was true, thus was frequently puzzled by the discrepancy between classroom history and romantic history. I was writing very bad short-stories, mostly modelled on those of 'Sapper', author of 'Bulldog Drummond', and wrapped in a layer of pompous pretentiousness. I also wrote some very blank verse. For my book reviews, I would go into the school library and read what *Time and Tide*, *The Spectator*, and *The New Statesman and Nation* said, and then I would concoct my own. This sounds extremely unscrupulous, and indeed it was, but all I can say is that at least it taught one to read more widely, it taught me standards beyond my own, and it gave a goal. And it also made me realise that although it was not difficult getting into print, it *was* difficult to write anything worthwhile, thus inducing a certain humility.

I got a scholarship to Oxford but I wasn't happy there. I realised almost at once that I wasn't a scholar. I didn't stay long and didn't take a degree. I have an impatient nature. I can't spend too long at any project. If I'm writing a sentence, my mind is already on to the next sentence. Half way through writing a book, I'm thinking about the next one. This is not what scholarship is about, and the themes which interested me and which I would have liked to have explored thoroughly, tended to be foreign themes: the rise of Fascism and Communism; the French Revolution; the reasons for Rome's collapse – but I was lazy, particularly about learning foreign languages. I was interested in what, in those days, I'd have called 'ideas' – I think, today, I would simply call them notions. I don't think I've ever had a single idea in my life, but I did realise that my limitations as a scholar could be used quite usefully for fiction. Many of my favourite novelists possessed enormous depth of feeling, and half-knowledge in a considerable number of diverse fields. I did not feel that Gorky, Woolf, R. C. Hutchison, Hemingway, *knew* as much as Aldous Huxley or Bertrand Russell. Today, if I'm writing historical novels, I take subjects which aren't particularly familiar. This leaves great areas for the imagination to move in. Of course, the drive to start a book must be strong feelings. I seldom know where these originate, not do I particularly want to know. I like life to preserve a certain amount of mystery. I like to pass a hole in the road and peer down and see important-looking people tinkering with wires and taps. For all I know they may be going to blow up parliament. They add excitement and colour to common existence.

At school, I would begin novels on a fairly big scale and give up after thirty or forty pages. This sounds unpromising, but it didn't occur to me, at fourteen or fifteen, that I wouldn't one day write serious fiction. The great figure for me at that period was a novelist almost totally forgotten today, Hugh Walpole, who was published in majestic-looking books by Macmillan: dark green volumes with golden lettering, generally of four or five hundred pages. F. R. Leavis was to call him, 'An utterly untalented purveyor of Book Society 'classics'.' My ambition was to write a book almost as good as the worst of Hugh Walpole, to be published by Macmillan, and to write a book of at least four hundred pages. I was like George Gershwin's father, who assessed the quality of music by its length – so *The Rhapsody in Blue*, which is nine minutes longer than *The Cuban Overture*, was therefore nine times as good. Indeed, all these ambitions were later realised: I think at least one of my novels is as good as the worst of Hugh Walpole's; I was published by Macmillan (disastrously); and I did publish at least one book of over four hundred pages. One lesson learned is that prayers get answered – but answered by somebody with a slightly sardonic or oblique sense of humour, and it would have been a great deal better in almost every case if they hadn't been.

I'd begun working before I went to Oxford. I'd got my scholarship a year before I should have done, having been sent in as a trial run. And much to my own annoyance I was taken away from school on the grounds that there was no point in spending more money as I'd already done what I was sent there to do. I did a bit of tutoring and a bit of school teaching. When starting the latter I was eighteen, and I was paid my term's fee in advance, which was ten pounds. There followed a common enough though disagreeable story – within two days the money had disappeared; I went to the headmaster in some irritation and said, 'Look, somebody's swiped my ten pounds.' The headmaster, by no means pleased with me, called the school together and declared that until somebody owned up there'd be no half holidays. This of course was a disaster, because even the staff had to work extra hours, and all the school cricket matches were cancelled. I was at once extremely unpopular. After about seven weeks of this misery, I put on an old coat that I hadn't worn for many weeks – and found, of course, the ten pounds had been there all the time. So then a rather interesting moral problem presented itself. I didn't have the nerve to announce my discovery, so we sweated out this miserable term to the end; and to this day, in Leicester Square, on Hampstead Heath, on Brighton Pier, old timers come up to me and say, 'I remember you. Weren't you responsible for that awful summer term...?' That was the start of a twenty-five year stint in teaching, which I found, from a writer's point of view, very useful. In teaching, I saw the unusual, the sad, the entertaining; could see the result, for better or worse – often for worse, of my work; I had long holidays; met some interesting, charming or disgusting people, both amongst the pupils and the staff; I could, to some extent, test my own beliefs. The real problem of life, I realised, was how to love not only the unlovable but the unspeakable. All this lasted until the early 1960s, when I'd had enough. Teaching had always seemed to me a job for the very young and enthusiastic, or for the very old and cynical, particularly the very old and cynical, who can make marvellous teachers. But there had come a time when I was neither, and I needed to recharge my batteries. I certainly didn't say, in any dramatic way, 'I'm no longer going to teach.' And if I had, there'd only have been a mild sigh of relief. But I merely drifted out of it, and never went back, although I do like it when I'm asked, and occasionally I am asked, to visit schools.

I always taught in private schools. Private education was something I'd known about; I knew the sort of people involved; I knew the ludicrous side of it and the attractive side; the pay was minimal, but while I was under forty it didn't really matter. I retain very mixed feelings about state and local authority education. The idea of local officials appointing teachers seems to me as absurd as the idea of the State appointing poets. Education controlled by the local authorities seems to me a contradiction in terms. The average local councillor knows nothing about education, and cares only for social engineering, a corruption of the imagination. Private education, which, after all, included A. S. Neill and Bertrand Russell, did offer more chance to experiment, more chance for small classes, more chance for escaping the examination racket, more chance for eccentricity. What I didn't like, and what no sane person could like, was that this was a matter of cash payment. Whatever the truth, I would not have been a success in any other system. I wasn't interested in promotion. I just wanted to introduce the age group I'd chosen, to world literature, world history, with as much humour, patience, tolerance, as I could muster, and to be left to get on with it. I've always been, in an unheroic way, an independent spirit, never taking kindly to regimentation or orders. At nearly all the schools I taught at, I was very much my own master – having appointed me, my employers assumed I could do a reasonably useful job. I enjoyed it enormously, some of my pupils became close personal friends. I don't think I was exceptionally competent, but I was an enthusiast, and managed to bring children's attention to certain books, films, events, landscapes and inscapes. I think it was Hugh Kenner who once said that teaching is an act of generosity. And this, I suppose, is one reason for writing. One has a conviction of something vital to communicate. But it's very difficult to achieve. I've only once or twice read a review of a book of mine where the reviewer has any idea of what I'm trying to say. Most of the fault is mine. I have a difficult style, and am always being told, in bad prose, how to write. There are occasional exceptions: Kenneth Graham, reviewing a novel I'd written, about one summer in Paris in 1794, wrote that the work was from an author who had obviously at one time or another been very excited by the paintings of Watteau and Brueghel. In forty years of having my stuff reviewed, that is almost the only interesting remark that anyone has ever made. And it was quite true, though neither painter was mentioned in the text. He'd cut away the surface area of the novel and reached the imaginative springs underneath.

I'm split about my own writing. There's a bit of my mind which says, 'Of course, you haven't had your due, and people don't take you seriously enough.' But another part is still a youth, amazed at ever getting into print, who knows, rather uneasily, that he's had a great deal more than his due, some luck, and a certain amount of favouritism.

My first book was a very, very bad book indeed, it had no starting-off flash of illumination, and its vision was vulgar. I simply wanted to write a book. It was called *I am the World*, and every day for months I slammed down the first things that came into my head. It went on and on – there was no particular reason why it should ever stop. I sent it to all the publishers beginning with A; all the publishers beginning with B; I got a brutal letter from Jonathan Cape, in person, but halfway through the Cs it was accepted, thanks to V. S. Pritchett, who for the first and last time in his life must have been out of his mind. It was scorned by the reviewers, and it was five years before I got anything else published. I used to go around public libraries taking it out and dropping it into Hampstead Heath ponds. It at least made me realise that I knew nothing about narration, dialogue, discipline, that I was giving all paragraphs and chapters equal weight in unreadable monotony.

The second book was more to the point. I wanted to write about the war (this was 1944) but I realised that what I really should be writing about was war as a perennial phenomenon, not only about that particular war. So I wrote *Enemies*, ostensibly about the Franco-Prussian war of 1870, near enough to modern times, directly related to both world wars, but sufficiently remote to avoid mere political points and arid journalism. It was seen from both sides, and I think it has unusual scenes, and, though conventional in form and very

long, I could republish bits of it without a feeling of great shame. I
had learned a little about how to use imagery. What I hadn't learned
was that one line of dialogue could cut out ten pages of description.

The third, called *Overseer*, was about Germany. I wanted to write
about Nazism, but again I didn't want to be too close to it, so I set
it in 1922 in a German provincial town. I aimed to show why an
abnormal political movement might emerge from apparently normal
families and individuals. Again it was of forbidding length. My
writing still suffered from having the same tone of voice throughout:
a riot, a duel, a scene of arson, would be written in exactly the same
way as an intimate conversation. I hadn't learned light and shade –
the work was too stiff, and dense with images (often of considerable
power) stuffed into incongruous contents.

Its successor was more in the right direction. The first three had
been totally humourless, though I myself am not a humourless
person. I set myself to write about what I'd had personal experience
of. *Broken Canes* was based on a school I was teaching in, rather to
the left of A. S. Neill. I set it back in the 30s and I realised I could
tackle a serious theme in a fairly light-hearted way.

That had minor critical success, but then I came unstuck. *A Verdict
of Treason*, was about fascism in English public schools, and though
it had good things in it, I wrote it too fast with insufficient respect
for the subject.

I produced too many books too fast, got flung out by my publisher
and had to find a new one. For the first time, I took the very remote
past, the fifteenth century. *The Tournament* started from an
unexpected bit of luck – I came across a passage in Huizinga's *The
Waning of the Middle Ages*: the passage wasn't important in itself,
but it turned a dramatic key for me. The theme of the novel was that
ideas, clothes, ceremony, ritual and so on, are at their most
spectacular at the moment that they've started to decline or to have
no further practical use. Tournaments were at their most spectacular
in the age of artillery when they'd ceased to have military
significance. That book got some attention here and indeed in
America, and showed me I could make a largely forgotten era
relevant to our own time. Of course there's always more than one
reason for deciding to write a book. In those days I was married,
and problems within the marriage, and realising that I was no longer
young, also came into the book. *The Tournament* took ten days to
write. Twice in my life I've written a novel in ten days, simply

because, apparently out of nothing, some fluke of reading or overhearing led to a vision which made the actual writing like copying off a blackboard.

I was still school-teaching and obsessed by the problem of violence. I was always looking for an ideal community, autonomous, cooperative, non-violent. It was the motive behind the school in *Broken Canes*, but I wanted a situation of fiercer tension and moment, so I took Germany just after the suicide of Hitler, and created a school for rehabilitating children in their early teens who'd reverted to barbarism: knifed someone, or denounced parents to the Gestapo, or killed a Jew; lost, perhaps damned, yet who had originally come from good homes. I tried to deal with the debate of war and pacifism; of how to deal with moral and physical hooliganism and debased heroism; of the degree of power a teacher should be allowed over his pupils. This was called *The Game in the Ground*, and was treated seriously by critics both here and in America (save by Conor Cruise O'Brien who compared it to St. Trinians with toothache).

Then, once more, I had several years of losing my way. In too many of my novels the parts were better than the whole. I had become only slowly interested in the chapter as a phenomenon with its own interior logic and dynamic; its rise and fall – something which the reader would take for granted, but which the writer can't. Some of these middle period books had good chapters, but they didn't add up to good books. I've always found writing about my own time much more difficult than writing about the past, partly because there's so much evidence, indeed too much evidence. Making sense of what's going on around one is much more difficult than working out one's attitude towards the fifteenth century, or the Secretariat of Attila the Hun, or Renaissance Morals.

I've never been very interested in politics, but there's an area where politics shades off into history, and that has always absorbed me. At school I won a prize for history. I chose Lord Acton's *Lectures on Modern History*, but when I got it, I found it ended in the eighteenth century and there was nothing modern about it. But there was a sentence in it which lasted: 'Thousands of humble Anabaptists suffered the same fate and nobody minded.' It didn't say what their fate was, and it didn't really explain who they were, but what particularly puzzled me was why nobody minded. It seemed unfair. The years went by, but I never forgot those unfortunates,

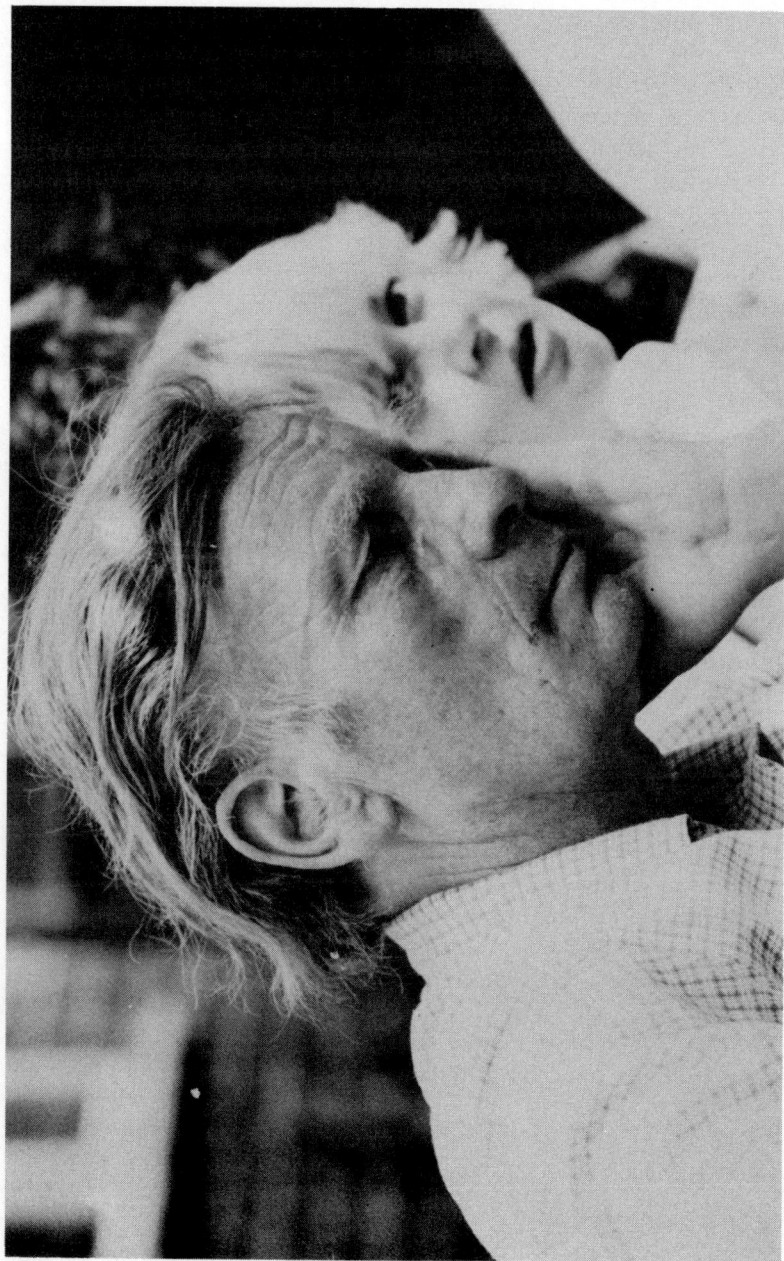

though never making much attempt to find out more. I'd read, in a
short-story by 'Saki', that a boy's favourite hen was suspected of
being a secret Anabaptist, but that didn't get me much further. But
when I was scratching around for a theme relevant to an attempt to
create an actual ideal community, I suddenly remembered the
Anabaptists. I found out that they had indeed been looking, not
merely for better government, but the perfect society, and had made
a fearful hash of it – they were the Bolsheviks of the sixteenth
century. They felt, with some reason, that not only had the Roman
Catholic church betrayed Europe, but Luther had too. They'd begun
as pacifists, but they didn't find that pacifism in German warfare
actually worked. Some of them marched off into battle naked,
feeling the Lord would protect them. This was inadequate
protection. They then went to the other extreme and became
ferociously militant. They set up their own kingdom under a
handsome young tailor, John of Leiden, and captured Munster in
Westphalia. John of Leiden divided the world into twelve dukedoms
with himself as absolute king, established polygamy, and abolished
sin by proclamation. He married twelve wives in public, killed more
than one of them with his own hands, and instituted a state of
terrorism which was finally put down with fanatic bloodshed by the
combined forces of the Protestants and Catholics. John of Leiden
and his two principal lieutenants were tortured to death on heated
thrones with red-hot crowns jammed over their foreheads, and the
cages in which their skeletons hung for centuries can still be seen
hanging from a spire of Munster cathedral. On this, I based a novel,
Friends of God. I can't claim it was a good book, but it suited the
darker side of my own predilections: showing how idealism can lead
to the most appalling hocus-pocus – that fair is foul and foul is fair.
It was a sort of *Macbeth* – a great swirling canvass; four hundred
pages of riots, mass movements, secret tribunals, sensational
proclamations, appalling cruelties, a wallowing in the ruins of Gothic
Europe. The subject matter should have been treated with much
more subtlety; but I have found that a number of readers have not
forgotten it.

I've always been interested in, not success itself, but the build-up
towards success and the way that success can be thrown away and
lost through mischance, boredom, incompetence, or too much
brooding. I wrote a novel, *The Lost Lands*, set in France in a period
when the Inquisition had just been founded. It was a way of studying

the nature of success; the nature of power; the role of religion; the range and limits of imagination; the role of class and the individual.

I've never been interested in fantasy. Alain-Fournier says, 'I like the fantastic only inside the real.' But I like fairy stories, and indeed have collected two books of fairy stories for children. It always puzzled me that most fairy stories didn't have any fairies in them, and then I realised that this was possibly due to a mistranslation in the thirteenth century. They seem to have been originally called 'fate stories'. Collecting folk-tales led me onto writing two further books. In *Lancelot*, I take the old story of the Saxons and Arthur and the Round Table very much in terms of a fate story; but it's simultaneously about the nature of historical reality. Lancelot says something like: 'I've always been puzzled about Arthur. He hadn't got any particular talent. I worked with him for thirty years and I never heard him make an interesting remark. I don't remember him doing anything particularly worth doing. I remember him stealing a pig once. But *he* got the reputation. Most of the work was done by people like me, as it nearly always is. Even *I* didn't do a great deal, and on the whole we failed. But I don't mind betting that in about five hundred years time I shall be totally forgotten, but the most extraordinary things will be told about Arthur, things which would have amazed him – mostly things he wouldn't even have approved of.' It aims to show how historical truths can get distorted: they can be connected up to ancient myths; they can turn off into legend; by mistranslation they can become downright lies. (Wellington is supposed to have said that Waterloo was won on the playing fields of Eton, but at the time he said it, there were no playing fields of Eton. What he actually said was, 'Gentlemen. I think I can claim that my spirit of enterprise was due to the tricks I used to get up to in the garden.' This was translated into French in the 1830s, and was translated back from the French into English in the 1850s and became what we now know it as.)

I followed on with *The Death of Robin Hood*, where I took the Robin Hood myth, starting with the bronze age forests of about 2000 BC and ending with the Munich Conference of 1938. It insists that, if a story is good enough, it will survive, but will be reinterpreted, re-enacted, by every generation with different parts emphasized. It will mean different things to different people, and yet mean something to everybody.

I also wrote a history of England for teenagers which got gratifying reviews, but reviews written by adults. I'd long ago given up teaching so I don't know what impact, if any, it had on children. The teaching of history was extremely bad in most schools I knew of, so I made an attempt to combine liveliness with truth. I wanted children to read it and say, 'I'd never thought of colour in that way, or armour quite in that way, or herrings in that way. It may not be true, but it's interesting, and now I must check it out in other books.' I've always had a bit of my imagination which is didactic, a residue of my school-teaching days, so I welcome the rare commission to write a non-fiction book. I published a history of England for adults some years ago, which begins in about 3000 BC and ends with the entry into the Common Market. It wasn't a particularly good book, and I had a very short time to do it in, but it drained off certain things which I wanted to say which otherwise would have got dragged into a novel (- and probably booted out again by the publisher).

In 1962 I had an unhappy love affair with a married woman. In the end she went back to her husband, as such women always do. I sat outside on a January night on Primrose Hill meditating: there were only two things to do. One, obvious and cheap and quick, was to commit suicide almost at once. The other, more difficult, more expensive, and more arduous, was to write a novel about it, giving myself the best lines, and getting my own back. She was quite famous, and so was her husband, so I had to be careful. So I wrote a novel called *The Story Teller*, about a man born in 1262 who in 1962 was sixty-two years old. He lives in Sweden during the Thirty Years War; in the Baltic in the fourteenth century; in Paris in the 1790s; in the Kaiser's and Bismarck's Berlin in the 1880s; and in Sweden in the 1930s and 40s; and throughout all these centuries she and I are having our emotional ups and downs, our repartee, false starts, aborted renewals. Of course, if it had remained mere revenge on an old friend it would have been a very bad novel. It probably is a very bad novel – but not bad in that way, because of course the unconscious took over.

Sometimes accidents happen. I was on a bus in Suffolk and I saw chalked on a barn wall, miles from anywhere, the number 367. I realised 367 meant something, but I couldn't make out what it was. When I arrived, there were only two books in my friend's cottage: the complete speeches of Winston Churchill, and Gibbon's *The Decline and Fall of the Roman Empire*. I didn't think Churchill, with all his merits, was going to help me here, but I rudely shoved aside my host and hostess, kept dinner waiting for hours and delved into *The Decline and Fall*. And I succeeded. 367 AD was the year of the alleged 'Barbarian Conspiracy'. England was besieged by the Scots from Ireland, the Picts from Scotland, the Franks and Vandals from Germany, and the Scandinavians. The Roman Empire broke down and there was no rule in England. The Picts besieged London, the Irish tried to burn Bath – total anarchy. After two years order was restored, and Roman Britain lasted for another seventy or eighty years. This interested me. The references to it are scanty. Archaeology tells us far more than any written documents – and that doesn't tell us very much. But it was enough for my purposes. What I was interested in is why people of one age will defend their city and in another age won't. Why was it that the Roman Empire, with all its resources, seemed not interested in defending itself? And this connected up to the problems of our own time, the perpetual problem of civilisation: how to keep people concerned with life, how to keep them public spirited. The Roman State was facing grave problems of unemployment, inflation, moral bankruptcy. To deal with this the emperors tried to keep society static. They legislated to make all jobs hereditary: if your father was a banker you were a banker; if your father was a slave you were a slave; if your father was a poet you were a poet. Wages and prices were pegged. As you can imagine, this didn't work for very long. I found it suggestive and relevant, finally tragic, and uncomfortably real.

I'm writing a novel at the moment about contemporary life, which is being very difficult indeed. I lay it aside, sometimes for a year, then go back to it, hoping in the meantime the unconscious has been doing some work. I don't mind this any longer, and am nearly always doing several things at once now. I used to think it really mattered if I didn't publish a book every week, but now one learns patience. I mean the patience of which Rilke talks, not in the sense of being passive, but actually working hard while waiting for the essential to happen. I used to get blockages, which would make me despair. I'd feel I'd never be able to write again. Now, I rather welcome them, because I realise that at the time you're most blocked in the consciousness, in the unconscious there's probably an immense amount seething around.

I have written an autobiography. I regret to say that my marriage only takes up a sentence. I married an extremely pleasant and intelligent woman, but the marriage, though it lasted for twelve years, was not finally a success. But in my private, self-centred imaginative world, that had no lasting importance. I don't think, if I'd been married eight times, or married not at all, it would have affected the sort of books I've written or the way I've written them. It's often the reverse. I find that writing books does affect one's social life, and, on the whole, it affects it badly. In order to get a particular sentence worked out and finished, you put the baby on the fire, you kick your wife into the garden, you burn the house down and start somewhere else where you can't be found. It's both a wide-ranging and exceptionally narrow life. It has affected certain love affairs, which have gone wrong entirely because of my own selfishness. But whatever was happening, even at the worst, when emotionally I was suffering because of what appeared, erroneously, as outrageous treatment from others, there was always one hour in the twenty-four when I could detach myself and complete the next chapter. Once I'm at a table, writing, my own personal relationships seldom interfere – or if they do, it's usually many years after the crisis. An exception was *The Tournament* where the duke and his duchess were very much myself and my wife; but that was only one of several themes.

I assume it's a very small public that I'm writing for. Not out of any feeling of elitism or snobbery, but simply because I've looked at my sales since 1942. I say what I have to say in what way seems to me appropriate. I don't like obscurity for the sake of obscurity. Possibly one gets more experienced as one gets older and one does manage to find a more simple language. I don't think I've been attacked in the last ten years as much as I used to be. On the other hand, what is complicated is that where one critic will attack another critic will praise.

I write in big notebooks, on the right-hand side only, keeping the left free for after-thoughts and revisions. I do a lot of the work while walking round the streets of London or walking fifteen or sixteen miles in the countryside with a notebook, and coming back at the end of the day and slotting things in. I see something and I realise it will fit in marvellously forty-five pages before. Or I overhear a line of dialogue on a bus or street and I think, this is exactly how my character would have spoken, so I cross out what she originally said and put in the stranger's remark. The left-hand side of the page is very important. The chief thing is to do a bit every day, whether I feel like it or not. It needn't be a lot. If you're basically rather lazy as I am, and don't particularly enjoy the moment of writing, you've got to have this rather puritan, self-disciplined way. Other people really enjoy writing, like Jo in *Little Women*, tearing away with the bit between her teeth and loving every minute of it. A certain regularity and rhythm is my answer.

I can't make a living from writing. I own my house (my savings as a school-teacher enabled me to do that). I let off most of it. I keep certain rooms, according to my income; if I've had a good year I can have more of the house for myself – if it's a bad year rather less. I live very simply. If you live alone you get by. If there were two of us it would be much more difficult. It means I can't turn down book reviewing. I've been book reviewing since the early 40's – Orwell was my first literary editor. Now, I don't do so much. I review for *The Guardian* and *The London Magazine*, occasionally for *The Financial Times*; but editors only send me books which they know I'm going to like. I don't have to write a line I haven't wanted to write – and that is luxury.

Tax men, I've always found perfectly reasonable. Partly, I suppose, because the sums of money involved are trivial. I have an excellent relationship with my agent who is a personal friend, whose judgement I respect, and we enjoy some laughter, some tennis, some drink together. Publishers are more tricky. As a non-best-seller I'm easily expendable. Twice, publishers have broken a contract and more or less said, 'You can sue us of course, but we're rich and you're poor, and you'll find that you won't get very far.' One of these was before I had an agent and I did nothing about it, but the last time it happened the agent insisted on £3,000 being paid and got it. Peter Owen, who issues my novels, has always been very co-operative, with little personal gain. On the whole, I can't imagine that publishers have actually made much money out of me.

I've had a bit more than my fair share of State support. The Art's Council have given me lots of cash, and they've twice contributed towards the cost of production of my books. I've got rather mixed feelings about this. If I'd had no support from the Arts Council it wouldn't have affected what I would have written. The books would have taken a bit longer to get into print, or might not have got into print at all, but I'd have written them. If a writer has something to say, he's going to say it. It's like a mushroom pushing through the concrete. I would find it very difficult to justify, on a public platform, somebody like me being given tax-payer's money. How far people should be asked to contribute to something which they don't like but which might be good for them, like my novels, or more convincingly, Covent Garden opera, is debatable. I tend to vary about this according to my mood.

I used to play a lot of cricket and squash and football. I still play tennis. I spend half the month in the country, walking, gardening, writing. I have a house there, inherited, not earned. I live a fairly gregarious life in the evening. I love the cinema. I don't often go to the theatre, I can't afford it, and it's not so easy to leave if you don't like it. A question I'm always asked in schools is, 'Do you have to have any talent to be a novelist?' (I always feel there's a lot of malice in this.) I think what they might be saying is, 'Do you have to be born with talent, or can you sort of invent it after having left school?' And the answer, I feel, is, 'Yes, if you whole-heartedly wish to, you *can* invent it.' Wandering round the streets of London or in the Suffolk fields or Yorkshire dales is important for me, providing I remain consistently alert. 'Without curiosity there can be no literature,' said Ezra Pound. Curiosity is protection, stimulant, weapon. As a child I didn't have as much curiosity as I have now. You need self-confidence too, and stamina. You may not feel that history would stop if you didn't finish your book, but you mustn't be too humble about it either. You've got to kid yourself that you have some vision, however unimportant, and something to say which is new and interesting and worth saying. And, I repeat, patience. Again, to quote Pound, 'I've seen young men and women of the utmost ability who've come to nothing because they've failed to calculate the length of the journey.'

* * *

E. M. Forster's *Passage to India*, once I got rid of it from the point of view of study for an exam, was important to me. The business of the Marabar caves corresponds to life as I've known it: there are certain things, impossible to precisely name, which do have important effects. Mrs Moore getting changed into a goddess by mob psychology seemed utterly convincing. Forster's *Two Cheers for Democracy* articulates much of my own feelings. I think it was C. B. Cox who said that Forster reminds us that human history is not really a contrast of extremes, but that a great deal of it consists of muddle.

Carlyle's *French Revolution* for me was a seminal book, not its
historical accuracy but for its atmosphere. It's a great prose poem. I
think of it as I think of *Macbeth*.

I still re-read Arnold Toynbee's *Study of History*, although I've
never yet met a historian who doesn't giggle or growl when I mention
it. But it did make me look, just as H. G. Wells's *History of the World*
did earlier, at the world in a way which made a great deal of the preoccupations of my fellow countrymen seem trivial. I've never lost my
predilection for the large scale, which can also mean the sensational,
the woolly-minded, the unscholarly.

I love the nineteenth century novels: such successes as Thomas
Mann's four 'Joseph' books. You see a very modern (in its day)
sensibility tackling one of the great stories, and producing a
historically, and philosophically fascinating account. But primarily it
is a marvellous feat of story-telling. I'm not a very effective story
teller myself, but I very much admire those who are.

Little Women, I read often, and I was always puzzled, and still am
puzzled, because that seems to me a marvellous story yet contains
some seven of the biggest bores of all fiction. And yet, the book, to
me, is a masterpiece.

Alain-Fournier's *Le Grand Meaulnes* takes me straight back to my
own adolescence: the mystery of life: the poignancy of it all; the sense
of adventure; the feeling that just around the corner is the magic
castle; or, in the turn of the way, life is going to be altered. It suggests
what is within reach, and yet practically inaccessible (like writing a
masterpiece).

Dickens is important to me. The whole of Dickens. The whole of
Hardy. The whole of Tolstoy. Rilke's poems. Flaubert's *Education
Sentimental*. I'm a perpetual re-reader, and there's a danger here: it
means that I'm not very adventurous about reading new stuff. I
certainly don't read as much new verse as I should. I'm certainly lazy
about reading short-stories. And I don't like reading modern novels
when I'm writing one myself; and as I nearly always am writing one
it means that I'm very out of date with the novelists younger than
myself, as most novelists now are.

* * *

If I didn't read novels and poetry I would think that humanity was far more homogenous than it actually is. I wouldn't take into account the infinite variety, not only of different personalities, but of personalities within a single personality. And the fact that psychologists are telling me the same in their books is not the same, because I find jargon unreadable. Literature shows me more vividly that nothing is either ordinary or extraordinary; it creates a marvellous balance between the inner and the outer; journeys to the moon, or the Stone age, a glance exchanged between two people at a party, all have their subtle connections. I think, though, that when I was a boy, we relied for instruction far too much on the book and far too little on the gramophone, the cinema, the graphic arts. Now, the book is released to its proper function: showing the inter-relatedness between people and things, people and people, this busy system of checks and balances within life and lives.

London, May 1984

NIGEL GRAY'S COMMENT.

Peter Vansittart must have been a remarkable teacher. He is witty, wise, stimulating and knowledgeable. He would make even the most severe critics of the public school system wish that their children could be educated by him or people like him. He is admirably eccentric, independent and unconventional (in his own words, 'a free spirit').

I first met Peter in the spring of '78. There were five of us sharing a platform, and beforehand we had to dine with the organisers in a hotel. It was not a good meal, I remember – a rather insipid, typically English affair. On the spectrum of poshness, Peter was way out on one end and I way out on the other (with Margaret Drabble just about above the fulcrum). But Peter and I, perhaps surprisingly, took to each other at once (much to the chagrin, it seemed, of assorted bureaucrats who were present).

Peter's Hampstead home is not a warm or comfortable place to be (it has the appearance and 'feel' of a poor bachelor's pad), but the good crack that is on tap there makes up for that. Peter Vansittart must be the ideal dinner party guest – which is just as well: I fear he would starve if it were not for the people who feed him in exchange for his marvellous company.

On one occasion when he came to us for dinner he was let down rather badly. Two many guests were crammed on a bench at our garden table. The bench collapsed, dumping Peter unceremoniously on the grass.

Since 1984, two more novels have been published: *Aspects of Feeling*, set in Britain between 1936 and 1986, one theme of which is the surrender by Britain of many thousands of anti-Communist Russians and Yugoslavs to Stalin after World War Two; and *Parsifal*, a novel which moves from AD 600 to AD 1945, re-telling and re-inventing the legend. He has also compiled two more anthologies, and written a memoir, *Paths from a White Horse*. At present he is compiling an anthology about the French Revolution, and working on a novel set in AD 275, entitled *The Wall*.

Peter Vansittart was born in Bedford on August 27th 1920.

Peter Vansittart's Book-Choice:

A Passage to India E. M. Forster   *Joseph in Egypt* Thomas Mann
Two Cheers for Democracy   *Joseph the Provider* Thomas Mann
   E. M. Forster   *Little Women* Louisa May Alcott
The French Revolution   *Le Grand Meaulnes*
   Thomas Carlyle   Alain Fournier
Macbeth William Shakespeare   *Bleak House* Charles Dickens
The Study of History   *Collected Poems* Thomas Hardy
   Arnold Toynbee   *The Cossacks* Leo Tolstoy
Joseph and his Brothers   *The Sentimental Education*
   Thomas Mann   Gustave Flaubert
Young Joseph Thomas Mann   The poems of Rainer Maria Rilke

Books by Peter Vansittart:

Novels:

I am the World   *The Lost Lands*
Enemies   *The Story Teller*
The Overseer   *Pastimes of a Red Summer*
Broken Canes   *Landlord*
A Verdict of Treason   *Quintet*
A Little Madness   *Lancelot*
The Tournament   *The Death of Robin Hood*
Orders of Chivalry   *Three Six Seven*
A Sort of Forgetting   *Harry*
Sources of Unrest   *Aspects of Feeling*
Carolina The Friends of God   *Parsifal*

For Children:

The Dark Tower   *Green Knights,*
The Shadow Land   *Black Angels*

Anthologies:

Voices from the Great War   *John Masefield's Letters*
Voices: 1870-1914   *from the Front*
                                     Happy and Glorious

History:

Dictators   *Vladivostok*
Worlds and Underworlds   *Flakes of History*

Memoir:

Paths from a White Horse